Advances in Computer Security Management

VOLUME 2

WILEY HEYDEN ADVANCES LIBRARY IN EDP MANAGEMENT

Edited by Thomas A. Rullo

Other Advances Series in the Library

ADVANCES IN DATA PROCESSING MANAGEMENT Volume 1

ADVANCES IN COMPUTER PROGRAMMING MANAGEMENT Volume 1

ADVANCES IN DISTRIBUTED PROCESSING MANAGEMENT Volumes 1 and 2

ADVANCES IN DATA COMMUNICATIONS MANAGEMENT Volumes 1 and 2

ADVANCES IN COMPUTER SECURITY MANAGEMENT Volume 1

ADVANCES IN DATA BASE MANAGEMENT Volumes 1 and 2

Advances in Computer Security Management

VOLUME 2

Edited by
MARVIN M. WOFSEY
Professor, Department of Management Science
The George Washington University

A Wiley Heyden Publication

JOHN WILEY & SONS
Chichester · New York · Brisbane · Toronto · Singapore

British Library Cataloguing in Publication Data:

Advances in computer security management—(Advances
    library in EDP management)
    Vol. 2
    1. Electronic data processing departments—
    Security measures—Periodicals
    I. Series
    658.4'78'05   HF5548.2

ISBN 0 471 26234 X

Typeset by Pintail Studios Ltd.
Duck Island Lane, Ringwood, Hampshire.
Printed by The Pitman Press, Bath, Avon.

CONTENTS

CHAPTER 4: Federal Legislation and Impact on   53
                  Security Management—
                  Peter S. Browne and Robert Y. Bigman

CHAPTER 5: Designing Secure Data Processing   73
                  Applications—
                  Peter S. Browne and Eugene F. Troy

LIST OF CONTRIBUTORS

ROBERT Y. BIGMAN, Systematics General Corporation, 1606 Old Ox Road, Sterling, Virginia 22170, U.S.A. (p. 53).

HERBERT S. BRIGHT, Computation Planning Inc., 7840 Aberdeen Road, Bethesda, Maryland 20814, U.S.A. (p. 173).

PETER S. BROWNE, Burns International Security Service, Inc., 320 Old Briarcliff Road, Briarcliff Manor, New York 10510, U.S.A. (pp. 53, 73 and 93).

ROBERT CAMPBELL, Advanced Information Management Incorporated, 1988 Opitz Boulevard, Woodridge, Virginia 22191, U.S.A. (p. 25).

CHARLES L. CAVE, Cave Associates, P.O. Box 2519, Reston, Virginia 22090, U.S.A. (p. 143).

WILLIAM C. GRAYSON, Bedford Group International, P.O. Box 3057, Crofton, Maryland 21114, U.S.A. (p. 161).

KENNETH L. KITTELBERGER, Information Systems and Networks, Inc., 5454 Wisconsin Avenue, Chevy Chase, Maryland 20815, U.S.A. (p. 1).

J. ROBERT McGRAEL, Management Dimensions Corporation, 185 East Garfield Avenue, Pomona, California 91767, U.S.A. (p. 203).

STANLEY S. MASHAKAS, U.S. Department of Justice, Washington, District of Columbia 20530, U.S.A. (p. 237).

TIMOTHY J. SALTMARSH, Information Systems and Networks, Inc., 5454 Wisconsin Avenue, Chevy Chase, Maryland 20815, U.S.A. (p. 93).

EUGENE F. TROY, Digital Analysis Corporation, P.O. Box 2850, Reston, Virginia, U.S.A. (p. 73).

JAMES R. WADE, Scott & Fetzer, 14600 Detroit Avenue, Lakewood, Ohio 44107, U.S.A. (p. 117).

J. T. WESTERMEIER, Abrams, Kovacs, Westermeier and Goldberg, 2nd Floor, 1735 K Street, N.W. Washington, D.C. 20006, U.S.A. (p. 39).

PREFACE TO THE WILEY HEYDEN ADVANCES LIBRARY IN EDP MANAGEMENT

Information, to be of value, must be timely, accurate, and accessible. By addressing each of these criteria, the *Wiley Heyden Advances Library in EDP Management* has proved to be a unique and valuable source of information for managers.

The timeliness of the material is maintained by issuing additional volumes within each series. These volumes build upon the base of previous ones to provide new insights and add topics of current interest. Because we continue to generate new ideas our readers receive the most up-to-date information.

The second attribute of useful information is accuracy. To create the *Wiley Heyden Advances Library in EDP Management*, we assign a separate editor to each volume as an expert in the field; that editor is responsible for the overall content of the volume. Each chapter is in turn developed by an expert in a specific area and then submitted to the volume editor for review. Wherever necessary, additional technical review support is obtained. Because of this detailed editorial and review process, a high degree of accuracy can be assured.

The third attribute that makes information of value is accessibility. This feature is the least commonly discussed and the most difficult of the three to accomplish. In fact the lack of easy accessibility to information was the main reason for developing the *Wiley Heyden Advances Library in EDP Management*. Our primary role as developers and managers of this base of material is to provide our users with the information they want in a form in which they can readily use it. This task is accomplished through the selection of relevant topic areas, maintenance of a consistent level of content, and organization of material in line with its intended use.

While we have achieved our timeliness, accuracy, and accessibility objectives, we strive to improve the library through the added dimension of communication with our end users. Thus we welcome any suggestions for improvement of our current series or expansion into new areas.

Thomas A. Rullo
Executive Editor

PREFACE TO VOLUME 2

The subject of computer security is a comparatively new consideration. In the earlier days of computer use the emphasis was on getting the work out of the computer. Furthermore, companies were not as totally dependent on the computer as many of them are today. Catastrophic events, such as the U.S. Air Force computer fire in the Pentagon, were viewed as freakish accidents, and the 'it can't happen here' feeling persisted.

It was not until the early 1970s that computer security was recognized generally as something that must be considered in the operation of a business, in the same manner as any other business risk. The steadily mounting number of computer disasters from fire, flood, bombs, theft, and other causes forced this change. Risk assessment became an integral part of computer planning, and the field of computer security boomed. As in any other new field, the pioneers came up with many innovations and new techniques.

This book is intended to summarize in detail the current status of the computer security field. Every effort has been directed toward obtaining people who have been and are concentrating on individual areas of computer vulnerability since they would be best able to describe the developments in that field and indicate what the trends are. The first chapter, as its title indicates, is a summary of the problems as they exist today. Kittelberger opens with a historical perspective, followed by summarized discussions of security as it is covered in the balance of the book.

In the second chapter, *Computer Security as a Management Issue*, Campbell brings to the fore the fact that top management cannot divest itself of security considerations by delegating them to people lower in the organization. Each level of management has a role to fulfill—top management to set the policy and provide the funds necessary to carry out that policy, middle management to devise the means of carrying out the policy, and lower management to implement these means. Failure of any level of management can result in negating the entire security system, and, as has happened in some cases, can ultimately force the company out of business.

As in any other new area, computer security violations are being tried under current laws, which have to be interpreted by the courts in terms of how they apply in a field not in existence when the laws were enacted. Westermeier discusses these legal interpretations. Copyright, the preemption doctrine, and trade secret protection all must be considered in safeguarding proprietary computer programs. Written contracts serve to allocate risk, and may provide protection against varying conditions. Risk assessment then becomes a two-edged sword. On one hand, it analyzes the risks and describes the means to minimize these risks. On the other hand, it serves to document negligence if these means are not employed. Laws, such as those concerning privacy and the Corrupt Practices Act of 1977, have necessitated additional security measures, and, finally, the burgeoning field of computer risk insurance should be considered.

Federal Legislation and Impact on Security Management indicates what the federal government has done to ensure the security of computer systems. Browne and Bigman portray the federal government's direct role in establishing requirements for the protection of federally owned computer facilities, systems, and data; and the indirect role in establishing regulations affecting the management of computer systems and data in the private sector.

In *Designing Secure Data Processing Applications* Browne and Troy not only point out the necessity of considering security requirements starting in the earliest stages of system design, but also delineate techniques to assure reliable and secure code. These techniques include structured programming and modularization. The chapter also covers various design and implementation tools, together with their advantages and disadvantages, and concludes with a section on quality assurance and testing.

In the chapter on *Data Processing Risk Assessment* Saltmarsh and Browne trace the history of this effort, and then discuss in detail the individual steps involved in one method of completing a risk assessment. Numbers of discrete approaches are geared toward measuring and evaluating risk in a data processing environment. This chapter discusses and lists the advantages and disadvantages of each approach.

In *Physical and Personnel Security Considerations for Data Processing Systems*, Wade opens with the location and design of the computer facility. It then gives ample coverage to access control and hazard protection. The chapter then examines different aspects of personnel hiring and control. In particular, the necessity for a clear, concise statement of company policy with regard to its position on securing company assets is emphasized.

Hardware and Software Security first covers the hardware and software objectives and procedural requirements of the ideal secure data processing system. Since no system is absolutely secure, Cave then examines the current status of hardware and software security, and discusses probable developments in the near future.

The special security problems inherent in telecommunications systems are discussed in *Vulnerabilities of Data Telecommunications Systems*. Grayson deals with transmission technologies such as Value Added Networks, microwave, satellite, and cable. 'Bugging' and 'tapping' techniques are described and prevention methodologies detailed.

The first part of *Modern Computational Cryptography* compares control table methods against cryptography. Bright then discusses different aspects of cryptographic concepts, ending with various methods of cryptanalytic attack and defense. Much of the material in this chapter results from the research and improvisations of the author.

In many large firms computer operations have encompassed the major paperwork of the company. The ability to revert to manual operations has disappeared. A disaster destroying computer operations and/or computerized records might well result in a complete stoppage of the company's operations. Since only about five consulting firms and very few business firms in the United States have actual experience in planning the actions necessary to recover after a disaster, very few companies are in a position to recover from a disaster. In *Disaster/Recovery Planning* McGrael furnishes detailed instructions concerning the preparation and implementation of such planning. The major segments covered are the initiation of the project, organization, plan structure and organization, gathering of the necessary data, development of the plan, and, finally, testing of the plan. This chapter should be required reading for all executives preparing company budgets. The reluctance to spend money for these efforts is fairly prevalent in private industry, although the federal government requires all federal computer installations to complete such a plan and to review it periodically.

In order to predict *Future Developments in Data Processing Security* it was necessary to predict future developments in computer hardware and software, communications, and the systems environment, and to forecast their impact on the security problem. Mashakas examines an architecture for security and the awareness of management with regard to the implications of lapses in security. It finishes with consideration of liability, standards of accreditation, authentication, internal auditing, personnel, and contingency planning.

Marvin M. Wofsey
Editor

Advances in Computer Security Management, Vol. 2
Edited by M. M. Wofsey
© 1983 John Wiley & Sons Ltd.

Chapter 1

SCOPE OF COMPUTER SECURITY PROBLEMS

Kenneth L. Kittelberger

Information Systems and Networks, Inc.

INTRODUCTION

The computer has unleashed countless opportunities for industrial growth, new applications, labor-saving accomplishments, and better decision-making. As various segments in the government and private sector have exploited these opportunities, dependency on computer-based systems has become almost universal. Commensurate with the growth of this technology and the consequent dependency on computer systems are the problems of detecting and preventing computer crime, planning for recovery from a host of disaster scenarios, and resolving a variety of other concerns. The development of complex, highly sophisticated systems that are capable of resource-sharing and wide geographic distribution has led to the requirement for a multi-faceted approach to the task of providing adequate and reasonable security.

The risks have increased with the increased capabilities of and dependence upon computer processing: interactive, on-line processing is replacing batch processing; the number of users has increased greatly; and users no longer need to be geographically adjacent to the computer (they can access the system from numerous remote locations). The potential losses (in monetary values) are larger, and the unavailability of processing may severely impact the continued functioning of the organization.

Dynamics of Risk

The risks to any organization's data processing function are dynamic in nature, in that the components of risk are in constant flux and vary from operation to operation. If risk is defined as 'the potential for future loss', where loss has both a frequency and intensity, the risk dependencies become more evident. The sources of these potential losses are a constant threat, and the likelihood of success depends on the level of vulnerability. Thus, the extent of potential losses is based on these threat-vulnerability relationships, which are constantly changing as conditions vary, from hour to hour, and day to day. It is essential that management understand and, more important, control the risk environments in which the EDP system must operate. This control is achieved by providing the proper degree of computer security.

The Issue of Computer Security

Not only does computer security concern itself with the physical protection of data processing facilities; it also addresses hardware/software functions, characteristics, and features; operational practices and procedures, accountability procedures, and access controls at the central computer facility, the remote computer, and the terminal facilities; the management constraints, physical structure, and devices; the personnel practices; the communications controls; contingency planning and disaster recovery techniques; and a multitude of subjects within these general categories, all of which are necessary in order to provide an acceptable level of protection in a computer system.

The objective of computer security, then, is to prevent unauthorized access to and use of (1) information being processed and produced and (2) the computer system resources; to ensure the continued availability of this information and the processing resources; and to comply with the legal protection requirements imposed upon management.

HISTORICAL PERSPECTIVE

The first generation of computers was a group of single-line or batch processors; that is, one program was executed while utilizing all the system resources. The computing resource was located where access was limited to a small population of operators, and security was primarily a matter of controlling physical access to the computer room.

The second generation of computers increased processing efficiency through the use of multiprogramming. This advance permitted more than one program to occupy the central processing unit and share resources. The remote location of input and output devices provided the capability of remote job entry and, when combined with multiprogramming, made security measures the responsibility of computer system technology. Unfortunately, security was not a design requirement until the mid 1970s.

The third generation of computers is characterized by increased performance and interconnection of multiple central processing units. This latter capability, when extended by remote terminals, increases the need for proper security by placing more reliance upon the technology of the hardware, software, and associated communications. Access authorization is no longer considered a matter of physical identification. Use of electronically transmitted passwords, development of complex user-identification schemes, and improvement in the reliability of communications media are essential aspects of ensuring that access to the computer utility is authorized.

Data Base Management Systems

The introduction of data base management systems and large-scale systems integration was a major step in providing computing power to the user community. No longer is it necessary for a programmer to develop a specialized program to retrieve or manipulate data. Personnel not under the direct authority of a data processing organization can access, add, delete, or change data and, in some cases, write programs. The levels of performance and efficiency necessary to provide readily available and conveniently located information are major objectives in computer systems today. Providing an environment which fosters a uniform level of security throughout a highly decentralized organization, with a variety of unique operating environments, therefore, is not a trivial task.

The availability of the computer resources has been further expanded by distributing computer mainframes and linking them together in networking configurations. Interaction between computers in a network environment no longer requires human initiation of such automated processes as decisions. These widely dispersed computer systems, referred to as automated decision-making systems, are based on preprogrammed parameters. Disbursements of large amounts of money, transfers of funds from one bank to another, and movement of goods from one location to another or to multiple locations is accomplished regularly without human intervention.

Distributed Processing

The introduction and exponential growth of mini- and microcomputers effectively distributes computer utility to a never-ending population of users and applications. Providing security in the distributed minicomputer environment requires many of the same controls needed for larger systems. However, the very fact that an organization may have tens or hundreds of minicomputers means that it increasingly relies on the human element. Each application and the type of data processed will be a major determinant of the level of security required. Each minicomputer system and terminal area must be viewed as an independent installation with unique security requirements.

Complexity

The growth of technology has made computer resources available to an ever-increasing proportion of the population. It is estimated that approximately 50% of the working population of the United States is involved in information processing. The demand for computer-based information systems has indeed wrought a highly sophisticated and complex society. The state-of-the-art has engendered highly specialized job classifications and skills in the data processing field. For example, one of the recent releases of the IBM VS Operating System contains some 2.9 million lines of assembly language code. Operating systems of this magnitude are not within the ken of one person. A major vulnerability exists simply in that no one person can completely understand the detailed functioning of such systems.

Asynchronous Processing

As more complex systems are developed, technology has provided the capability to process asynchronously. In today's systems, many diverse processes are executed simultaneously in a random order. Many interactions taking place at millionths and billionths of a second make it impossible for most of us to comprehend, much less assure, a flow of control in such an environment.

To realize the highest levels of performance and efficiency of complex systems requires sophisticated computer-based evaluation systems. When one considers that efficiency and performance are major design goals of computer systems, it is unsettling to realize that it is now necessary to use computer technology to determine how to achieve performance goals. Security, on the other hand, has not been a design objective. Security requirements are normally added to a complex system as an afterthought. Reliance on operating systems and hardware to provide reasonable security is not sensible. Complexity, in and of itself, is a major aspect of vulnerability.

Resource-Sharing

Multiprogramming, multiprocessing, and networking have extended computer capability to many application areas. The computer is shared by many organizational users, and data proprietary to one owner must now be isolated from unauthorized persons by the technology of computer hardware and software. The term generally applied when separate systems are electronically interconnected is resource-sharing. This feature provides the opportunity for a penetrator to use one computer mainframe to attack or exploit another in the network.

The system is vulnerable because the number of processes, the amount of information, and the population of users has increased dramatically. As with the complexity issue, performance and efficiency are the major design goals. Security has only recently become a design requirement.

Perceptions

Every computer system has vulnerabilities which can be exploited. The security problem is usually viewed in terms of protecting against exploitation. Until recently, much of the data processing community believed that security in the data processing environment was a nuisance factor, and security, per se, did not directly aid the performance of an organization's daily work. Today, various segments of the user community are realizing that the *lack* of secure systems not only inhibits the performance of an organization's functions, but also jeopardizes its very existence.

As the perception of the problem has changed, so has the solution. In the past, the retrofit of security into systems was believed to be a viable approach. Now it is recognized that security must be a design requirement.

Defining security requirements involves understanding the inherent vulnerabilities of a computer system that are in part due to its technology, development, and implementation. A major step in this process is understanding what data are worth protecting, by regulation or management decision. It is also necessary to understand the value of information to would-be perpetrators, as well as to the agency or corporation.

SECURITY AS A MANAGEMENT ISSUE

> Much has been written about computer security, and everyone agrees that it is a very important subject in today's business world. The increasing importance of the computer in business requires that a Data Processing Manager be aware of his responsibilities to protect the company's valuable computer resources. But all too often, there is greater emphasis on getting the work out, and less on computer security. Many managers display the 'it can't happen to us' attitude, and do not recognize the fact that they are particularly vulnerable to sudden, unexpected loss.
>
> Jack P. Curry
> Vice President
> Ranier Bank
> Seattle, Washington

In the four years since Mr. Curry made this statement, security awareness on the part of most data processing professionals has changed immeasurably. The industry is constantly reminded of the consequences of security weaknesses, through the news media, mailings, seminars, and conferences and, painfully, through the number of computer-related crimes being perpetrated; paralleling the rapid growth in computer technology, albeit lagging slightly behind, has been the development of several technical security advancements, from physical access to software access controls. In addition, a plethora of security consulting firms has evolved to provide security services. The net result has been that management has gradually realized that information systems are a valuable resource, generally possessing numerous security flaws and subject to a number of threats from many sources. That management has become aware of these security issues is progress.

However, recognition of the problem is only the first step. Effective security procedures must be devised and implemented in an orderly manner.

In spite of management's recognition of today's computer security issues, most organizations have failed to respond sufficiently to either externally imposed requirements or internally developed policies and standards. Protective measures typically are applied in a haphazard, inconsistent, and perhaps costly manner. EDP security practices are often not effective because they are not properly implemented and enforced. Many corporations today face a high probability of financial loss due to increased levels of EDP risk exposure. The proper response to such increased risk exposures is a comprehensive EDP security program developed and directed by a formal corporate function responsible for protecting the organization's EDP resources.

Often claiming that they cannot afford an effective computer security program, many corporations choose to accept the risk. Such firms are playing a deadly game of Russian roulette. Instead, they should be balancing the costs of various levels of computer protection against the tremendous potential risks involved. It has been often stated that an institution or business that cannot afford adequate computer protection cannot afford a computer operation. A corollary is that any institution or business that does not have adequate computer protection will not have a computer operation very long.

IMPLICATIONS OF FEDERAL LEGISLATION

Over the past several years, the federal government has enacted into law a variety of major acts relating to the issue of privacy and computer security. Most prominent of these are the Foreign Corrupt Practices Act of 1977, the Privacy Act of 1974, and the Electronic Funds Transfer Act of 1980.

The key provision of the Foreign Corrupt Practices Act states that all publicly held companies that report to the SEC shall '. . . make and keep books, records, and accounts, which in reasonable detail, accurately and fairly reflect the transactions and dispositions of the assets of the issuer'. Assets include the computer system itself and the data it contains, as well as all other forms of assets. Internal controls over company assets may demand control over the computer systems on which we have come to depend.

Perhaps the key here is 'reasonableness.' No single definition yet explains what constitutes reasonable detail. In early 1981, SEC chairman Harold M. Williams stated that 'Reasonableness depends on an evaluation of all the facts and circumstances.' He further added that while the best or most effective control measure need not be employed, the one selected must be reasonable under all circumstances. Failure of corporate management to implement adequate security controls to protect their data processing resources leaves them liable to their shareholders for damages.

In contrast to the Foreign Corrupt Practices Act, which protects the stockholders of a company, the Electronic Funds Transfer (EFT) Act is a federal consumer protection law. It is concerned with all institutions providing EFT services. Liability is only for actual damages that can be proved. Thus, losses incurred from a breakdown in the computer or communication system operations or from a breach in security may be claimed.

The Privacy Act of 1974 established a number of procedural requirements regarding the collection, storage, protection, and dissemination of individual personal data. Perhaps the key element in the Act as it pertains to data processing is the protection of Privacy Data from unauthorized disclosure and use. Federal data processing systems contain vast repositories of personal data; and under the provisions of the Privacy Act, they are liable to the individuals concerned for failure to protect that data from unauthorized persons and use.

Just as the federal acts apply to federal government operation, states are enacting laws (based in large part on the federal acts) which will apply to companies and state agencies.

> Management must be ready for these regulations upon their operations. The concerns of the private sector go well beyond the personal information disclosures covered by privacy legislation. The very viability of a company may depend on the security of sensitive information having to do with future plans, expansion of markets, proprietary secrets, financial conditions of the company, and so on. If these types of information are stored in a computer-controlled information system, their protection becomes as significant to the company as personal information may be to the individual.
>
> In summary, security can never be 100 percent, because what human ingenuity can devise, other human ingenuity can penetrate. Security measures, then, must be devised which would make penetration of a computerized information system so expensive as to make such activity unprofitable. By 'expensive' we mean to include the consequences of being apprehended. The new computer crime bills enacted in several states provide for severe penalties, including conviction of felonies with attendant long jail sentences and heavy fines.[1]

RISK ASSESSMENT

It is the responsibility of management to protect and preserve the assets of the organization. As concerns the data processing facility and the data stored, processed, and produced there, a large set of factors can contribute to its protection. It is universally recognized that no data processing installation or computer system can ever be made completely secure against data disclosure, physical damage, unauthorized access to data, or interruption of services. Through the use of risk assessment techniques, however, it is possible to determine which particular combination of security measures will provide a reasonable level of security at an acceptable cost.

Risk assessment is a widely accepted procedure for estimating the anticipated or expected loss from some adverse event. It has a history of use in risk management investment decisions and in insurance risk calculations. Applied to EDP systems, risk assessment is a systematic, quantitative, and qualitative procedure for estimating the exposure of an EDP resource to a given threat, and for evaluating the level and the allocation of security safeguards. EDP 'resources' in the broad sense include equipment, facilities, software, and data, all of which are continuously available. Thus, risk assessment is a determined attempt to organize the EDP security problem around a set of established procedures for estimating risks, for evaluating the needed level of computer security, and for selecting cost-effective safeguards.

Risk assessment, which deals with a unique set of resources and conditions, is an assessment of the security profile of a specific facility or system. For a risk assessment to fulfill its purpose, it must present a comprehensive description of threats at a particular place or to a specific system, at a specific time, with known and documented existing conditions. For instance, a risk assessment performed on an EDP facility with no off-site storage available and no terminals permitting remote processing would have little relevance after the facility established off-site storage facilities or installed an interactive distributed processing system.

Realizing the importance, but lack of scientific precision, of risk assessment, a formalized step-by-step approach must be taken in collecting pertinent data, analyzing the results and implications of many variables, and preparing the final report for management. Risk assessment is an art, not a science. In computing risk exposures, the risk analyst attempts to predict future events. The specific ingredients required for a risk assessment will differ from facility to facility or from system to system (for example, the scope of the assets analyzed or the types of threats included).

In the past, management decisions to implement or do without various security measures have generally been made on a subjective basis following an actual security incident or event. Now, however, the complexity of data processing systems and the legal requirements imposed by the Foreign Corrupt Practices Act and privacy legislation have caused this method of decision-making to be outdated, inaccurate, and generally unusable. In many organizations, the risk assessment process has replaced the former subjective method of safeguard selection.

A risk assessment attempts to strike an economic balance between the impact of risks and the cost of protective measures. The analysis shows the current security posture, then assembles the basic facts necessary for the selection of adequate, cost-effective safeguards. A risk assessment provides management with information on which to base decisions, e.g., whether it is best to prevent the occurrence of a situation, to contain the effect it may have, or simply to recognize that a potential for loss exists. Because a risk assessment is the basis for such decisions, its findings of loss or damage must be presented, whenever possible, in a quantitative fashion.

A number of other methods available for inspecting, testing, or evaluating security are penetration attempts, vulnerability studies, security audits, checklists, and questionnaires. Although they may be an adjunct to a risk assessment, none of them can be a substitute because their purposes are different and they do not consider the key elements of damage, likelihood of occurrence, or cost of recommended controls.

Conducting a risk assessment offers the following benefits:

1. Gives guidance on the amount of resources to spend on each security measure. Permits scarce resources (people, money, equipment) to be allocated where payoffs are highest.
2. Alerts management to near-term risks with unacceptable economic, political, social, or ethical consequences.
3. Pinpoints the need for corrective actions.
4. Directly relates objectives of the security program to the functions of the organization.
5. Increases security awareness at all organizational levels.
6. Results in criteria for designing and evaluating contingency plans for backup operation, recovery from a disaster, and ways to deal with emergencies.

The limitations of a risk assessment are threefold:

1. Risk assessment deals with future events; making predictions of both loss and occurrence rates is extremely difficult, if not impossible in some cases. However, the risk assessment provides a means of ordering the relative importance of various perceived or actual threats and gives management a better perspective of the overall situation.
2. The information upon which the risk analyst bases predictions is imperfect. However, this limitation is not severe provided that the risk analyst utilizes reasonable estimates in performing the calculations and adequately documents the assumptions and findings.
3. Risk assessment is an analytical process with a large number of variables, many of which are unique to the environment under consideration, either in their individual natures or the manner in which they interrelate. For this reason, no single methodology within the general state-of-the-art is broadly applicable to all risk management environments.

PHYSICAL SECURITY AND PERSONNEL PRACTICES

Physical security and administrative controls are the foundation of any computer security program and in many instances parallel user requirements for assurances of physical protection. They are a necessary, but not sufficient, condition to provide protection against data loss, modification, or destruction. In addition, tangible assets of equipment, supplies, and documentation must be protected by physical means. Any software protection is operative only through a setting of employee awareness, good personnel practices, administrative security proce- dures, and physical access restrictions. A secure operating system is useless if anyone can obtain sensitive data by walking into an open tape library or by bribing an employee. Not only do computer centers and data terminal areas contain assets of extremely high value; they also include technical and/or administrative controls over data which can be defeated by permitting unrestricted physical access to central computers or communication devices.

Degree of Controls Needed

No algorithm exists for calculating the degree of control that a computer center may need, for this formula is a function of data sensitivity and risk. The type of protection at a given site is usually predicated upon a thorough analysis of two factors:

1. The impact of loss, which is a measure of the importance and value of the physical facilities as well as the data processed within them.
2. The vulnerability or susceptibility of the location to given threats of natural hazards (flood, storm, earthquake, volcano), accidents (fire, power interrup- tions, environmental failure, telecommunications interruptions, human errors), and intentional acts (vandalism, unauthorized use, denial of service, theft).

Physical Security Principles

The establishment of an adequate physical security environment within the data center is an important part of achieving a secure data processing environment. This security can be achieved through adherence to the following basic physical security principles:

1. Physical security protection provided through in-depth application of a series of barriers and procedures, including continual surveillance (human or electronic) of the protected area.
2. Positive physical access controls established to prevent unauthorized entry into the data center and other critical areas which support or affect the operation of computer equipment or the processing of data by this equip- ment.
3. Effects of disasters such as fire, storms, and floods prevented, controlled, or minimized to the extent economically feasible by the use of detection equip- ment, extinguishing systems, and well-conceived and tested emergency plans.
4. Continued stability of environmental support systems provided by adequate physical protection and aggressive procedural controls.

Personnel Practices

Security is only as strong as the weakest link. Even in a computer facility with strong physical, technical, and other administrative controls, the people who program, operate, maintain, or access the EDP system are generally the weakest link in the security chain. However, numerous protective measures can be implemented to strengthen this vital link; these measures can be broadly viewed as personnel practices.

1. Procedures must be implemented for changing or withdrawing all access media (i.e., passwords, keys, badges, combinations) upon termination or reassignment of employees. Employees about to be terminated must not be permitted access to the data processing facilities after receiving their termination notice.
2. All positions which normally permit incumbents to access the computer facilities, its software, or data itself should be so designated, and requirements for background screening established for different levels of access (e.g., operators, programmers, users). The need-to-know concept must be established at all levels.
3. Separation of duties, rotation of duties, and enforced mandatory vacation periods are practices that help to discourage fraudulent activities.
4. Security awareness training must be continuous to ensure that employees challenge unescorted visitors, remain attentive to disgruntled employee activity, and are observant of potential security vulnerabilities.

Personnel security is concerned not only with the integrity of the internal data processing staff of managers, analysts, programmers, and operators but also with external problems involving users, competitors, criminals, disgruntled former employees, contractors, and 'friends' of data center employees. A combination of physical site, software, and procedural security measures, together with improved internal data center hiring and personnel policies, will serve to reduce the external threat considerably. Security is everybody's business, and all employees must know their responsibilities.

HARDWARE AND OPERATING SYSTEMS

Over the years, as the computer industry evolved, hardware and operating software design objectives were rarely oriented toward security authorization controls and audit trails. The reason is quite obvious. Controls tend to inhibit efficiency, and the users of computing power have been far more interested in efficiency than in control. However, as the impact of system failure and computer abuse has become well known, the need for control and security mechanisms is forcing computer manufacturers, software designers, and users to give careful consideration to the architectural elements of systems security. Security features in hardware have been implemented from the time that systems shared more than one user job in memory during a given time. The security was designed so that one job would not inadvertently destroy or affect another. As systems evolved to multiprogramming and multiprocessing, the integrity problems became more complex to handle. At the same time, serious security issues were raised.

Hardware Mechanisms

Hardware-based controls are normally designed to prevent inadvertent system integrity problems caused by wrong address references in a multiprogrammed environment. The two basic mechanisms are memory protection and privileged instructions. Other, more sophisticated approaches are beginning to appear as security and control become design issues.

Independent of the hardware architectures are basic security-related requirements, which should be reviewed whenever choosing or evaluating given hardware. This factor is especially important when reviewing minicomputers or word processing units.

1. Access privilege verifications and memory bounds checking should be performed when access to the system or file occur, or during data transfers between memory and storage devices. Control measures within this area include terminal identification, communication or I/O channel identification, message validation, and other validation or accuracy checks.
2. Hardware/processor architecture design should include equipment controls whose purpose is to ensure functional correctness. Simple integrity features, such as parity characters and hardware validity checks, enhance system security and also help protect against equipment malfunctions.
3. The integrity of hardware protection mechanisms should be verified either periodically or continuously. This check would include software monitoring techniques, maintenance logging, and subsequent review and analysis by systems engineering personnel.
4. It is highly desirable that access and entrance to the supervisory or executive mode be hardware controlled by means of identification and authorization verification implemented in microcode.

Hardware security features provide, as fundamental protection, mechanisms against unauthorized access to the system and the contents of data files.

Since the inclusion of hardware security features will be predicated upon or limited by such factors as architecture design, system sophistication, type of computer (mini versus large frame), and performance degradation, other compensatory security measures may be applicable. Compensatory actions would include but not be limited to:

1. Utilization of software techniques.
2. Operational policies and procedures.

3. Manual control and review procedures.
4. Audit review program.

Operating System Mechanisms

Hardware security features do not operate in a vacuum, but are implemented through the operating system software. The trend is to take more and more of the physical machine handling functions out of the hands of the operator and move them into the operating system software or firmware. As a result, many of the inherently susceptible areas for security breaches are being reduced because of less human handling.

It is the operating system that assigns resources and supervises actions within a system, and a number of functions provide this management and control. Some of the more relevant functions for purposes of security and integrity are:

1. Executive routines.
2. Job control language.
3. Scheduling routines.
4. Resource allocation.
5. Communications functions.
6. Dispatcher routines.
7. Memory allocation.
8. I/O routines.
9. General-purpose utility routines.

When evaluating operating systems, certain key elements are essential to operating system security.

1. *Isolation.* This feature is the basic and fundamental principle of security. Users must be protected from each other, from the system, and from themselves, through the use of software, hardware boundary and register mechanisms.
2. *Identification and Authentication.* A remotely accessed computer system should be equipped to identify all individual users and substantiate that the user is, in fact, who he claims to be.
3. *Controlled Access.* The concept of controlled access implies that each properly identified user is permitted by the executive or control software to access system data and resources to which he is authorized, but not more. File access authorizations, security profile mechanisms, and terminal access limitations are software techniques that can be used to control or restrict user access. Other known techniques include user passwords, terminal identification, and communications channel identification.
4. *Operating System Integrity.* The security of most general-purpose computer systems depends in some degree on the integrity of the system control

program. Ideally, it should be stored in read-only memory and protected by software controls so that a program operating in user mode is prevented from performing unauthorized executive functions.

5. *Residue Clean Out.* A beneficial system software feature is the erasure of data residue in memory segments or on-line storage areas prior to reallocation by the central program.

6. *Audit Trail.* It is highly desirable for the system software to be capable of identifying, reporting, and assigning accountability for potential compromises. A history log or audit trail containing a record of system transactions related to the accessing or modifying of sensitive data or internal protective features can facilitate the study of system activities that may be questionable or suspicious.

COMMUNICATIONS/NETWORK SECURITY

The fastest growing expenditure in most corporate and governmental organizations is that for data communications. In the early and mid-1970s, data communications was perceived as being the relatively straightforward analog path between computers and their remote batch or time-shared asynchronous terminals. The evolution to true distributed data processing, made possible by microprocessor technology, has caused most organizations to rethink the role of communications functions and to put increasing emphasis on the integration and expansion of telecommunications services.

In a distributed environment, the concept of a node could encompass either computational devices or terminals. The interface devices (modems, concentrators, or multiplexors) which facilitate communications through protocols, transmission facilities, and even networks may be dissimilar or incompatible. Depending on the nature of the interface, it can be thought of as part of the host system, the communications link, or remote station.

In most environments, implementation of data communications service adds an order of magnitude in terms of complexity. The addition of an in-house network, the interfacing to a myriad of common carrier or value-added networks, the dialogue between two computer systems, and even the relatively simple enhancements of Remote Job Entry (RJE) or time-sharing provide an immense amount of complicated protocol, requirements for error controls, need for high reliability, and dependence by users on multiple systems and vendors. Most of the complexities arise from the following factors:

1. Computers can control multiple communications systems, lines, and ports.
2. Any given communications line can be shared by many terminals.
3. Any given communications system can be shared by many computers.
4. The provision of communications service by many vendors other than the phone companies presents a wide choice of possibilities with complex sets of cost and service trade-offs.

5. The expense of implementing a major in-house network makes the consideration of specialized vendors of value-added communications services an attractive choice; but local control is lost, and the organization must rely on the vendor(s).
6. The need to link many dissimilar operational functions such as word processing, electronic mail, teleconferencing, scientific or engineering data processing, or business data processing across many locations and among different computers makes the interfacing decision of primary concern.
7. The requirement to share data among different organizational entities adds technical complexity and explicit considerations of authority and responsibility.

In many cases the data communications function is asked to solve these issues via technology, when often the problems are behavioral and organizational in nature.

Security Issues

The two primary determinants of systems security requirements are the extent of shared resources and the degree of complexity. Data communications systems are designed to increase the accessibility of data by means of multiple access paths and widespread geographic distribution. Thus, such systems become excellent targets for security breaches, and the risk of given system failures increases.

In addition to providing increased opportunities for failure or for masking of security breaches, many data communications systems present the additional problem of misrouting sensitive data. In many commercial time-sharing systems, the 'port intrusion' problem is given top priority, and all such instances are treated as serious security breaches. In addition, except for classified government networks, little thought has generally been given to the intentional insertion of clandestine code into communications software to subvert data. Given the complexity of such hardware/software systems, such acts of industrial espionage could be accomplished with ease.

Other factors relating to the need for effective communications security are:

1. The transmission links are usually under vendor control, yet are susceptible to the same physical or logical security intrusions as the primary company facility.
2. Most communications equipment, except for major concentrators or processors, is located in unattended or insecure facilities.
3. Additional threats, not normally considered as part of computer security, can subvert a communications system. These threats will be described later.
4. Some basic design deficiencies make the security of a given system quite tenuous. For example, dial-up access to a time-shared computer system is inherently insecurable.

5. The traditional attitude of most managers and technical specialists is that the risks are trivial. This problem is compounded by the fact that most cases of industrial espionage through breaches of communications security are not publicized.

The preceding factors would suggest that the communications security problem is severe, yet generally underestimated.

It should be noted that the usual threats facing computer systems also can apply to data communications systems. Natural hazards such as storms, earthquakes, and floods can affect data communications facilities, which in this case includes intermediate switching points and control modes. Accidents such as fire or human errors can as easily affect a telephone company facility as an in-house computer center. Finally, acts of computer sabotage, manipulation of software, and tampering with data, can apply in a communications environment as easily as in a main computer center.

The myth that communications security is not an issue and the fact that the technology is new lead to a syndrome of 'undercontrol'. Thus, systems are designed without management, administrative, or technical control procedures. Audit trails to show message routing and disposition are many times inadequate. Marking, tracing, and evaluation of lines, ports, and patch-panels make channel and port identification somewhat problematical and difficult to control. Physical access controls to many sensitive areas are nonexistent. Password management and other access control software are often inadequate at best. Finally, despite attempts to provide redundancy and fail-safe operation, every system has bottlenecks, wherein a single-point failure could mean disaster.

APPLICATION SYSTEM DESIGN

Security concerns should be an integral part of the planning, development, and operation of a computer application. Unfortunately, as is the case in so many manual operations that have been converted to automated systems, certain manual security control techniques are eliminated. However, even in an automated environment it should be expected that security control objectives would remain essentially the same. In actuality, the requirements for security controls increase dramatically as an organization converts to an on-line or data base processing environment.

Each application system should utilize security controls which, under given circumstances, provide for adequate measures to ensure the accuracy, completeness, security, auditability, and validity of data processed. The selection of those controls depends on the sensitivity of the data accessed, processed, or produced, the degree of harm that can result from unauthorized actions, and the vulnerabilities existing in the environment in which the application operates.

'While the selection of controls is still an art based on experience and good judgment, it is possible to make this selection if it is not overly constrained by poor planning for security'[2] or by an inadequate definition of what the application is supposed to do. The life cycle of a computer application consists of three identifiable phases: requirements, or initiation; development; and implementation, or operation. After some period of operation, the system undoubtedly will have to undergo a revision, and the life cycle is then repeated. Security concerns must be included in each of these phases.

Observing security and control requirements over the entire system life cycle is of critical importance from two standpoints. First, since security controls are introduced in the original design, their long-run implementation costs are normally less than when systems are retrofitted. Second, since the security controls are a part of initial specification, protection against losses exists for a longer period of time. From a systems architecture viewpoint, it is much more difficult to design security after-the-fact and quite often it is not nearly as effective, or complete.

Any system, to provide a fundamental level of security, should reflect certain attributes, which may be manifested in whole or in part by several types of security measures: administrative, physical, and technical. These attributes are briefly explained:

1. *Identification.* All users, data, programs, transactions, outputs, and other system elements and resources should be uniquely and adequately identified. Such identification is necessary for the other security attributes to be present.
2. *Authorization.* Mechanisms must be present to authorize (i.e., approve) the access of users, programs, terminals, and transactions to system resources, such as transactions and data.
3. *Access Control.* Technical, physical, and administrative mechanisms are needed to control access within the system in accordance with the authorization process.
4. *Controllability.* The system must be designed and constructed in such a way that its various components (e.g., transaction modules, programs, operating system interfaces, and data base) can control fully the data or capabilities they share with each other.
5. *Integrity.* The system must perform its designated functions, and *only* those functions, correctly and consistently, within time constraints and exactly according to specifications. This restriction implies integrity requirements for data, programs, and the processing capability itself.
6. *Recoverability.* The system must be designed and operated in such a manner as to enable timely recovery from loss of data or processing capability due to the entire range of minor (e.g., power fluctuation) to catastrophic (e.g., fire) threats.
7. *Auditability.* Activity within the system and at its interfaces must be identifiable and accountable.

Each security requirement must be stated in concrete terms, with a specific metric so that management will know when and whether the requirement is being met.

CRYPTOGRAPHY

Crypotography is not well understood by most computer professionals, and with good reason. It is deeply involved with esoteric areas of mathematics, including number theory. Most of the technology has evolved under deep military secrecy, and few articles or papers with a computer orientation have been written for non-mathematicians. However, it is a sufficiently important subject to deserve textual treatment, at a level of detail necessary to discuss its concepts and to allow the reader to understand its use.

It has been noted that the choicest targets for passive eavesdropping of communications traffic may not be the military or diplomatic traffic of governments, but the large companies or banks that transfer billions of dollars of funds via satellite and other data communications services. Information about such topics as clients, markets, and movement of energy resources, can be used and manipulated much more easily and more profitably than a few funds' transfer transactions can be comprised. In addition, the only way to secure sensitive internal data from a very large body of systems professionals is to encrypt the files. Home-brewed, software-based encryption schemes generally do not work.

The basic premise for encryption is that certain information being used should be secure from disclosure. To keep this information inviolate, it is transformed into a new form which can be read only by someone in possession of additional, secret information, called a 'key'.

The original information is called 'plaintext', which is transformed into 'ciphertext' by applying an invertible transformation ('encipherment').

The recipient 'deciphers' the ciphertext with the inverse transformation to obtain the original plaintext.

The transformation used is chosen from a family of related transformations (a 'cryptographic system') by designating a 'key'. The set of all possible keys is called the 'keyspace'.

When evaluating a cryptographic system, it is generally assumed that the opponents know the system (which is usually difficult to change in the field), but not the key (which is usually easily changed). Indeed, 'breaking' a cryptographic system consists of determining what key was used.

Data Encryption Standard (DES)

Given the obvious need to provide adequate cryptographic methods for securing computer data and traffic, the National Bureau of Standards requested that industry supply algorithms, which were subsequently evaluated. An IBM algorithm was selected and published as the DES in January 1977. This standard commercial cryptographic system is probably the only standard encryption technique that is likely to be implemented in unclassified hardware in the foreseeable future.

DES has been attacked by critics as being too trivial, or even breakable under certain conditions. However, despite certain design properties which might reduce an opponent's search time, no feasible cryptanalytic technique for breaking DES has yet been found. Exhaustive key searching would be conceivable only with a specialized computer system, searching the keyspace of 10^{17} keys daily and costing in excess of $20 million.

Of more interest is that DES is available in devices marketed by several vendors. Implementation choices range from complex communications devices down to a single chip costing less than $100. DES is now used in bank funds transfer systems, in private company networks, in electronic mail systems, in manufacturing processes, and in personnel and payroll systems.

As the security of the system is no better than the security of the key, the sender and recipient(s) must exchange the key in a way that is presumably more secure than the cryptographic system. Suppose that secure key exchange is impractical; what then?

'Public Key' System

The concept of the 'public key system' is an attempt at solving this class of problem by eliminating the need to exchange keys on an individual pair basis; it has nothing to do with the type of encryption actually used to secure the message, which could be DES, Caesar cipher, or the good old Secret Decoder Ring. What is needed is the magic that will allow perhaps a single item to serve as a key for everyone that one needs to talk with, something about which he can publicly announce. 'Use this when you talk to me, and your messages will arrive here encrypted in a way that only you and I can decrypt.'

It is not quite as magical as it sounds. A number of public key systems have been proposed. The basic idea is usually to create an algorithm that can be split into two parts; then, using a private key, each individual generates a public key. 'When I send a message to you, I appropriately use both your public key and my private key to encrypt, and when you decrypt it, you use my public key and your own private key to decrypt.'

Just any old algorithm is not going to work, and defining the 'right kind' of algorithm is quite difficult. Not only must the keys work as described in the preceding paragraph, but no one must be able to determine what the private keys are by fooling around with the public keys. Generally these algorithms tend to be 'easy' to compute (encrypt), but hard to invert (decrypt) without some additional information. For example, it is easy to multiply two large primes, A and B, to form the product, C, but it is hard to factor C into A and B without knowing either A or B.

To date, no one appears to have gone beyond the paper algorithm stage, at least in the unclassified literature. Such systems will soon be tried, as they appear to be simple to implement (if you understand the mathematics), and are of high value in electronic mail and distributed data processing. As these techniques are also related to the idea of an 'electronic signature', more and more pressure is being exerted to get this type of system satisfactorily tested and implemented as a commercial reality.

EDP AUDITING

The necessity for adequate EDP security, internal controls, and procedures plus soundly practiced accounting procedures, has increased the need for an awareness of the effects which computers engender. The computer's impact varies depending on the level of complexity of the computer system and the sophistication of the applications being processed. The more that diverse manual procedures are placed in computers, and the more unavailable the procedures are for review, the more complicated the auditor's work becomes.

The objectives of auditing have not changed, but the environment within which they are sought has. In turn, auditors must adjust their thinking, modify their approaches, and tailor their reviews to fit the current environment. This custom approach involves a basic knowledge of EDP equipment, organization, and functions. It also requires a new breed of auditor—the EDP auditor, who provides the knowledge and specialities to perform EDP audits.

Nature of Auditing

Auditing is an independent appraisal activity within an organization that provides a review of operations as a service to management. It is a managerial control which functions by measuring and evaluating the effectiveness of other controls. Most audits can be classified into three general types: financial, compliance, and managerial.

The financial audit, enmeshed in financial records and accounting transactions, has its core in the question:

'Do the financial statements (i.e., the consolidated balance sheet and related statements of income, stockholders' equity, and changes in financial position) present fairly the financial position of the entity?'

The compliance audit takes policies and standards as given and then asks, 'Are we doing things right?' It is really asking whether we are going by the book.

The management audit is highly skeptical and potentially radical. It asks, 'Are we doing the right things?'

Scope of EDP Auditing

EDP auditing does not and cannot fall neatly into one of the three 'pure' categories. The combination of managerial effectiveness and the finance and accounting functions is a vital area for any organization, and one rich in complexity and detail. But is it an area of concern for the EDP auditor? The answer is yes, because specific application systems—such as accounts receivable—can be examined from the standpoint of improving financial results through better cash management and funds flow. In other words, several accounting and financial management systems are present in any organization. Each of them was designed and implemented to meet certain objectives. The EDP auditor should be equipped to find out whether these objectives are being met.

The extent to which on-going operations in the finance and accounting function conform to established policies, standards, procedures, and principles becomes an area of interest for the EDP auditor as part of a general controls review, especially in dealing with:

1. Organizational issues and separation of duties.
2. Personnel practices.
3. System controls for data, documents, and dollars.

An area of prime interest for the EDP auditor is management's adherence to regulations, policies, and standards across the entire spectrum of EDP activities. Moreover, the EDP auditor should be sufficiently independent to call into question the relevance and utility of the very standards and controls used as the compliance benchmark.

In the last analysis, the bringing together of the triple facets of financial, compliance, and managerial auditing forms the true realm of EDP auditing. It is here that the three objectives of protecting assets, monitoring compliance, and improving performance interact.

Noting that system security deals with protecting information, programs, and resources, the EDP auditing function is one of the most powerful tools available to management to ensure that systems are used properly and to provide the type of control necessary to oversee the entire information flow.

CONTINGENCY PLANNING

Because of the increasing organizational dependence upon the continued availability of data processing and data communications capability, most organizations cannot afford extended interruptions of their information processing systems. Surveys have shown that some organizations are imperiled after even a two-day disruption of their computer center. Reversion to manual processing often becomes nearly impossible if the organization's data processing facilities are non-operational. The process of recovery from an interruption of service can be complex and difficult; without a detailed plan, it may even be impossible.

Organization for recovery from a catastrophic occurrence and development of a computer center contingency plan should be undertaken prior to the need for such a plan. Since 100% security can never be provided, it is imperative that a high level of backup and recovery capability be established. Effective plans must be devised, tested, maintained, and updated for each computer center as well as for the remote processing sites.

Backup and Recovery Strategy

An EDP contingency plan should be embodied in a single document which frames the steps to be taken and the decisions to be made in the event of a disaster that disables the organization's computing resources. Such a plan would encompass short- and long-term recovery, both on-site, at a temporary alternate site, and at a new permanent or semi-permanent EDP facility. Priorities should be identified and employees should be trained in the use of the plan. This plan should be all-encompassing, leaving little to guesswork as that would result in hasty decision-making under crisis conditions. The plan must be sufficiently detailed so that the responsible personnel have no doubts as to the specific actions they must take. It should periodically be tested by simulating a disaster and exercising the steps contained within it. Finally, it must be revised, following a test, in order to correct the deficiencies.

Short-Term Recovery

Most EDP facilities are subject to everyday short-term outages, from several minutes to several hours. Jobs require rerun, and records must be recreated. While many occurrences of these outages can lead to considerable expense, they are controllable through the use of routine software and hardware recovery procedures. A larger problem that confronts the facility manager, however, is the question of short-term delays in processing.

A short-term contingency can be defined in terms of time. Normally, 24 hours or less is a baseline short-term contingency. These contingencies can result from such things as a power interruption, minor damage to a computer's logical circuitry, or disruption from a minor fire. The thrust of a short-term recovery effort is therefore to minimize the effects of these contingencies and to allow recovery to take place at the site experiencing the problem. It is the task of the on-going security program, on the other hand, to keep these contingencies from erupting into major disasters where possible.

Short-term recovery plans may be entirely an EDP function, as when an operator error or data error is involved. In the case of a power interruption, the delay may not be predictable and the extended contingency plan may need to be placed in motion. In any case, the short-term plan should separate the predictable short delays from the possible long-term ones, and it should invoke the respective procedures. The short-term recovery procedures should be able to restore all EDP assets and information to their original states quickly and inexpensively. Various threats, such as small water leakages and minor fires, should be evaluated in terms of their delay effects. It is important to defend against the short-term contingencies that chronically beset an EDP facility or system, and to prevent acute small contingencies from growing into larger ones.

Long-Term Recovery

Planning for a lengthy interruption of the EDP function requires much more effort than would be expended in the short-term case. A lengthy interruption is likely to curtail the organization's mission effectiveness and is therefore intolerable. A backup and recovery plan is a realization that an extended delay cannot be tolerated since alternative EDP processing will need to be used in the event of a disaster.

Failure Scenarios

A number of different scenarios can reflect what could occur at or to a computer center to create the need for backup and recovery actions. For the purposes of a general ranking, failure scenarios can be grouped into three basic categories:

1. Common failures (likely to occur regularly).
2. Uncommon failures (unlikely to occur regularly).
3. One-time failures (unlikely to occur more than once).

Actions which can be taken to mitigate the effects of the failure scenarios focus on two basic strategies: preventive measures and recovery plans. These strategies should be developed so that the most applicable can be implemented in time of need.

Preventive Measures. These measures serve to ease recovery from a fault, failure, or disaster, and are inherent in the system design. For backup and recovery purposes, preventive actions can be categorized in four major areas: design of software and systems, disaster plans, duplication of system components, and an on-going measurement program.

Planning for Recovery. Preparation of a recovery plan should enable personnel on the scene at the time of an assumed disaster to make decisions concerning what steps to take to restore services and recover from the emergency situation.

Objective

Contingency planning should provide information system management with the procedures that describe appropriate responses to an emergency situation at any location. The procedures themselves can never be completely detailed for any and all future emergencies. However, they should serve to minimize the impact of an emergency by providing an orderly operations plan for dealing with the disaster conditions. The intent is to anticipate the requirements common to emergencies and to provide a set of essential capabilities. This plan will allow selection of appropriate sequences of actions in response to a particular crisis.

REFERENCES

1. Enger, N. L., and Howerton, P. W.: *Computer Security.* New York, AMACOM, 1980, p. 18.
2. *Guidelines for Security of Computer Applications.* Federal Information Processing Standards (FIPS) 73, U.S. Department of Commerce, National Bureau of Standards, June 30, 1980.

Advances in Computer Security Management, Vol. 2
Edited by M. M. Wofsey
© 1983 John Wiley & Sons Ltd.

Chapter 2

COMPUTER SECURITY AS A MANAGEMENT ISSUE

Robert Campbell

Advanced Information Management Incorporated

Is computer security an important issue? Is it important enough to be brought before senior management for action, or should it be viewed as a technical matter to be resolved by data processors? These and similar questions have been debated for years without resolution. A clearer understanding of the problem and management's role in confronting the problem finally seems to be emerging.

The problems with the security of computer systems, that is, the inability of the technology to provide secure computers and the similar inability of users and operators to protect these insecure computer systems adequately, is one of the most vexing issues surrounding the technology. The importance of the computer security issue has not been recognized enough, although the increase in seriousness of the problem closely parallels the advance of data processing itself. The past three decades have seen the role of the computer grow from a technical curiosity to an administrative support tool, and then to an integral part of important business systems. The extent of reliance upon computers to perform vital business functions now makes it imperative that management give adequate attention to matters related to the security of sensitive and critical operational systems.

Senior management is becoming increasingly aware of their heavy reliance upon the technology. A recent study by the Financial Executive Research Foundation reported that the 'aspect of internal control that troubles executives most is the increasing dependence on computers. . .'. A small 1980 survey of executive attitudes on computer security, solicited from selected Fortune 1000 executives in conjunction with a major international computer security and fraud control conference, revealed that the majority of those executives responding felt that computer security was a serious corporate problem and that computer abuse and misuse are fairly widespread. Management is expressing growing concern over the role of computers in the business function. At the same time, this concern has yet to be translated into the degree of management involvement that many believe is necessary to deal with the problems adequately.

THE NEED FOR MANAGEMENT INVOLVEMENT

The need for strong management involvement in matters of security involving sensitive and critical computer systems can be understood by analyzing potential risks and resource impacts caused by lack of security.

The Nature of Risk

Computers control and process sensitive organizational data. If secret information stored in a computer system is compromised, who sustains the loss? Not the data processing function, but the overall organization and owners of the data sustain the loss. If sensitive personal information in an automated system is compromised, who sustains the loss? Again, not the data processing function but the individuals to whom the information belongs are the ones who lose. If corporate assets are embezzled or defrauded using an automated system, who sustains the loss? Again, it is not data processing but the business function as a whole. Finally, if the computer center or facilities are destroyed or disabled, who sustains the loss? In all of the loss situations just described, the only one that directly impacts the data center resources is the overall organization. This relationship is the primary reason why initial security precautions instituted by data processors will center primarily around physical protection of the data center. Again, because data processing perspectives have focused on direct loss of data processing capability, they have not normally seriously considered the impact upon important business functions—where the real losses are incurred.

Processing Loss

The key factor is the potential loss's impact upon the entire business organization. As businesses become more dependent upon computers, evidence suggests the potential for considerable loss in the event of delayed or denied processing. Studies on the extent of impact, such as that conducted by the University of Minnesota in 1978–1979,[1] indicate that critical business functions decay rapidly upon loss of data processing support. The Minnesota study concluded that, on the average, critical functions cannot continue more than 4.8 days after a catastrophe that disables the data center. Some industry groups are less tolerant of failure than others (e.g. financial businesses reach a critical point in only 2 days, distribution firms in 3.3 days). These figures are averages, however, and may not be representative of true impact. For example, while the critical point in the insurance industry group is an average of 5.6 days, the process of selecting applicants for issuance of policies drops to 50% of effectiveness in approximately 2 days, and effectively ceases in $3\frac{1}{2}$ days after the loss of processing.

Because lack of security has such strong potential impacts upon the organization, it is clearly in the best interests of the organization for senior officials to be actively involved in managing the security problem. Experience has shown all too often that, due to lack of awareness of the potential of the problem, senior management is not involved, thus leaving data processing personnel to make decisions regarding the risk when it is not their prerogative.

FUNCTIONS OF MANAGEMENT

Even in these days of enlightened knowledge about the problems of computer security there is still a great lack of understanding and appreciation for the role of top management in addressing these problems.

The Role of Top Management

In addition to establishing the mission of the business, charting its course, and generally functioning at the strategic level, top management is also responsible for recognizing, analyzing, and directing actions necessary to address serious problems. Depending upon the gravity of the problem, it may be handled at a lower level and never brought to top management for resolution. This practice, unfortunately, allows for serious misjudgment at lower levels, as is the case with the current level of understanding of the computer security problem, so that top management is rarely made aware of the serious potential of the problem.

A key role for top management, then, is to ensure the existence of a control system which will enforce adequate reporting and accountability for lower-level actions. While lower-level problem solving should take place at lower levels of the organization, senior management should also be made aware of the existence and resolution of the problem. In this manner, the top level of management can monitor the state of the business and be attuned to the development of serious problems. In those organizations where top management has not yet addressed the computer security problem, it is likely that the facts regarding its seriousness and its potential impact upon the organization are available but have not yet been brought to the attention of top management. The 1980 Financial Executive Research Foundation report on the state of internal controls in U.S. corporations bears this idea out in its finding that 'Corporate managements often believe that their data processing operations are much more tightly controlled than do either the heads of internal audit or the managers of data processing'.[2] The issue, then, is whether or not the computer security problem is serious enough to be brought to the attention of top management.

The Role of Middle Management

In addition to discharging those responsibilities within its assigned level of authority, middle management serves as a conduit for situations and information that should be brought to the attention of top management. Additionally, middle management acts to interpret and pass downward guidance and instructions in support of top management planning, policymaking, and objective setting activities. Middle management is a vital link in management's reporting system for monitoring and enforcing its control and accountability mechanisms. While 'management-by-exception' is essential in order to keep top management from becoming immersed in day-to-day activities, top management must have clearly defined standards (e.g., information thresholds) for its control and accountability mechanisms, or the process will not work. 'Management-by-exception' becomes 'management-by-deception' as vital indicators of potential problem areas and strayings of the business occur. Middle management shows a natural tendency to 'filter' information going up the chain to top management. An important function of middle management, therefore, is to support the information needs of top management in terms of problem recognition, analysis, and decision-making.

PLACEMENT OF THE COMPUTER SECURITY FUNCTION

Regarding the potential impact on the corporate organization of breaches of computer security or the loss of data processing support, the long-standing arguments for imbedding the computer security function deep within the data processing organization (i.e. under the data center manager) quickly fail the tests of logic. In defense of these arguments, senior management has contributed to prolonging the debate and thus the problems of computer security because of a basic conflict-of-interest situation that they have created for data processing management. Security has been relegated to a minor position, understandably, because data processing success is measured almost exclusively in terms of standard productivity measures. Quoting again from the Financial Executive Research Foundation Study:[2] 'the success of the data processing staff is most often measured in terms of its ability to respond quickly to user needs . . . providing ease and speed of access' to computer systems. Unless proper emphasis has been given to computer security when measuring data processing effectiveness, even placing the computer security official under the senior data processing manager (a position coming more into acceptance) is not without jeopardy for top management.

Therefore, despite increasing recognition of the desirability of placing the computer security function high in the data processing organization, senior management and data processing must accommodate one another in determining the effect of security upon system development and operation costs and traditional performance measures. While unquestionably a well-developed, highly controlled, designed-for-security system costs a great deal more to develop, it also provides a high payoff in efficiency, effectiveness, productivity, and security over the life cycle of the system.

The first argument in this discussion is that, generally speaking, security expertise is not a part of the data processing manager's portfolio of qualifications. As a result, the data processing manager is not equipped to deal with these problems without qualified advice and assistance. As a matter of fact, the notion of security and its implications for the data processing function, in terms of access to data processing facilities and services, is foreign to most data processing personnel.

The point is that the placement of the data processing security function is no longer an issue; it is a problem of serious concern to management. Thus, this important function should be placed accordingly in the organization.

INCREASING DEMANDS FOR MANAGEMENT ACCOUNTABILITY

Organizational management is being increasingly held accountable for its actions in running that organization. This attention is coming from primarily interests outside of operating management. Consumer interest groups, stockholders, boards of directors, and external auditors are the main sources of direct attention to management activities, Legislation, such as the Foreign Corrupt Practices Act, is also focusing attention on the actions of management and holding them accountable. In the midst of these trends has come a major change in the role of the auditor. Whereas the auditor's major function used to involve review of the financial activities of the business for conformance with accepted accounting principles and practices, the auditor has broadened this perspective to include the overall management of the organization and the business decisions being made by that management.

This trend toward increased accountability on the part of management has had a marked impact on the nature of business management. A driving force in this movement has been the Foreign Corrupt Practices Act (FCPA) of 1977. Enacted by Congress in response to several highly publicized cases where major U.S. corporations had bribed foreign officials in order to obtain contracts, the FCPA placed requirements upon publicly held corporations to implement controls to prevent or detect unauthorized use of corporate resources for bribery, among other things. Since senior management itself was the target of this legislation, it fell upon the external auditor to assess the presence and effectiveness of those controls. The short-term effect of the FCPA has been to highlight a serious lack of basic control and accountability throughout most major business systems. They found that the heart of most of these systems is the computer. Both the computer and its systems have been found to be generally unauditable for purposes of establishing the required degree of control and accountability. The FCPA imposes potential corporate as well as individual liability for violation of its provisions.

This increased need to protect corporate assets is highlighted by Michael J. Comer of London, England. In his book, *Corporate Fraud*,[3] Comer points out that fraud losses have more serious impact than is generally recognized because the loss of assets by fraud has a multiplied effect upon both future sales and profitability. A loss by fraud directly reduces corporate assets—assets that may be 'turned over' several times during the course of a year. For example, a business which turns its assets 20 times per year could have turned $1,000,000 lost through an uninsured fraud into $20,000,000 in additional sales. The relationship between the asset structure of a business and its ability to use those assets to generate sales is straightforward, and one of the reasons so much emphasis is being placed upon management's responsibility to protect business assets and stockholder interests. The key point is that fraud losses are not costs of doing business to be expensed in the profit and loss statement, but are direct attacks against the asset structure of the business.

Within the context of management's responsibility to manage and safeguard the assets of the corporation are serious implications which bear directly upon the security of the data processing function and its ability to control and safeguard these assets.

POTENTIAL MAGNITUDE OF LOSS

Recent instances of spectacular loss of corporate assets have demonstrated the potential impact of inadequate control and security within systems supporting important business functions. The fact that banks, with their highly touted controls, can be billed to the extent of $10 to $20 million per incident should be fair warning to senior management that the lack of control and accountability and the resultant potential for loss are serious enough to warrant their attention. Management should know that control and accountability of the bulk of the corporation's assets have been turned over to the computer—with varying degrees of effectiveness.

The potential for disruption of business operations through denial of an organization's data processing capability also poses a liability to senior management. Organizational management generally feels that the company's systems are much better protected against catastrophic failure than they actually are.[4] As dependence on these systems increases, so does the potential for loss. Generally severe cost penalties are incurred for any significant interruption of data processing support. These penalties are not well understood, however, and, depending upon the financial strength of the organization, could even be responsible for the demise of the organization.

While management may express concern over the security and survivability of these systems, their lack of full awareness and understanding of the issue has generally caused them to treat it as a technical problem to be left to the specialists to address. Management must be made aware that it is a serious corporate problem, affecting the whole organization, and that this problem is not well understood, in terms of impact, even by the technicians.

BROAD ORGANIZATIONAL INVOLVEMENT REQUIRED

The potential for loss due to inadequate computer security is a problem that affects virtually the entire organization. The computer security issue is so complex that the problem-solving process may require the involvement of much of the business organization. Not only must data processing be involved; it will also be necessary to draw upon the expertise of such areas as industrial security, personnel management, fire and safety, facilities management, procurement, legal, and auditing in order to design adequate protections into the physical, technical, and administrative aspects of computer security. Key to understanding the potential impact of security problems and defining specific requirements for security is the involvement of the functional users or proponents of these automated business systems. Unless the users put forth statements of potential impact and general requirements for security (i.e. sensitivity of their data and processing; criticality of processing), data processing will have neither the motivation nor the direction required to respond adequately.

The complexity of the response required and the number of corporate activities having a share of the total response dictate senior management involvement. That level of management exercising control over all of the organizations that must interact in order to address these problems affectively will often be the chief operating officer of the organization or his principal assistant. Only this level of management can assess the full impact of these problems and assign responsibilities for corrective action. The old debate as to whether computer security is a data processing or a security problem is moot; it is a serious problem and one that requires the attention of senior management, who must make decisions regarding corrective actions. In discharging its responsibilities, management must bring its organizational resources to bear by assigning roles and specifying responsibilities. It is important that both primary and supporting responsibilities be clearly identified.

SERIOUS RESOURCE IMPLICATIONS EXIST

Not only does the computer security problem have grave potential impact upon organizational resources; so does the cure. The basic lack of security, control, and accountability in sensitive and critical business systems may be so severe as to require significant allocation of resources to correct. The potential outlay is so large that, when confronted by the possible drain upon its resources, data processing will of necessity opt to minimize the dangers and settle for technical or less than optimal solutions. This attitude is easy to understand; since the problem affects the entire organization, the costs of solving the problem should be borne by the entire organization. Where data processing has brought the problem to the attention of senior management and presented comprehensive action plans for their consideration, management has been more inclined to share the burden.

Because inadequate attention has generally been paid to security, control, and accountability problems, a great deal of 'catching up' has to be done. Physical, technical, and procedural improvements, to include development of expensive contingency plans, major analysis and redesign of application software controls, as well as improvements to physical security, all require outlay of resources. While hard data on the cost of security are not readily available, one authority estimates that up to 5% of the annual data processing budget would not be unreasonable.[5] In a related area, another widely quoted source estimates that as much as 25% of the audit staff's resources should be assigned to EDP audit responsibilities.[6] This resolve on the part of the audit function ought to be similarly reflected in the resources allocated by data processing to the security, control, and accountability problems.

The resource aspects of the computer security problem will be one of the most important and controversial issues to be resolved. Significant resources will be required to address these security problems effectively. Where do they come from? One reason that data processing has failed to push for resolution of computer security problems has been the inclination of management to view it as strictly a data processing problem. The prospect that, due to lack of understanding of the problem, management would force or mandate data processing action strictly from within its own resources has caused many to ignore the problem—and rightly so. To attempt to force resolution of computer security problems, which are really organization-wide problems, will not work. Trying to squeeze solutions out of existing data processing resources and programs will not succeed. Since it is a serious organizational problem, the resources to resolve the problems must come from general organizational resources.

A MANAGEMENT CONTROL PROCESS

Because of the wide variety of organizations involved in addressing the problem, the serious potential resource implications, and the large number of security-related tasks which will need to be accomplished, some type of management control process is needed. In discharging its basic responsibilities for planning and control, some type of formal plan and program for implementing computer security should be developed by management.

Computer security is not a one-time concern. Because there are no guarantees or assurances against serious breach of security, it must be continuously monitored and improved carefully and deliberately. It is not possible to do everything at once when attempting to improve security. While the initial activities in a formal security program will create a surge of resource requirements, there will still be longer term needs. The most practical way to respond to these needs is to address them over a period of time, in order of priority. This approach calls for formalizing these requirements into an organizational plan and program.

The extent of potential loss, the involvement of a broad range of organization resources, and the need for a sustained level of effort dictate that senior management play a strong role in the development and implementation of a formal organizational computer security plan and program. The lack of senior management involvement in the approval process cycle for this program indicates failure to present the issue properly and will likely adversely affect the organization's ability to sustain the program.

In evaluating the manner in which the organization has addressed its computer security problems, external auditors will be looking for evidence of careful consideration and measured response on the part of management. In evaluating compliance with the provisions of the Foreign Corrupt Practices Act, for example, the auditors will be evaluating management's actions in this area and looking for the presence of a control mechanism which will help assure management of the change process while imposing accountability upon organizational management. The formal computer security program and plan is that mechanism.

COMPUTER SECURITY POLICIES AND GUIDELINES

Heightened awareness of security problems and organizational commitment to security-improved control of sensitive and critical systems all require coordinated and cooperative effort on the part of data processors, users, and other special support areas throughout the organization. Besides the establishment of formal roles and responsibilities in implementation of a computer security plan and program, management must ensure that other control and coordination activities are taken. The most important of these actions involves the development and promulgation of responsive policies and guidelines regarding computer security.

Perhaps the most effective way for management to express its resolve and ensure consistency of response, these formal policies and guidelines form the keystone of any organizational effort to deal effectively with computer security problems and issues. The promulgation of such guidelines represents an important step in the top-down development of an effective organization effort. This expression of management intent should take place early in the process through issuance of formal policy directed at the security of important business systems. More detailed policies and guidelines can follow, possibly as part of the formal plan and program of activities. Both are important for ensuring a uniform, consistent, and coordinated response by the organization.

THE ROLE OF MANAGEMENT IN LONG-TERM SECURITY PROBLEMS

One of the most important aspects of management involvement in the computer security problem is its ability to bring about change. The history of data processing is well into its second decade of concern over documented weaknesses in the technology's ability to provide adequate security. Improvements in the security of these systems have been largely cosmetic and geared only to the perceived needs of the market. Thus far, vendors have not viewed security as a marketable aspect of their product lines, as they have generally not seen economic viability in investing in significant security improvements.

Just as data processing has been opting to accept computer security risks in the past, when it has not been its prerogative, today's danger is that these attitudes have been conveyed to data processing vendors in the form of requirements, resulting in an understatement of the needs of users and managers. The predictable gap between the needs of the ultimate consumer and the functional users for security, social good notwithstanding, and the ability of the applied technology to satisfy those needs stands to grow larger unless management is actively involved in dealing with these issues.

THE PEOPLE ASPECT OF THE PROBLEM

'Computers don't steal; people do', 'A computer will only do what it's told to do', and other well-worn phrases reflect the underlying source of the abuses and misuses of computer systems—the people who design, build, operate, and use the computers and their systems.

As appreciation for the sensitivity and criticality of these systems increases, so does recognition of the need to restrict access to them. Privileged access must be restricted to fewer people and, the more privileged this access, the more trustworthy the person must be. This concept has long been accepted in the federal government, particularly the defense organizations, for protection of classified information. It is only recently that the federal government has accepted this position regarding its sensitive and critical computer systems and it has established a requirement for a background review of persons in 'trusted' positions in data processing.

At the same time, this traditional approach to personnel reliability and security has come under increasing attack from legislation and the popular movement toward greater protection of the individual's right to privacy. There are and will continue to be increasing problems in the old background investigation and review process upon which the government and some businesses have depended so heavily in the past. However, the need for some type of personnel reliability program for positions of trust will always exist.

In dealing with the people aspect of the problem, two basic ingredients support individual misuse or abuse of a computer system: motivation and opportunity. Managers dealing with the security of sensitive and critical computer systems must realize that personnel security and reliability programs deal only with the motivational aspect—attempting to predict future behavior based upon past experience—and that state-of-the-art in personnel reliability programs has 'gone about as far as it can go' without moving into areas that are increasingly considered intrusive and a violation of individual privacy rights. Future emphasis must shift to the 'opportunity' side of the equation and the development of controls which will effectively deter or deny individual opportunity to misuse or abuse sensitive or critical systems. State-of-the-art in this area is primitive at best.

THE IMPORTANCE OF CONTROLS

This gap in the adequacy of organizational controls has been heightened by increased application of and dependency on computerized systems to support vital business functions. The computer has made it possible to 'make mistakes at lightning speed'. Internal and external audits, focusing upon financial accounting practices, have long drawn attention to problems of financial controls. While the obligation to maintain accurate records and an adequate system of controls has been recognized for a long time, the Foreign Corrupt Practices Act established this requirement in law.

The purview of audit is expanding to encompass review of broader aspects of corporate management practices, extending management's accountability for protection of a corporation's assets into an evaluation of basic management decisions and its system of control and accountability for organizational operations.

This trend is highlighting deep and serious problems existing in organizational control, especially that aspect which has been entrusted to computerized systems. The audit function, boosted by the legislative thrust of the Foreign Corrupt Practices Act, has become the primary agent of change in the area of internal control.

However, it must be understood that the development and implementation of effective control and accountability mechanisms is an essential function of management, and not of an auditor. The auditor's responsibility is limited to determining whether controls are present and, if present, how effectively they are working.

To deny individual opportunity for abuse or misuse of a computerized system requires a carefully developed and implemented control structure which will:

1. prescribe strict procedures.
2. enforce individual accountability for adherence to these procedures.
3. demonstrate reasonable assurance that misuse will be detected.

In prescribing a control structure to protect corporate resources (which, incidentally, includes information), control processes, authorities, and checks and balances must be carefully designed.

The difficulty in implementing controls in an automated environment is highlighted by some of the examples, given next, of tried and proven pre-automation control objectives which automation has managed to overcome:

1. Accounting Control: Never allow the same person to create, authorize, and enter a transaction.
   Computerized Corollary: Automate data at its source, thereby creating, authorizing, and entering a transaction in one step.
2. Accounting Control: Accounts in one department must agree with totals maintained in another department.
   Computerized Corollary: Create loosely structured, transaction-driven data based systems that permit update of the data base from multiple entry points.
3. Accounting Control: Segregate check authorization from check writing and require two signatures of authorized signers on each check.
   Computerized Corollary: Use preprinted forms of automated check-signing machines to sign checks authorized for issue by the computer.

Quite often the definition of the control will suffer in its implementation in an automated system. One trend, based upon the influence of the auditors and recognition of control weaknesses, is toward development of strong internal control groups, reporting to high company officials. These groups are appearing in organizations where management has recognized the need for controls and realized its responsibility (not the auditors) for developing and implementing these controls.

DETECTION AND PROSECUTION OF FRAUD

One of the most perplexing problems resulting from today's complex automated environment deals with the detection and prosecution of fraud. Serious weaknesses throughout the cycle of use of automated systems hamper the ability to deal with computer-related fraud: poorly designed controls, difficulty in protecting systems in an automated environment, limited ability to detect abuses and misuses, difficulty in collecting evidence admissible in court on abuses and misuses, and lack of legislative tools appropriate to the prosecution and conviction of persons committing computer-related crimes.

Many of these shortcomings are not being addressed in earnest by government and industry because of a perceived lack of concern and stated need on the part of system users. One of the greatest responsibilities of senior management is to recognize the shortcomings presented and to ensure that a statement of corporate need is conveyed to those in government and industry who are capable of bringing about necessary improvements in the technology, the law, and application of both.

The increasing problem of white collar crime demands that businesses deal quickly and effectively with perpetrators of such deeds. The same is true of those that use the computer or its systems as instruments of crime. Despite the difficulties in prosecuting computer criminals, the deterrent value of attempting to prosecute is great. With each attempt, and the accompanying investigation, the corporation will learn a great deal about its system controls and safeguards, monitoring and detection capability, and evidence-gathering techniques, which will enable it to improve its posture. This improved posture, combined with increased knowledge of needed improvements to be conveyed to appropriate government and industry organizations, will help bring about these improvements.

In summary, computer security is an important issue for management because of the potential for loss to the whole organization as a result of abuse, misuse, or denial of use of sensitive and critical computer systems. High-level management involvement in addressing computer security problems is necessary because of increasing demands for management accountability for proper control of organizational resources and the potential magnitude of the loss. The problems of computer security have no easy solution—they promise to be with us for a considerable period of time. During this period, solutions are going to require broad organizational involvement, considerable assignment of resources, a formal organizational program and management control process, and strong organizational computer security policies and guidelines. Senior management is the only element in the organization capable of quickly and effectively dealing with these needs. All other approaches, historically, are marginally effective, are debilitating to organizational resources, and lack sustaining power.

The history of computer security shows great difficulty in getting management to address these computer security problems. However, the nature of the problem meets all of the standards for senior management involvement: a serious problem with no obvious organizational solution and significant potential future impact.

Senior management must address the problem and—discharging its responsibilities to plan, organize, direct, control, and coordinate—define organizational solutions.

Special aspects of the problem that are deserving of directed attention concern the placement of the computer security function, dealing with the personnel aspect of the problem, giving attention to the development and implementation of controls over sensitive processes, and prosecuting vigorously those attempting to abuse or misuse these sensitive systems.

Finally, the key to resolving long-standing, industry-wide problems in the security of automated systems lies in involving senior management. The industry is well into its second decade of awareness of serious problems in this area. Unfortunately, the prognostications of the early researchers into computer security are coming true. The types of abuses that were predicted are happening, and they are a warning of more serious problems. Solutions will not be found until they are demanded by senior management. The problems are likely to deepen until management becomes truly involved.

REFERENCES

1. *An Evaluation of DP Machine Room Loss and Selective Recovery Strategies*, Graduate School of the University of Minnesota, March, 1979.
2. *Internal Control in U.S. Corporations: The State of the Art, 1980*. New York, Financial Executive Research Foundation, p. 356.
3. Comer, M. J.: *Corporate Fraud*. Maidenhead, England, McGraw-Hill Book Company (U.K.) Limited, 1977.
4. *Internal Control in U.S. Corporations: The State of the Art*, Financial Executive Research Foundation, 1980.
5. Martin, J.: *Security, Accuracy and Privacy in Computer Systems*. Englewood Cliffs, N.J., Prentice-Hall, Inc., 1973, p. 8.
6. Mullen, J. B.: Developing an EDP Audit Staff. *In EDP Auditing*. Pennsauken, N. J., Auerbach Publishers, Inc., 1979, p. 3.

Advances in Computer Security Management, Vol. 2
Edited by M. M. Wofsey
© 1983 John Wiley & Sons Ltd.

Chapter 3

LEGAL IMPLICATIONS OF COMPUTER SECURITY

J. T. Westermeier

Abrams, Kovacs, Westermeier and Goldberg, P.C.

Legal considerations affect computer security in many different ways. If a program directed at safeguarding computerized information resources is to be effective, it should be designed to take full advantage of the legal protection available. This policy generally requires an understanding of the traditional legal means for protecting intellectual property—patent, copyright, and trade secret protection. It also must be remembered that contracts are an important aspect of computer security. They need to be drafted with computer security concerns in mind so that the security risks involved in varying contractual relationships can be managed more effectively. Furthermore, risk analyses conducted for computer security purposes need to consider legal requirements and potential legal exposures; otherwise, the analyses will not be complete. The likelihood of recovery or assessment of liability, and the consequences which may result therefrom, are important considerations in the development of a complete risk assessment.

This chapter will discuss some of the major legal considerations affecting computer security.

SAFEGUARDING COMPUTERIZED INFORMATION

The need for information security has grown for many reasons, including the incredible expansion of the scope and value of such information, the tremendous increase in the financial rewards available for the exploitation of computerized information resources, and the new and developing techniques available to the people and companies bent on misappropriating computerized information resources. Advances in computer and communications technology have made the theft of such information easier, more difficult to detect, and more profitable. Thus, today, more than ever, computer security programs have to be designed to take maximum advantage of the legal protection available for computer programs, computer data bases, and other valuable information resources for which protection is sought.

The traditional means at law for protecting intellectual property usually involve patent, copyright, and trade secret protection. While a comprehensive computer security program should use a combination of copyright and trade secret protection, and possibly even patent protection, the form(s) of protection chosen will differ depending on the circumstances.

As a general proposition, copyright protection should be used for computerized data bases, computer programs, and related documentation which are made available to third parties outside the originating organization. On the other hand, trade secret protection should be used to safeguard computerized information resources which are maintained only for internal use or are disclosed to parties outside the originating organization only under carefully controlled conditions.

Copyright Protection

On December 12, 1980, the Computer Software Protection Act of 1980, Public Law 96-517 was enacted.[1] Under this statute, computer programs are expressly subjected to the full coverage of the Copyright Revision Act of 1976, which became effective on January 1, 1978. This Act makes it clear that computer programs are copyrightable works if the statutory requirements for a copyright are met.

The Federal Copyright Office will accept computer programs, data bases, and other works first published in computer-readable media for copyright registration. However, before a work is entitled to copyright protection, several requirements must be met. The work must be a writing by an author, and it must be original. The word 'original' does not mean that the work is novel or unique, but that it originates with the author. All that is required is that the author contribute something more than a 'merely trivial' variation. The author must contribute something that is recognizably his own.

The copyright protection available for computerized information resources does not exceed the protection that is available to other works protected by copyright. Copyright protects the expression of an idea—not the idea itself. The actual process or methods embodied in a computer program are not within the scope of the copyright laws. Different expressions of the same idea written in different programming languages may each qualify for a separate copyright if the necessary originality and creativity are present.

Prior to 1978, the Copyright Office had classified computer programs as 'books'. This practice meant that the program had to be 'published' in order to obtain copyright registration from the Copyright Office. Upon publication, i.e., the distribution of copies of the work to the public, however, other persons would have available, and theoretically were free to adopt, the ideas expressed in the program, although they could not copy the program itself. Indeed, others might well have been free to use the information contained in a copyrighted data base, although they would not be entitled to make copies. Copyright protection for software thus may often have been viewed as illusory, and would create but little incentive to publish when, as a practical matter, only text copying was actionable.

But under the law as it has existed since January 1, 1978, it has also been possible to copyright computer software, including data bases, as published or unpublished literary works. Now, protection without publication can only be achieved under certain circumstances and involves at least some degree of subtle risk. Still, copyrighting software as an unpublished work appears to provide the luxury of both the protection afforded by copyright law and, at least to some extent, by trade secret law except when the remedial actions available against those misappropriating trade secrets are preempted by the federal copyright laws.

Registration at the Copyright Office is *not* a prerequisite to copyright protection. Copyright in a work subsists from its creation, though certain statutory incentives to register the work do exist. The right to have an infringer pay reasonable attorney's fees is one such incentive. Another incentive to registration at the Copyright Office is that statutory damages, which generally range from $250 to $10,000 in the court's discretion, can be recovered from infringers in lieu of actual damages and profits. One further incentive is that, with certain minor exceptions, no action for infringement can be instituted until copyright registration has been obtained.

For computer programs being registered as unpublished 'non-dramatic literary' works (published only in machine-readable form), only the first 25 and last 25 pages (or equivalent units) of the computer program need be filed. In addition to the deposit, registration requires filing a properly executed registration form, together with the applicable statutory registration fee of $10 per work. These forms, together with explanatory materials, are available without charge from the Copyright Office. Simply write to Register of Copyrights, Library of Congress, Washington, DC 20540.

Prior to 1978, notice of copyright was an essential formality to secure copyright protection. For example, in *Data Cash Systems, Inc.* v. *JS&A Group, Inc.*,[2] the court held that since the software developer had failed to include a copyright notice on the Read-Only-Memory (ROM) version of a computerized chess game program developed prior to 1978, copyright protection was not secured and copyright infringement therefore did not take place. Now the failure to include the notice of copyright will not be fatal to securing copyright protection, provided: (1) the publication of the copyrighted software without the notice has not been widespread; (2) registration has been made before or is made within five years of the publication without notice and a reasonable effort is made to add notice to all copies distributed within the United States, and (3) the publication was made in violation of an agreement to publish only with notice.

Even though the failure to provide notice will not, in many cases, prove catastrophic, notice of copyright is highly desirable because 'innocent' copiers are protected by the statute. Notice of copyright should be provided in the first 20 steps of the computer program. The notice should be included on all versions and adaptations of the copyrighted software. It is further recommended that all documentation reference the computer programs as copyrighted works. Output routines can further provide that results are generated from a copyrighted computer program. If the software developer is relying on the copyright provisions for unpublished works, the notice should so indicate.

Preemption Doctrine

Until recently, trade secrets were used either as complementary copyright protection or as the sole form of protection for software. Indeed, the preferred mode of software protection for small software developers called for use of licensing agreements premised on trade secret protection with very limited access to the source code listings for the licensed programs. However, enactment of Public Law 96-517, which expressly brought computer programs within the ambit of federal copyright protection, clearly extended to computer programs the copyright act's preemption of state law, which grants rights that are 'equivalent' to any of the federal copyright rights, as to works which are fixed in a tangible medium of expression and which come within the subject matter of copyright. Congress indicated in the legislative history of this preemption provision that the common law rights of trade secrets remain unaffected as long as the cause of action contains an element, such as breach of trust or confidentiality, that is different in kind from copyright infringement.

Preemption has serious implications for software protection schemes used in computer security programs, especially since unauthorized copying is the most common form of software piracy. If an unauthorized copying of a computer program occurs, the proper remedy is probably a copyright infringement action rather than an action for misappropriation of trade secrets even if trade secret protection was relied upon.[3] The right to copy is expressly covered by the copyright laws, which preempt any state claims that may have previously been available to redress unauthorized copying of proprietary software.

Even though copyright protection is certain to play an increasingly greater role in the protection of computerized information resources, trade secret protection may still be used effectively.

Trade Secret Protection

Unlike the law of patent and copyright, trade secret law is largely grounded on the common law. Secrecy is the essence of this form of protection. While an exact definition of a trade secret is not practicable because of variances in the treatment accorded trade secrets under state laws, the following definition has generally been adopted:

A trade secret may consist of any formula, pattern, device or compilation of information which is used in one's business, and which gives

him an opportunity to obtain an advantage over competitors who do
not know or use it.[4]

Compilations of technical information, price information, cost information,
computer programs, data bases, and other groupings of data have been afforded
trade secret protection under this definition. While the information for which trade
secret protection is sought should have some special value of intrinsic worth, it
may be nothing more than a mechanical or process improvement upon generally
known information, a special combination of generally known elements, or a compilation of generally known data.

Some of the factors that may be considered in determining whether unpublished
computerized information resources qualify as protectible trade secrets are:

1. The extent to which the information is known outside the originating
   organization.
2. The extent to which it is known by employees and others involved in the
   organization.
3. The extent of measures taken by the organization to guard the secrecy of the
   information.
4. The value of the information to the organization.
5. The amount of effort or money expended by the organization in developing
   the information.
6. The ease or difficulty with which the information could be properly acquired
   or duplicated by others.

The information should then be analyzed from a protectability perspective. The
extent of the secret information and its permanence should be considered. If only
a minimal amount of secret information is present, it may be unnecessary to
implement a comprehensive information security program. Similarly, if the information's secret character is likely to be short-lived, it may be inappropriate to try
to safeguard such information using methods for the protection of permanent
secrets.

Access to the information must also be considered. Can access be limited to a
few or must many employees have access to the information? Access should also
be analyzed from an organizational perspective. Is the secret information centrally
situated or is it widely dispersed throughout the organization? It may be possible
to limit restrictions to that part of the organization's offices where the secret information is located or it may be appropriate to reorganize consistent with minimizing the dispersion of secret information.

The next step is well known to computer security specialists; however, the
importance of the risk analysis in light of the law of trade secrets is usually not
fully appreciated. After reviewing the nature of the organization's computerized
resources and operational considerations applicable to them, vulnerabilities
should be analyzed. The program to safeguard these information resources should

be designed so as to block the most vulnerable disclosure possibilities while interfering as little as possible with operational activities.

All forms of disclosure must be analyzed, the risks of disclosure in each vulnerability situation carefully considered and appropriate safeguards adopted. Where have you heard this idea before? Maintenance of trade secret protection is thus another reason for conducting a risk analysis.

A successful program to safeguard information resources requires the implementation of a number of precautionary measures. The program should include educating the employees in the importance to them of making the information security program a success, and in new developments in the law of trade secrets and the copyright laws.

The following procedures are recommended for information security programs:

1. Restrict access to areas where trade secret information may be found to those with a need to go there.
2. Restrict access to trade secret information to those with a need to know, which includes restricting access to computer data bases and proprietary computer programs.
3. Mark all documents containing trade secret information 'Confidential' and indicate the information to be the property of the organization. These confidential markings should be included on all media in which such information is stored.
4. Restrict circulation of visitors to areas necessary for purposes of the visit. All visitors should be escorted by a qualified employee.
5. Maintain logs showing who had access to trade secret information, when and for how long, so that a audit trail of accountability is provided.
6. In areas where trade secret information is used or discussed, the contents of waste baskets should be burned or otherwise destroyed.

Because the legal definition of trade secret is so imprecise; it is very important that organizations relying on trade secret protection, in whole or in part, implement procedures which clearly treat computerized information resources that may qualify for such protection as secrets.

Computer security audits should assure that trade secret and copyright protection are being used properly and to the full extent applicable.

DOCUMENTATION STANDARDS

One purpose served by system documentation is to demonstrate that the system has been penetrated if and when a penetration occurs. As such, documentation needs to be viewed from a legal evidentiary perspective. What documentation is needed to prove that a computer crime or abuse took place? If it is assumed that a penetration took place, can it be proved? What other documentation would be helpful? Breaches of computer systems usually must be proven by indirect circumstantial evidence. Effective computer security practices call for complete documentation which has been developed with the legal system in mind.

It is important to recognize also that while computer printouts are normally admissible in a court of law as business records under the rules of evidence, such computer-generated records may be deemed inadmissible if sufficient documentation is not available to satisfy a court that the sources of information, method and time of preparation were such as to justify admission of the record.[5] Furthermore, even if admitted into evidence, the probative value accorded computer-generated records and reports may depend on the procedural safeguards designed into the system to assure the integrity and accuracy of the record or report proferred as evidence and the documentation available to demonstrate the use of such safeguards. Thus, computer-generated evidence submitted by organizations which follow sound computer security practices and can demonstrate that they do will most likely be credited with greater evidentiary value than organizations which have inadequate computer security programs.

CONTRACTING

The importance of written contracts to computer security is often overlooked. A written contract serves to allocate risk and may provide protection against varying contingencies.

All vendors and third parties who have access to computer facilities should be bound, to the extent possible, by non-disclosure agreements designed to protect the confidentiality of information. Likewise, key employees who have access to valuable information resources should execute employment agreements containing non-disclosure and, in some circumstances, non-competition covenants.

When an element of risk is identified, ask whether the risk can be shifted or minimized by written contract. Protection, for example, may be provided against system failures and the imposition of legal liability under different circumstances.

NEGLIGENCE

Any discussion of the legal considerations affecting computer security would be incomplete if the potential liability for failing to maintain adequate computer security were not addressed. In the absence of strict liability, such failures will most likely be covered under the branch of law called negligence.

Legal liability for negligence generally requires the presence of four elements. First, there must be a legally recognized obligation for a person to perform to a certain standard of conduct so that others are protected against unreasonable risks. This first element establishes the duty that someone owes to another as a minimum under given circumstances. What this duty requires in terms of minimal conduct will differ from situation to situation, system to system depending on the risks and circumstances. The standard of care with respect to computer security practices is evolving rapidly. Methodologies, procedures, and practices have been accepted by the industry, and are continually being improved.

The second element that must be present for a negligence action is a failure to conform to the required standard which is established for a given set of circumstances applicable to a system.

The third element requires a reasonably close connection between the conduct in question and the resulting injury. At law this element is often referred to as proximate causation.

The fourth element involves the injury itself. The resulting injury must be an actual loss or damage to the interest of another. In other words, the injury has to be ascertainable. The injury should be subject to economic quantification for the imposition of legal liability premised on negligence grounds.

While none of these four elements can properly be stated without the other three, negligence law is founded on the concept of a required standard of conduct—the standard of care a reasonable person would exercise under the circumstances of a particular case.

This objective standard imposed by society is stated in general terms to cover all forms of conduct under any circumstances. It recognizes that unreasonable danger to others or property can be brought about by behavior which lacks the due care required by the circumstances.

Professional negligence adds several other considerations to the liability formulation. The standard-of-care or duty-to-others element requires that the professional demonstrate certain minimum skill, knowledge, and ability. These considerations pertain to the professional's special competence which is not part of the learning of ordinary man. Key to the concept of professional liability in this context is the existence of a reliance relationship which is brought about because an ordinary man is not able to resolve his problem without trusting and relying on the professional. Thus, in some situations where the user or customer of data processing services is relying on computer security specialists, the specialist may be adjudged by professional standards in determining potential liability. Where an omission or error is brought about by a mechanical error instead of a judgmental error, the courts are more likely to assess liability against the computer specialist for failing to demonstrate the minimum skill, knowledge, and ability that a computer security specialist should have exercised under the circumstances.

The concept of risk analysis which is fundamental to computer security today has direct relevance to determining whether negligence is present. This form of risk analysis requires that the gravity and probability of injury be balanced against the utility and type of conduct which an injured party may claim could have been performed to avoid the injury. The procedure was aptly explained in 1947 by Judge Learned Hand in a case which had nothing to do with reliance on computerized systems—*United States* v. *Carroll Towing Co.*[6] This case involved a bargee's liability for failure to watch over a barge which broke away from a pier after another barge's crew had shifted its mooring lines. The unattended, runaway barge ran into a tanker causing it to lose its cargo and sink.

Under these circumstances, Judge Learned Hand indicated that the barge owner's duty to provide against resulting injuries, as in other similar situations, is a function of three variables:

1. The probability the barge will break away from its moorings.
2. The gravity of the resulting injury.
3. The burden of adequate precautions.[7]

The relationship among these variables was expressed in the following algebraic terms:

If the probability be called P; the injury L; and the burden, B; liability depends upon whether B is less than L multiplied by P; *i.e.*, whether $B < PL$.[8]

This $B < PL$ formulation can be appropriately applied to computer security questions. To determine the relevant PL, the computer security specialist focuses on potential losses. If the cost of protecting against the risks found in this analysis is less than the 'PL', the failure to implement the safeguards under such circumstances may result in legal liability being assessed in the event the risk occurs and losses are sustained as a result thereof.

This potential liability places management in a tenuous position. If a company conducts a computer security review which identifies risks and action to reduce these risks, and then fails to implement the recommended precautionary measures, it would appear to be in grave danger of potential legal liability for mismanagement. Corporate management may be vulnerable to a stockholders' derivative suit premised on negligence under these circumstances.

The same liability formula applies to the work performed by computer security specialists. For example, in the event the security review fails to identify risks, and management relies on the review to its detriment by not implementing precautionary measures that should have been adopted, the computer security specialist could be liable for losses sustained as a result of the failure to identify the particular risk situation or failure to recommend adequate safeguards. In view of the potential liability in this area, computer security specialists should make every effort to be as thorough as possible.

Thus, in the area of computer security two principal liability scenarios should be considered. One is the potential liability of the computer security specialist for failing to conduct an adequate security review. The other is for the company which fails to maintain adequate security. This failure could be especially dangerous in the situation where management knew or should have known what to do, but failed to act.

PRIVACY LAWS

Privacy laws may profoundly affect policies, practices, and procedures covering the collection, maintenance, use, and disclosure of personal information.

System security should be planned and implemented with these privacy laws and proposed privacy legislation in mind. Every effort should be made to prevent the misuse of individual information and promote system security.

The Freedom of Information Act,[9] Fair Credit Reporting Act,[10] Bank Secrecy Act,[11] Trade Secret Act,[12] Family Educational Rights and Privacy Act,[13] Fair Credit Billing Act,[14] Equal Credit Opportunity Act,[15] Privacy Act,[16] Right to Financial Privacy Act,[17] and Privacy Protection Act of 1980[18] apply across the board to the federal government, to certain local governmental entities, and to selected members of the private sector. In addition to these federal statutes, state privacy laws and certain common law principles may be applicable to computer security. Under the common law, privacy actions are generally covered under tort law premised on one of the following causes of action:

1. Intrusion upon one's physical solitude or seclusion.
2. Publication of private facts about an individual.
3. Creation of a false image by untrue or defamatory publication.
4. Appropriation of one's likeness for commercial purposes.[19]

In 1977, the Privacy Protection Study Commission transmitted to the President and to Congress its final report containing recommendations for legislation, administrative action, or voluntary adoption of various requirements and principles deemed appropriate to protect the privacy of individuals.[20]

Even though Congress has been slow to enact privacy legislation affecting computer security in the private sector, prudent computer security practices include consideration of the 'fair information practices' provided by the Privacy Protection Study Commission. Data collection methods and procedures should be examined in light of the objective of minimizing intrusiveness in individual record-keeping. Processing procedures and safeguards should be reviewed for the purpose of promoting fairness in the way individuals are treated. The system should be designed to assure that individual information is not used or disseminated in a manner which is inconsistent with the expectation of confidentiality applicable to such individual information. Consideration of these principles should avoid costly redesign efforts in the future.

FOREIGN CORRUPT PRACTICES ACT OF 1977 (FCPA)

The FCPA requires all companies which must register with the Securities and Exchange Commission to develop and maintain effective systems of internal accounting for their domestic as well as their international business operations. In this connection the use of the term 'Foreign' in the title is a misnomer since the requirements of the Act apply to SEC-registered companies without regard to whether business is conducted abroad.

The FCPA requires that these mandatory internal accounting controls provde 'reasonable assurances' that: (1) access to the company's assets and execution of transactions are in accordance with management's authorization, (2) accountability for assets is maintained, and (3) transactions are recorded as necessary to permit preparation of certified financial statements. Directors and officers are charged with the responsibility for compliance with the FCPA requirements. The failure to comply, whether intentional or as a result of negligence, can result in individual liability and the assessment of substantial personal penalties.

The corruption controls specified in the FCPA are likewise important for computer security purposes. If firms fail to meet these internal auditing requirements, they lack the necessary safeguards to protect against computer crime and abuse.

INSURANCE

Computer security specialists should be knowledgeable about offerings in ADP insurance. While too few legal judgments are available and too little experience has been gained with claims resulting from the risks involved in ADP systems to develop actuarially sound ADP insurance policies, several insurance policies are available.

The first data processing insurance policy was offered by the St. Paul Fire and Marine Insurance Company, Inc. in 1961. The St. Paul policy is a broad, all-risk insurance package for ADP equipment, data, and media, extra expenses, and business interruption coverage. Under this policy, damage caused by deliberate or accidental harm to ADP equipment, data, or media by the insured's employees may be covered. In addition, breakdowns may be covered. The business interruption insurance provisions cover monetary losses due to total or partial closing of business operations due to direct physical loss to the ADP equipment, data, or media, the building, or the air conditioning or electrical systems on the premises. This policy does not cover losses or damages resulting from a change in electric power supply, such as interruption, power surge, or brown-out, if the change originates more than 100 feet away from the building containing the ADP equipment. It also does not cover losses caused by fraud, dishonesty, or crimes committed by the insured company, or its partners, officers, directors, or trustees. The Home Insurance Company offers coverage similar to that provided in the St. Paul's policy. The Chubb Group of Insurance Companies also offers this type of insurance coverage. It is possible to extend this coverage in most cases to cover the professional liability resulting from the negligent acts, errors, or omissions of data processors.

There are many innovative developments in the insurance area which computer security specialists need to know about. In 1980 St. Paul introduced its Mini-Computer policy, which covers values up to $250,000.

The Chubb Group of Insurance Companies has developed a computer theft policy. This policy was developed for a special client of Chubb's. Under this policy two separate forms of computer theft are insurable, computer theft of property and/or computer theft of proprietary information. Computer theft is defined for purposes of this insurance policy as the intentional and unlawful taking of money, securities, or other property through use of the insured's computer located at the insured's premises.

While only a few of the Chubb computer theft policies have been sold (approximately 10), it is clear that more emphasis on this form of insurance will occur. In view of the growing dependence on computer technology and the emphasis on sound risk management practices, the insurance industry is certain to play an increasingly greater role in computer security.

OTHER LEGAL CONSIDERATIONS

Numerous other potential legal considerations, such as labor, tax, and antitrust requirements, may affect the risk assessment for a given system under appropriate circumstances. All of these matters should be included in the overall risk assessment if they are appropriate.

In conclusion, legal considerations are an important aspect of computer security. They must be included in the design and implementation of a computer security program if the full measure of protection under the law is to be achieved and potential liability minimized.

REFERENCES

1. Public Law 96-517 amends section 117 and Title 17 of the United States Code, in relevant part, as follows:

> Notwithstanding the provisions of section 106, it is not an infringement for the owner of a copy of a computer program to make or authorize the making of another copy or adaptation of that computer program provided:

> (1) that such a new copy or adaptation is created as an essential step in the utilization of the computer program in conjunction with a machine and that it is used in no other manner, or
> (2) that such new copy or adaptation is for archival purposes only and that all archival copies are destroyed in the event that continued possession of the computer program should cease to be rightful.

> Any exact copies prepared in accordance with the provisions of this section may be leased, sold, or otherwise transferred, along with the copy from which such copies were prepared, only as part of the lease, sale, or other transfer of all rights in the program. Adaptations so prepared may be transferred only with the authorization of the copyright owner.

2. 203 USPQ 735 (N.D. Ill. 1979), *Aff'd on other grounds*, 208 USPQ 197 (7th Cir., 1980).
3. *E.g., Avco Corp.* v. *Precision Air Parts, Inc.*, No. 79-275-N (M.D. Ala., decided September 4, 1980).
4. Section 757(b), 2d Restatement of Torts.
5. Rule 803(6), Federal Rules of Evidence.

6. 159 F.2d 169 (2d Cir., 1947).

7. 159 F.2d at 173.

8. 159 F.2d at 173. For a discussion of the *Carroll Towing Co.* case, *see* Westermeier, DP and the Law—Don't Neglect Negligence, 16, *Data Management*, **42**, March 1978, and Westermeier, Legal Considerations Affecting Information Management, *Information & Management*, **May 1979**. Additional discussion of the principles may be found in Westermeier, Nuclear Near-Disaster Should Shake Risk-Ridden DP, 17, *Data Management*, **30**, June 1974.

9. 5 U.S.C. §552.

10. 15 U.S.C. §§1681-1681t. Applies to consumer reporting agencies. It limits information collection, provides a right of access and correction, and limits dissemination and use.

11. 12 U.S.C. §§1829b, 1953, 31 U.S.C. §§1051-1122. Applies to financial institutions. It limits information collection, use, and dissemination.

12. 18 U.S.C. §1905. Creates criminal liability for employees of the federal government who unlawfully disclose proprietary information. Trade secret protection in this context is a form of corporate privacy.

13. 20 U.S.C. §1232g ('The Buckley Admendments'). Applies to educational institutions (Dept. of Education funded). It provides for right of access and correction, limits use and dissemination, and contains notice provisions.

14. 15 U.S.C. §§1666-1666j. Applies to creditors. It limits use and dissemination.

15. 15 U.S.C. §§1691-1691e. Applies to creditors. It limits information collection.

16. P.L. 93-579 (Dec. 31, 1974), 5 U.S.C. §552a. Limits federal government's ability to collect data, provides for right of access and correction, limits disclosure and use, and establishes notice requirements.

17. 12 U.S.C. §§3401-3422. Applies to financial institutions. It limits use and dissemination and establishes notice requirements.

18. Public Law 96-440 approved October 13, 1980. Provides First Amendment privacy protection by limiting investigative authority to search and seize materials possessed by person who has purpose of disseminating information to the public.

19. See generally, Prosser, *Law of Torts* 829 (3d Ed. 1964); Westermeier, The Privacy Side of the Credit Card, 23, *Am. Univ. Law Review*, **187**, 1973.

20. See Westermeier, Privacy Report to Alter Relation of Business to Individual, 15, *Data Management*, September 1977.

Advances in Computer Security Management, Vol. 2
Edited by M. M. Wofsey
© 1983 John Wiley & Sons Ltd.

Chapter 4

FEDERAL LEGISLATION AND IMPACT ON SECURITY MANAGEMENT

Peter S. Browne and Robert Y. Bigman

Systematics General Corporation

The purpose of this chapter is to describe the role the federal government has played in establishing security requirements for computer systems. The objectives of these requirements have been to protect computer facilities, systems, and data from destruction, damage, data modification, delay, and disclosure. Data disclosure as it relates to the privacy of individuals has been of particular concern to many. This concern has resulted in a number of legislative acts to protect information about individuals.

The majority of the federal requirements for computer security, enacted as acts, regulations, and directives, concern the secure management of government-owned or government-operated computer systems. However, the legislative branch has also enacted acts that impact the operation of computer systems in the private sector. For example, the legislative branch has considered specific computer crime laws for a number of years. Currently, comprehensive computer crime laws have been enacted only at the state level. A federal computer crime law currently awaits a subcommittee's decision on its fate. Supporters of such a computer crime law want detailed federal legislation that defines what a computer crime is and establishes specific penalties for such crimes. The heart of the proposed legislation involves the use of computer systems to commit fraud and embezzlement. No one doubts that these crimes exist and are increasing. The growth of computer technology has resulted in such advancements as data communications, distributed networks, minicomputers, microcomputers, and, more recently, home computers. These advancements, state the supporters of federal computer crime legislation, necessitate the enactment of such legislation. A federal computer crime law has gained broad-base support, and many believe that such a law is forthcoming.

The intent of this chapter is not so much to discuss what laws have been enacted through federal legislation, but rather to discuss what the government has done to ensure the secure management of computer systems. Focus is on the role of the Defense Department, the Office of Management and Budget, the General Accounting Office, and Congress. This chapter is divided into two sections. The first section describes the direct role the government has played in establishing requirements for the protection of federally owned computer facilities, systems, and data. Both the executive and legislative branches of government have been involved in enacting regulations, acts, and directives. This section will describe how concern for computer security management originated with the need to protect classified information and how computer security concepts from the national security environment have provided the framework for government-wide policy concerning computer security. This section will also discuss federal actions that have affected government computer systems by necessitating the release of some information while requiring the special protection of other information.

The second section describes the indirect role the government has played in establishing regulations affecting the management of computer systems and data in the private sector. The term indirect is used in light of the lack of a comprehensive federal computer crime law. In this respect, the federal government has not dealt with privately owned computer systems in a comprehensive manner, but has become involved in regard to specific issues like credit reporting and corporate internal accounting activities. It is believed that these issues will form the basis for a comprehensive computer crime law, but until one exists, the federal government's involvement in private sector computer security management can only be termed 'indirect'.

DIRECT ROLE LEGISLATING FEDERAL COMPUTER SYSTEMS

The executive and legislative branches of government became principally involved in the secure management of federal computer systems in the late sixties and seventies. Before this only sporadic and very general requirements were established. Most of these requirements dealt with issues of physical and administrative security. It was up to the individual agencies to develop specific computer security policies. Because there was no outstanding mandate to do so, and also because the government was just beginning to realize how to use the benefits of computer technology, computer security took a back seat. However, there was an exception.

Early Computer Security Regulation

In the late fifties, the Department of Defense officials began to question the security posture of these new powerful computing machines that concentrated large volumes of data in little space. Their concern centered around the processing, storage, and dissemination of classified information. Up to this point the Executive Office of the President, the Defense Department, the Atomic Energy Commission, and the Intelligence community had established specific policy dealing with the secure management of classified information for manual systems. What was needed were requirements for the processing of such information in computer systems.

Historically, computer security legislation first emerged as policies in various functional areas where the handling of classified national security information was involved. The basis for such policies was Executive Order 12065 [10] and its predecessors (e.g. E.O. 11652, 1972; E.O. 10501, 1953). Although none of these Executive Orders qualify as 'computer security policy documents' the Department of Defense implemented these orders through computer security policies dealing specifically with national security information in the ADP environment and directly with Special Access Programs. Special Access Programs outlined the roles and responsibilities of individuals working in an ADP facility and set criteria for establishing who had access to computer systems and data.

Executive Order 12065 was used as the foundation for other policies and directives in defense-related establishments. USSAN Instruction 1-69, 'Implementation of NATO Security Procedure (U)', in turn implements NATO RESTRICTED Document C-M (55) 15 (Final), 'Security Within the North Atlantic Treaty Organization', March 8, 1955. Enclosure 'C' of this document contains a Section X, 'Protection of Classified Information Handled and Stored in Automatic Data Processing Systems', which applies to all NATO commands and member nations.

The Director of Central Intelligence promulgated computer security policies for the protection of 'intelligence information using Executive Order 12065.' The basic Director of Central Intelligence Directive and associated 'Computer Security Regulation' set forth computer security policy requirements for ADP systems and networks that process 'intelligence information', and these requirements apply to both government and contractor ADP systems and networks.

The Department of Defense and the Intelligence communities' ADP security policies have basically dealt with three areas. The first area involved policies to control personnel working directly with computer systems and data. Special clearance procedures, access authorizations, duty separation, forced vacations, and other practices were used to prevent the disclosure and/or manipulation of computer-processed data. The second area involved policies to provide for a secure physical environment in which to operate classified computer systems. Special access systems and procedures were developed and special computer centers were designed to increase secure data processing. Environmental controls, like air conditioning, raised floors, false walls and ceilings, fire control, and humidity controls, were implemented to provide for a safe data processing environment. The third area, and a very important one, was administrative/procedural controls. These controls involved detail procedures for processing classified information. Many times, one system was dedicated to the processing of classified information. These policies, initiated primarily in the fifties and early sixties, provided a basis for contemporary computer security policies. They were designed to provide control over the first- and some of the second-generation computer systems. Hardware and software controls were mostly absent from these systems since computer system vendors placed little or no emphasis on internal controls.

Contemporary Computer Security Regulation

As computer systems became more and more complex, offering increased data processing benefits, their use expanded not only in the defense environment but also throughout the government and private industry. The increased benefits came at the cost of increasing vulnerabilities. From a relatively secure single central processor running batch operations, a gigantic leap was made by the introduction of asynchronous computer systems with multiple channel operating systems. These systems allowed a computer to handle multiple users at one time. The introduction of interactive on-line computer terminals facilitated the use of multiple operating system channels. These computer systems offered dramatically increased capacity by means of direct or removable storage media. Distributed networks began to gain acceptance and small data communications networks were also established.

The existing federal legislation was insufficient to provide for a secure data processing environment in contemporary systems. The vendors, second- and third-generation computer systems offered great possibilities, but they also offered a number of operating system and hardware vulnerabilities, not to mention the physical and administrative/procedural flaws involved in network environments. As before, the first federal entity to respond, at a regulatory level, to these new and dangerous vulnerabilities was the Department of Defense and the Intelligence community. The Department of Defense issued a number of computer security regulations that expanded on the policies discussed earlier. DOD Directive 5200.28, issued in 1972, provides a comprehensive policy for the secure management of all defense-owned or defense-operated computer systems. The focus of the directive is to provide a policy for the unique problems posed by shared computer systems. Other salient features of the directive are:

1. A detailed policy on investigations and clearance of Defense personnel for access to classified information.
2. The requirement to incorporate physical, hardware/software, and administrative/procedural security features from the beginning of the design.
3. The requirement to plan computer security through the use of life cycle management.
4. The requirement to audit and evaluate all aspects and features of the computer security program.
5. The requirement to protect personal information in the same manner as classified information.
6. The requirement to provide for documentation of security specifications.
7. The requirement to provide risk assessments of all computer facilities.
8. The requirement to procure only those computer systems that have a specified level of security commensurate with the sensitivity of the information they will process.
9. The requirement to develop, implement, and test contingency plans.

The directive also called for all these requirements to be part of a comprehensive computer security program that all defense components must establish. The ADP security program policies impact not only DOD components but also those ADP systems processing classified information among the 11,000 contractors in the newly established Defense Industrial Security Program.

Non-Defense Computer Security Regulation

The Defense Department promulgated a series of regulations (based upon 5200.28) which clearly put defense and its contractors far ahead of other executive level agencies. Most other agencies were making full use of computer technology with only very general and limited policy guidance on computer security. A number of computer fraud and embezzlement incidences in the middle seventies caught the eye of many in Congress and the General Accounting Office. Action soon followed.

Interest in computer security matters by Congress stemmed from a broader concern for the effective management of computer and information resources (e.g. enactment of the 1965 Brooks Act, P.L. 89-306), and the growing awareness over the past decade of the value and sensitivity of non-defense federal ADP programs and services. The Privacy Act, to be discussed in detail later in this chapter, was an early milestone (in the seventies) that specified protection of personal data. Since many federal personnel and other data systems with personal data are automated, the Act led to increased emphasis on the use of computer security measures *per se*.

More comprehensive concern for computer security, as such, was reflected by the publication of three reports on federal computer security in the spring of 1976 by the General Accounting Office (GAO), an investigative and auditing arm of the Congress. These reports were 'Improvements Needed in Managing Automated Decisionmaking by Computers Throughout the Federal Government', April 23, 1976; 'Computer-Related Crimes in Federal Programs', April 27, 1976; and 'Managers Need to Provide Better Protection for Federal Automatic Data Processing Facilities', May 10, 1976. Shortly thereafter, the Chairman of the Senate Committee on Government Operations (now called the Senate Committee on Governmental Affairs), Senator Ribicoff, announced that he had directed the Committee staff to conduct a preliminary inquiry into the problems associated with the areas highlighted by GAO. The Committee subsequently issued two studies dealing with computer security. The first, entitled 'Problems Associated with Computer Technology in Federal Programs and Private Industry— Computer Abuses,' reviewed some of the major issues and problems, and it included the three 1976 GAO studies cited above. A 1977 follow-up report by the committee staff included recommendations: (1) that the Office of Management and Budget (OMB) direct federal agencies to put into effect appropriate computer security controls and safeguards and (2) that federal agencies improve coordination of computer resource protection efforts, develop additional computer security standards, and establish personnel security policies.

Based partly on the foregoing, Senator Ribicoff also introduced the 'Federal

Computer Systems Protection Act of 1977'. S. 1766. With no final action in the 95th Congress, the 'Federal Computer Systems Protection Act of 1979' (S. 240 and H.R. 6196) was introduced by Senator Ribicoff. The bill in essence would make it a crime to use or attempt to use a computer with intent to defraud or obtain property falsely and to embezzle or steal property. On November 6, 1979, the Senate Judiciary Subcommittee on Criminal Laws and Procedures referred an amended version of the bill to the full Committee for consideration. As mentioned earlier in this chapter, the bill is still under consideration.

Office of Management and Budget Circular No. A-71, TM No. 1

July 27, 1978, is a watershed data in understanding the impact of federal legislation on computer security. OMB Circular No. A-71 provides comprehensive computer security requirements for federal government data and applications processed by government or contractor computer systems. The promulgating document called for each executive branch department and agency to provide OMB with an implementation plan. To oversee program implementation and specifically review department/agency implementation plans, OMB established an *ad hoc* team in December of 1978. These reviews continue today. Naturally this directive caused a shock wave throughout executive branch departments/agencies, as they scattered to satisfy this new requirement.

The complete OMB A-71 Directive is included at the end of this chapter. Following is a summary of the important facets. Pay attention to the similarity between this document and the areas covered by the Defense Department's 5200.28 discussed earlier.

OMB Computer Security Program Minimum Requirements

The OMB-directed computer security program requires, 'at a minimum', each federal department and agency to:

1. Assign responsibility for the security of each computer installation operated by or on behalf of the agency *to a management official* knowledgeable in data processing and security.
2. Establish personnel security policies for all federal and contractor personnel involved in the design, operation, or maintenance of, or having access to data in federal computer systems.
3. Establish a management control process to assure that appropriate administrative, physical, and technical safeguards are incorporated into all new computer applications and significant modifications to existing applications (for applications deemed 'sensitive', this includes: prior definition and approval of security specifications and the conduct, approval, and certification of design reviews, and application systems tests).
4. Conduct periodic risk analyses for each computer installation operated by or on behalf of the agency (at least one every five years).

5. Assure that appropriate security requirements are included in the specifications for the acquisition or operation of computer facilities or services (the above-cited management official must review, approve, and certify the sufficiency of these requirements).
6. Conduct independent periodic audits or evaluations and recertify the adequacy of the security safeguards of each operational sensitive application (at least every three years).
7. Assure that appropriate contingency plans are developed and maintained to provide for the continuity of operations should events occur which prevent normal operations; and to periodically review and test these plans.

OMB Tasking for Additional Requirements

In support of the program, OMB has further tasked the following agencies as indicated below:

1. The Department of Commerce to develop and issue computer system security standards and guidelines.
2. The General Services Administration to issue policies and regulations for the physical security of computer rooms and assure that security requirements are included in agency procurements.
3. The Office of Personnel Management to establish personnel security policies for federal personnel associated with computer systems.

Supplemental Central Agency Policy

Pursuant to the above OMB tasking, the Office of Personnel Management (OPM) has already promulgated federal personnel security policies in this area, and the General Services Administration (GSA) has apparently fulfilled their tasking as well. The National Bureau of Standards, an agency of the Department of Commerce, has published a substantial number of computer security guidelines and is engaged in standards development efforts.

Office of Personnel Management

On November 14, 1978, OPM issued their Federal Personnel Manual Letter 732–7, 'Personnel Security Program for Positions Associated with Federal Computer Systems' (subsequently incorporated into the Federal Personnel Manual). Pursuant to the responsibilities assigned by TM-1, OMB A-71, the bulletin was the first step in establishing personnel security policies for screening all individuals participating in the design, operation, or maintenance of federal computer systems or having access to data in federal computer systems, to include both employees and contractor personnel. OPM Bulletin No. 732-2, January 11, 1980, further set forth authorities for investigating contractor personnel and procedures for requesting such investigations from OPM.

With regard to federal employees, the OPM guidance established criteria for designating personnel position sensitivity 'to be viewed separately, but in addition to the more traditional relationship to the national security' as currently employed under E.O. 10450.

General Services Administration

GSA actions included amendments to the following documents:

1. *Federal Property Management Regulations.* Amendments (e.g. FPMR Amendment F-42) were published in August 1980. The amendment to *FPMR Part 101-35* provides government-wide security management guidance for the protection of ADP and telecommunications systems and facilities. This new subpart contains the policy provision that 'Federal agencies shall ensure that an adequate level of security is provided for all ADP and telecommunication systems and services, including those provided by contractors', and then defines and describes associated requirements and responsibilities. The amendments to subpart 101-36.7, 'Environment and Physical Security', provide guidelines to federal agencies on the environmental and physical security of ADP facilities.
2. *Federal Procurement Regulations.* Amendments (FPR Amendment 210) published in October 1980 included the following which are pertinent to computer security:

   Section 1-4.1104 added the requirement that an agency's computer security requirements be included in the agency's procurement requests to GSA.

   Section 1-4.1107-21 prescribes government computer security requirements in connection with solicitations, contracts, and contract administration.

The Right to Privacy Act of 1974

Before the enactment of OMB A-71, TM No. 1 the only other government regulation that affected the management of federal computer systems is the Right to Privacy Act of 1974. The act was the result of increased public concern over the enormous amounts of personal information that the government possesses. Of specific concern was the use of government computer systems that process, store, and disseminate such information. Political abuses and the effects of 'Watergate' were contributing factors in the enactment of the act in 1974. Specifically, the act called for the special control of computer data that either directly or indirectly makes reference to personal concerns of U.S. citizens. The act is summarized below.

The Right to Privacy Act of 1974
(5 USC Sec. 552a)

Basic idea: Agencies *may not* release certain information *unless* it falls within one of eleven excepted categories.

1. An agency may not release any record to any person or agency relating to an individual except upon written request or consent of the individual.

2. Excepted categories in which case records *may be* released include the following releases:

a. To agency's own personnel who need such records to perform other duties.
b. As required under FOIA.
c. For a routine use (i.e., for a purpose compatible with the use for which the record was collected).
d. To Bureau of Census for planning purposes.
e. To a person who has provided prior written assurance that it will only be used for statistical purpose.
f. To National Archives where records have historical value.
g. To federal and state law enforcement authorities upon written request and specifying portion of record sought and law enforcement activity for which it is sought.
h. To person showing compelling need relating to health or safety provided that notification is transmitted to individual.
i. To Congress.
j. To Comptroller General in the course of performing duties of the GAO.
k. Pursuant to Court Order.

The Privacy Act of 1974 is implemented within the Executive Branch primarily through Office of Management and Budget (OMB) Circular No. A-108, 'Responsibilities for the Maintenance of Records About Individuals by Federal Agencies', as amended (i.e. Transmittal Memorandum No. 5 to OMB Circular A-108, August 3, 1978). The Circular defines responsibilities for implementing the Privacy Act 'to assure that personal information about individuals collected by federal agencies is limited to that which is legally authorized and necessary and is maintained in a manner which precludes unwarranted intrusions upon individual privacy'. Relative to this report, the Circular applies to all federal agencies and requires the head of each agency to 'establish reasonable administrative, technical, and physical safeguards' for protecting personal information subject to the Act, to include such information handled by EDP and such information handled by government contractors.

PRIVATE SECTOR COMPUTER SECURITY LEGISLATION

The federal government has not enacted any legislation that directly deals with the management of private sector computer systems. Nonetheless, contractors who process government information in their computer systems must satisfy government requirements (e.g. the Privacy Act of 1974).

Congress has, however, passed legislation that indirectly affects the management of computer systems by directly regulating the way firms keep records and administer internal control of funds and transactions. The Foreign Corrupt Practices Act of 1977 is just such legislation.

The Foreign Corrupt Practices Act of 1977

The Foreign Corrupt Practices Act (FCPA) of 1977 administered by the Security and Exchange Commission was enacted to prevent corrupt payments, 'bribes', to foreign officials. The law covers all transactions, not just those related to foreign payments. In order to determine whether any such transactions have occurred, a publicly held company is required to keep accurate records and to maintain internal control systems to safeguard a company's assets against unauthorized use or disposition. Assets include the computer system itself and the data it contains as well as all other forms of assets. Management must establish and maintain controls to provide 'reasonable' assurance that:

1. Transactions are executed by authorization of management only.
2. Transactions are recorded for financial statement and asset accountability.
3. Access to assets is by management authorization only.

A problem resulting from a data processing performance failure or misuse of an internal system might be evidence that a publicly held company's internal controls are weak, with the result that a business may be in violation of the law, even though no corrupt or fraudulent events have taken place. Internal controls over company assets may depend on control over the computer system.

No regulations exist to provide operational guidance as to the extent of the required controls. However, it is the responsibility of corporate managers and directors to assure that these internal controls exist and function in a defined and predictable fashion. Corporate management can be held individually responsible for losses ('bribes') resulting from deficient internal controls. Personal liability for non-compliance can result in a fine of $10,000 and/or five years' imprisonment. There has yet to be a lawsuit against an individual of a corporation based upon the statutes of the FCPA. The essential parts of the FCPA are included at the end of this chapter.

The only other body of legislation that affects, again indirectly, the management of private sector computer systems is the Fair Credit Reporting Act, 15 USC SS 1681. This act defines when and what type of personal information may be released about an individual, specifically financial information. Again, no direct reference is made to the management of computer systems. However, since most of this type of information is stored and processed by computers, sufficient processing and dissemination controls must be present to assure that only the proper information is released.

In summary, the government has directly responded to needs of safeguarding federal computer systems and data. Based upon the regulations promulgated by the Department of Defense, the government enacted comprehensive regulations dealing with all aspects of computer security. Office of Management and Budget Directive A-71 Transmittal Letter No. 1 and the Privacy Act of 1974 represents Omnibus policy for the security of government computer systems. While at face value this directive represents an important step, enforcement is another question. The General Accounting Office has begun to audit government data centers for compliance with A-71. For the most part the results have not been good.

The government has yet to respond to the issue of computer security management in the private sector. The lack of federal computer crime legislation has left this issue largely up to the states that have such laws. A federal computer crime law is currently under consideration. The Foreign Corrupt Practices Act indirectly represents federal involvement in computer security management. This act holds corporate managers and directors personally responsible for sound internal control of their corporate assets (e.g., computer systems).

BIBLIOGRAPHY

Security Requirement for Automatic Data Processing (ADP) Systems, Department of Defense Directive 5200.28, December 1972.

Information Security Program Regulation, Department of Defense Regulation DOD 5200.1-R, December 1978.

Security of Federal Automated Information Systems, Transmittal Memorandum No. 1 to OMB Circular No. A-71, Office of Management and Budget. Executive Office of the President, Washington, D.C. 20503, July 27, 1978.

Responsibilities for the Maintenance of Records About Individuals by Federal Agencies, OMB Circular No. A-108, Office of Management and Budget, Executive Office of the President, Washington, D.C. 20503, July 1, 1975, as amended (Transmittal Memorandum No. 5, August 3, 1978).

National Security Information, Executive Order 12065, The Federal Register, July 3, 1978.

Security Requirements for Government Employment, Executive Order 10450, April 27, 1953, as amended.

Managers Need to Provide Better Protection for Federal Automatic Data Processing Facilities, U.S. General Accounting Office, Washington, D.C., Report F6MSD-76-40 (May 10, 1976).

Staff Study of Computer Security in Federal Programs, Committee on Government Operations, U.S. Senate, February 1977.

The Foreign Corrupt Practices Act, Public Law 95-213-95th Congress, 1977.

July 27, 1978 CIRCULAR NO. A-71
Transmittal Memorandum No. 1

TO THE HEADS OF EXECUTIVE DEPARTMENTS AND ESTABLISH-
MENTS

SUBJECT: Security of Federal Automated Information Systems

1. *Purpose.* This Transmittal Memorandum to OMB Circular No. A-71 dated
March 6, 1965 promulgates policy and responsibilities for the development and
implementation of computer security programs by executive branch departments
and agencies. More specifically, it:

a. Defines the division of responsibility for computer security between line
operating agencies and the Department of Commerce, the General Services
Administration, and the Civil Service Commission.
b. Establishes requirements for the development of management controls to
safeguard personal, proprietary, and other sensitive data in automated
systems.
c. Establishes a requirement for agencies to implement a computer security
program and defines a minimum set of controls to be incorporated into each
agency computer security program.
d. Requires the Department of Commerce to develop and issue computer
security standards and guidelines.
e. Requires the General Services Administration to issue policies and regulations for the physical security of computer rooms consistent with standards
and guidelines issued by the Department of Commerce; assure that agency
procurement requests for automated data processing equipment, software,
and related services include security requirements; and assure that all
procurements made by GSA meet the security requirements established by
the user agency.
f. Requires the Civil Service Commission to establish personnel security policies
for federal personnel associated with the design, operation or maintenance of
federal computer systems, or having access to data in federal computer
systems.

2. *Background.* Increasing use of computer and communications technology
to improve the effectiveness of governmental programs has introduced a variety of
new management problems. Many public concerns have been raised in regard to
the risks associated with automated processing of personal, proprietary, or other
sensitive data. Problems have been encountered in the misuse of computer and
communications technology to perpetrate crime. In other cases, inadequate
administrative practices along with poorly designed computer systems have
resulted in improper payments, unnecessary purchases or other improper actions.

The policies and responsibilities for computer security established by this Transmittal Memorandum supplement policies currently contained in OMB Circular No. A-71.

3. *Definitions.* The following definitions apply for the purposes of this memorandum:

a. 'Automated decisionmaking systems' are computer applications which issue checks, requisition supplies, or perform similar functions based on programmed criteria, with little human intervention.
b. 'Contingency plans' are plans for emergency response, back-up operations, and post-disaster recovery.
c. 'Security specifications' are a detailed description of the safeguards required to protect a sensitive computer application.
d. 'Sensitive application' is a computer application which requires a degree of protection because it processes sensitive data or because of the risk and magnitude of loss or harm that could result from improper operation or deliberate manipulation of the application (e.g. automated decisionmaking systems).
e. 'Sensitive data' are data which require a degree of protection due to the risk and magnitude of loss or harm which could result from inadvertent or deliberate disclosure, alteration, or destruction of the data (e.g. personal data, proprietary data).

4. *Responsibility of the heads of executive agencies.* The head of each executive branch department and agency is responsible for assuring an adequate level of security for all agency data whether processed in-house or commercially. This includes responsibility for the establishment of physical, administrative and technical safeguards required to adequately protect personal, proprietary, or other sensitive data not subject to national security regulations, as well as national security data. It also includes responsibility for assuring that automated processes operate effectively and accurately. In fulfilling this responsibility each agency head shall establish policies and procedures and assign responsibility for the development, implementation, and operation of an agency computer security program. The agency's computer security program shall be consistent with all federal policies, procedures, and standards issued by the Office of Management and Budget, the General Services Administration, the Department of Commerce, and the Civil Service Commission. In consideration of problems which have been identified in relation to existing practices, each agency's computer security program shall at a minimum:

a. Assign responsibility for the security of each computer installation operated by the agency, including installations operated directly by or on behalf of the agency (e.g. government-owned contractor operated facilities), to a management official knowledgeable in data processing and security matters.

b. Establish personnel security policies for screening all individuals participating in the design, operation, or maintenance of federal computer systems or having access to data in federal computer systems. The level of screening required by these policies should vary from minimal checks to full background investigations commensurate with the sensitivity of the data to be handled and the risk and magnitude of loss or harm that could be caused by the individual. These policies should be established for government and contractor personnel. Personnel security policies for federal employees shall be consistent with policies issued by the Civil Service Commission.

c. Establish a management control process to assure that appropriate administrative, physical and technical safeguards are incorporated into all new computer applications and significant modifications to existing computer applications. This control process should evaluate the sensitivity of each application. For sensitive applications, particularly those which will process sensitive data or which will have a high potential for loss, such as automated decisionmaking systems, specific controls should, at a minimum, include policies and responsibilities for:

(1) Defining and approving security specifications prior to programming the applications or changes. The views and recommendations of the computer user organization, the computer installation and the individual responsible for the security of the computer installation shall be sought and considered prior to the approval of the security specifications for the application.

(2) Conducting and approving design reviews and application systems tests prior to using the systems operationally. The objective of the design reviews should be to ascertain that the proposed design meets the approved security specifications. The objective of the system tests should be to verify that the planned administrative, physical, and technical security requirements are operationally adequate prior to the use of the system. The results of the design review and system test shall be fully documented and maintained as a part of the system test; an official of the agency shall certify that the system meets the documented and approved system security specifications, meets all applicable federal policies, regulations and standards, and that the results of the test demonstrate that the security provisions are adequate for the application.

d. Establish an agency program for conducting periodic audits or evaluations and recertifying the adequacy of the security safeguards of each operational sensitive application including those which process personal, proprietary or other sensitive data or which have a high potential for financial loss, such as automated decisionmaking applications. Audits or evaluations are to be conducted by an organization independent of the user organization and computer facility manager. Recertifications should be fully documented and maintained as part of the official documents of the agency. Audits or evaluations and recertifications shall be performed at time intervals determined by the agency, commensurate with the sensitivity of information processed and the risk and magnitude of loss or harm that could result from the application operating improperly, but shall be conducted at least every three years.

e. Establish policies and responsibilities to assure that appropriate security requirements are included in specifications for the acquisition or operation of computer facilities, equipment, software packages, or related services, whether procured by the agency or by the General Services Administration. These requirements shall be reviewed and approved by the management official assigned responsibility for security of the computer installation to be used. This individual must certify that the security requirements specified are reasonably sufficient for the intended application and that they comply with current federal computer security policies, procedures, standards, and guidelines.

f. Assign responsibility for the conduct of periodic risk analyses for each computer installation operated by the agency, including installations operated directly by or on behalf of the agency. The objective of this risk analysis should be to provide a measure of the relative vulnerabilities at the installation so that security resources can effectively be distributed to minimize the potential loss. A risk analysis shall be performed:

(1) Prior to the approval of design specifications for new computer installations.

(2) Whenever there is a significant change to the physical facility, hardware or software at a computer installation. Agency criteria for defining significant changes shall be commensurate with the sensitivity of the information processed by the installation.

(3) At periodic intervals of time established by the agency, commensurate with the sensitivity of the information processed by the installation, but not to exceed five years, if no risk analysis has been performed during that time.

g. Establish policies and responsibilities to assure that appropriate contingency plans are developed and maintained. The objective of these plans should be to provide reasonable continuity of data processing support should events occur which prevent normal operations. These plans should be reviewed and tested at periodic intervals of time commensurate with the risk and magnitude of loss or harm which could result from disruption of data processing support.

5. *Responsibility of the Department of Commerce.* The Secretary of Commerce shall develop and issue standards and guidelines for assuring security of automated information. Each standard shall, at a minimum, identify:

a. Whether the standard is mandatory or voluntary.

b.   Specific implementation actions which agencies are required to take.
c.   The time at which implementation is required.
d.   A process for monitoring implementation of each standard and evaluating its use.
e.   The procedure for agencies to obtain a waiver to the standard and the conditions or criteria under which it may be granted.

6. *Responsibility of the General Services Administration.* The Administrator of General Services shall:

a.   Issue policies and regulations for the physical security of computer rooms in federal buildings consistent with standards and guidelines issued by the Department of Commerce.
b.   Assure that agency procurement requests for computers, software packages, and related services include security requirements which have been certified by a responsible agency official. Delegations of procurement authority to agencies by the General Services Administration under mandatory programs, dollar threshold delegations, certification programs, or other so-called blanket delegations shall include requirements for agency specifications and agency certification of security requirements. Other delegations of procurement authority shall require specific agency certification of security requirements as a part of the agency request for delegation of procurement authority.
c.   Assure that specifications for computer hardware, software, related services or the construction of computer facilities are consistent with standards and guidelines established by the Secretary of Commerce.
d.   Assure that computer equipment, software, computer room construction, guard or custodial services, telecommunications services, and any other related services procured by the General Services Administration meet the security requirements established by the user agency and are consistent with other applicable policies and standards issued by OMB, the Civil Service Commission and the Department of Commerce. Computer equipment, software, or related ADP services acquired by the General Services Administration in anticipation of future agency requirements shall include security safeguards which are consistent with mandatory standards established by the Secretary of Commerce.

7. *Responsibility of the Civil Service Commission.* The Chairman of the Civil Service Commission shall establish personnel security policies for federal personnel associated with the design, operation or maintenance of federal computer systems, or having access to data in federal computer systems. These policies should emphasize personnel requirements to adequately protect personal, proprietary, or other sensitive data as well as other sensitive applications not subject to national security regulations. Requirements for personnel checks imposed by these policies should vary commensurate with the sensitivity of the

data to be handled and the risk and magnitude of loss or harm that could be caused by the individual. The checks may range from merely normal reemployment screening procedures to full background investigations.

8. *Reports*. Within 60 days of the issuance of this Transmittal Memorandum, the Department of Commerce, General Services Administration and Civil Service Commission shall submit to OMB plans and associated resource estimates for fulfilling the responsibilities specifically assigned in this memorandum. Within 120 days of the issuance of this Transmittal Memorandum, each executive branch department and agency shall submit to OMB plans and associated resource estimates for implementing a security program consistent with the policies specified herein.

9. *Inquiries*. Questions regarding this memorandum should be addressed to the Information Systems Policy Division (202) 395-4814.

FOREIGN CORRUPT PRACTICES ACT OF 1977

PUBLIC LAW 95-213—95th CONGRESS
(Approved December 19, 1977)

An Act to amend the Securities Exchange Act of 1934 to make it unlawful for an
issuer of securities registered pursuant to Section 12 of such Act or an issuer
required to file reports pursuant to Section 15(d) of such Act to make certain payments to foreign officials and other foreign persons, to require such issuers to
maintain accurate records, and for other purposes.

TITLE I–FOREIGN CORRUPT PRACTICES

Sec. 101. This title may be cited as the "Foreign Corrupt Practices Act of
1977"

Accounting Standards

Sec. 102. Section 13(b) of the Securities Exchange Act of 1934 (15 U.S.C.
78q(b) is amended . . . by adding at the end thereof the following:

'(2) Every issuer which has a class of securities registered pursuant to section
12 of this title and every issuer which is required to file reports pursuant to section
15(d) of this title shall—

'(A) make and keep books, records, and accounts, which, in reasonable detail,
accurately and fairly reflect the transactions and dispositions of the assets of the
issuer, and

'(B) devise and maintain a system of internal accounting controls sufficient to
provide reasonable assurances that–

'(i) transactions are executed in accordance with management's general or
specific authorization;

'(ii) transactions are recorded as necessary (I) to permit preparation of financial
statements in conformity with generally accepted accounting principles or any
other criteria applicable to such statements, and (II) to maintain accountability for
assets;

'(iii) access to assets is permitted only in accordance with management's
general or specific authorization; and

'(iv) the recorded accountability for assets is compared with the existing assets
at reasonable intervals and appropriate action is taken with respect to any
differences.'

Note: The remainder of Sec. 102 lists exemptions for national security matters.

Foreign Corrupt Practices by Issuers

'Sec. 103(a) The Securities Exchange Act of 1934 is amended by inserting after
Section 30 the following new section:

'Sec. 309A. (a) It shall be unlawful for any issuer which has a class of securities registered pursuant to Section 12 of this title or which is required to file reports under Section 15(d) of this title, or for any officer, director, employee, or agent of such issuer or any stockholder thereof acting on behalf of such issuer, to make use of the mails or any means or instrumentality of interstate commerce corruptly in furtherance of an offer, payment, promise to pay, or authorization of the payment of any money, or offer, gift, promise to give, or authorization of the giving of anything of value to—

'(1) any foreign official for purposes of—

'(A) influencing any act or decision of such foreign official in his official capacity, including a decision to fail to perform his official functions; or

'(B) inducing such foreign official to use his influence with a foreign government or instrumentality thereof to affect or influence any act or decision of such government or instrumentality,

in order to assist such issuer in obtaining or retaining business for or with, or directing business to, any person;

'(2) any foreign political party or official thereof or any candidate for foreign political office for purposes of—

'(A) influencing any act or decision of such party, official, or candidate in its or his official capacity, including a decision to fail to perform its or his official functions; or

'(B) inducing such party, official, or candidate to use its or his influence with a foreign government or instrumentality thereof to affect or influence any act or decision of such government or instrumentality, in order to assist such issuer in obtaining or retaining business for or with, or directing business to, any person; or

'(3) any person, while knowing or having reason to know that all or a portion of such money or thing of value will be offered, given, or promised, directly or indirectly, to any foreign official, to any foreign political party or official thereof, or to any candidate for foreign political office, for purposes of:

'(A) influencing any act or decision of such foreign official, political party, party official, or candidate in his or its official capacity, including a decision to fail to perform his or its official functions; or

'(B) inducing such foreign official, political party, party official, or candidate to use his or its influence with a foreign government or instrumentality thereof to affect or influence any act or decision of such government or instrumentality, in order to assist such issuer in obtaining or retaining business for or with, or directing business to, any person.

'(b) As used in this section, the term "foreign official" means any officer or employee of a foreign government or any department, agency, or instrumentality thereof, or any person acting in an official capacity for or on behalf of such government or department, agency, or instrumentality. Such term does not include any employee of a foreign government or any department, agency, or instrumentality thereof whose duties are essentially ministerial or clerical.'

(b)(2) Section 32 of the Securities Exchange Act of 1934 (15 U.S.C. 78ff) is amended by adding at the end thereof the following new subsection:

'(c)(1) Any issuer which violates section 30A(a) of this title shall, upon conviction, be fined not more than $1,000,000.

'(2) Any officer or director of an issuer, or any stockholder acting on behalf of such issuer, who willfully violates Section 30A(a) of this title shall, upon conviction, be fined not more than $10,000 or imprisoned not more than five years, or both.

'(3) Whenever an issuer is found to have violated Section 30A(a) of this title, any employee or agent of such issuer who is a United States citizen, national, or resident or is otherwise subject to the jurisdiction of the United States (other than an officer, director, or stockholder of such issuer), and who willfully carried out the act or practice constituting such violation shall, upon conviction, be fined not more than $10,000, or imprisoned not more than five years, or both.

'(4) Whenever a fine is imposed under paragraph (2) or (3) of this subsection upon any officer, director, stockholder, employee, or agent of an issuer, such fine shall not be paid, directly or indirectly, by such issuer.'

Note: Sec. 104 parallels Sec. 30A with 'domestic concerns' replacing 'issuers'.

Sec. 104(c) Whenever it appears to the Attorney General that any domestic concern, or officer, director, employee, agent, or stockholder thereof, is engaged, or is about to engage, in any act or practice constituting a violation of subsection (a) of this section, the Attorney General may, in his discretion, bring a civil action in an appropriate district court of the United States to enjoin such act or practice, and upon a proper showing a permanent or temporary injunction or a temporary restraining order shall be granted without bond.

(d) As used in this section:

(A) any individual who is a citizen, national, or resident of the United States; or (b) any corporation, partnership, association, joint-stock company, business trust, unincorporated organization, or sole proprietorship which has its principal place of business in the United States, or which is organized under the laws of a State of the United States or a territory, possession, or commonwealth of the United States.

(2) The term 'foreign official' means any officer or employee of a foreign government or any department, agency, or instrumentality thereof, or any person acting in an official capacity for or on behalf of any such government or department, agency, or instrumentality. Such term does not include any employee of a foreign government or any department, agency, or instrumentality thereof whose duties are essentially ministerial or clerical.

(3) The term 'interstate commerce' means trade, commerce, transportation, or communication among the several States, or between any foreign country and any State or between any State and any place or ship outside thereof. Such term includes the intrastate use of (A) a telephone or other interstate means of communication, or (B) any other interstate instrumentality.

Note: Title II improves the disclosure requirements of ownership of securities.

Advances in Computer Security Management, Vol. 2
Edited by M. M. Wofsey
© 1983 John Wiley & Sons Ltd.

Chapter 5

DESIGNING SECURE DATA PROCESSING APPLICATIONS

Peter S. Browne
Burns International Security Service, Inc.

Eugene F. Troy
Digital Analysis Corporation

The recognition of the 'software problem' over the last decade has resulted in much attention being focused on the development of quality software. Software has become the predominant factor in the cost of present and future computer systems, accounting for about 60% of the system development cost and steadily rising. A major difficulty of software systems is complexity; as complexity increases, lack of discipline and adequate control results in high cost, unresponsive systems, slippage of schedules, and problems in operation and maintenance.

This chapter will discuss both the techniques for better control over the software development process and the progress that has been made over the last decade in techniques for achieving higher quality software through disciplined engineering approaches, and explicit consideration will be given to both accounting controls and security in application systems.

CHARACTERIZATION OF THE SOFTWARE PROBLEM

The major problems in software development can be characterized as high development cost and inadequate performance when completed. Large software projects may fail completely or be subject to severe time delays and large cost overruns. Studies in the early 1970s by Barry Boehm discovered systems that had unpredictable behavior, exhibited hard-to-correct errors, were poorly documented, and were unresponsive to user requirements. In addition, these systems were almost impossible to maintain because the programming practices resulted in code which was incomprehensible. Thus it became apparent that the quality and dependability of the software development process needed improvement. An appropriate set of standards and procedures for all phases of the software development life cycle, coupled with effective project management techniques, can result in considerable success in developing high-quality software.

Programming Policies, Standards, and Procedures

A disciplined engineering approach to software development begins with the establishment of policies, standards, and procedures. These guidelines form a continuum, ranging from the general to the specific. Their effective use enables management to plan, direct, and control the software development activities effectively and efficiently. Following are several reasons for utilizing a well-organized, disciplined structure based upon sound policies, standards, and procedures.

1. Policies provide management directives for who, when, why, and where activities are to be performed. They may range from a national policy or act of federal legislation to a company or organizational policy.
2. Standards identify and establish the norms against which performance can effectively be measured. The imposition of standards is a difficult task, and care must be exercised in assuring that they are not arbitrary and capricious. Reasonable standards will be followed and will thus be effective; irrational and rigid standards will be ignored. In areas where standards cannot be effectively established and used, reasonable guidelines can provide an appropriate solution.
3. Procedures provide a systematic step-by-step process on how to perform the work in an orderly manner.

Characteristics of Quality Software

The utilization and adherence to sound policies, standards, and procedures will help attain high-quality software. The desired characteristics of high-quality software include, but are not limited to, the following fundamental goals:

Reliability

This feature refers to correct operation (with respect to its specification) of the software and the ability of the software to recover from errors. The software must work under all circumstances defined in the specification of its behavior and must not contain any unspecified and undocumented interactions with its environment.

Modifiability

This term refers to the ability to make changes in a controlled manner, modifying the relevant portions while leaving the rest of the system intact. This characteristic is difficult to achieve for several reasons. The effects of changes on the total software system are often hard to predict. Changes become necessary for so many different reasons, including augmenting the capabilities of a system, removing discovered errors, improving a system's run-time performance, or transferring a system to a new environment with different operating characteristics.

Understandability

This fundamental characteristic is related to and is a prerequisite for all the other desired goals. If the software can be understood by individuals other than the developers, the ability to determine whether it is operating correctly is possible. It also significantly eases the task of modifying and maintaining the software once it has been developed and is in a production environment.

Efficiency

This attribute refers to the software's utilization of system resources. An efficient software system is a desirable characteristic; yet it sometimes causes difficulties by being considered too early in the design phase, to the detriment of all the other characteristics. An efficient system which is unreliable, full of errors, and difficult to maintain is not a desirable software product; neither is a system which operates correctly but is grossly inefficient.

THE SYSTEMS LIFE CYCLE

The systems life-cycle concept is an approach to the development process that attempts to ensure the specifications of user requirements, the design, development, and implementation of systems. Its goals are to deliver computer systems on a schedule, within budget, and to the user's satisfaction. One of the attributes of following a rigorous life-cycle approach is that computer systems are invariably better controlled, more secure, and less vulnerable.

Basic Concepts

The systems life cycle consists of several distinct phases of activity relating to final implementation of a system. These phases are systematically planned, organized, and controlled, with detailed documentation an essential element.

Of the various approaches, many are very detailed and specific. However, all of them follow a similar pattern. An overview of the basic phases follows, with the specific security ramifications then discussed.

The major phases of a typical systems development life-cycle program are:

1. Project definition and survey.
2. System requirements definition.
3. Computer system design.
4. Application software development.
5. System installation.
6. Post-installation review.

These items are not meant to establish an absolute standard; they are presented to be illustrative of one approach or to allow a basis for discussion of the impact of security in this process.

Project Definition and Survey

This step consists of a problem analysis to determine the nature of the problem, related business issues, economics, and the appropriateness of a computer-based solution. It should include security and data sensitivity impacts and issues and, in measurable terms, requirements for controls.

System Requirements Definition

This step defines in detail the user or agency requirements which must be met and the specific functions the system must perform. It also considers practical current (and expected near-term future) technology. It defines the functional requirements of the proposed system in order to select a viable design strategy, and to set system acceptance criteria. These criteria include controllability and auditability requirements.

Computer System Design

This step involves providing a technical blueprint for the data design, system packaging, and program designs to most effectively meet the system's functional performance, including security requirements.

Application Software Development

In this step, modular construction, integration, and thorough testing for compliance with the system's functional and performance requirements is accomplished.

System Installation

Installation in the target operational environment, user personnel training, and acceptance testing are complete in this phase.

Post-Installation Review

This final important stage, usually neglected, includes an analysis of costs/operations/benefits underlying a major system's venture to assure a level of actual user satisfaction or use of the system, and its design goals.

Security Implications

Many considerations of security are present within the life-cycle concept described previously.

In the project initiation phase, compliance with law, the regulatory environment, and company policy in terms of security, privacy, and controls must be considered in this initial stage of systems specification. In addition, security considerations are imposed by generally accepted accounting practices and various policy directives. Further constraints of existing facilities, computer services, and manpower may well limit the degree of security control possible.

System requirements definitions must explicitly consider risks to the proposed system. Once risks are defined, then basic user requirements relating to access, integrity, recoverability, and auditability need to be specified. (These topics are discussed later.)

During the detailed design phases, the technical controls must be considered and designed, and the administrative and procedural aspects of implementing control made explicit.

In the development and installation phase, the designed security controls are coded, tested, written, and installed in the user environment. Testing must account for all possible conditions of use, including overload or situations where all the system of human resources may not be available.

SPECIFYING SECURITY IN THE DEVELOPMENT OF SYSTEMS

The most significant activity in terms of cost-effectiveness is to define security requirements and design applications for systems during the initial phases, rather than wait until design is completed.

Sources of Security Requirements

A key success element of security relates to the initial definition of security requirements. It is not possible to provide adequate protection 'after-the-fact'. Therefore, the principal objective of any security effort must address three basic components:

1. Externally imposed security requirements affecting DP systems can be derived from both outside and inside the organization. For example, most corporations are affected by the privacy laws, government regulations, the SEC, and other regulatory bodies. In addition, legal obligations may also include a requirement to meet certain criteria to enforce a level of protection, such as generally accepted accounting principles which affect those systems handling or controlling financial assets.

2. Internally imposed security requirements come from two sources. The first relates to internal rules or policy that relate to security and protection. The second source arises from a detailed consideration of risks.
3. Constraints as imposed by technology, system limitations, or policy may force design requirements on certain processes. For example, a requirement to process in only one data center facility may affect a possible security requirement to distribute certain data near its source so as to facilitate backup and recovery.

In the requirements definition process, these overall considerations will contend with each other and be analyzed in order to develop a concise set of functional security requirements for consideration in the design process. The requirements will also cover the areas of access control rules, integrity requirements in terms of processing capability, backup and recovery, system availability, and procedural interfaces.

Basic Security Requirements

Security requirements for a system under development must be based on the specific operational, legal, and technical environment in which the system will exist. Although many types of security measures are fundamental requirements for all systems, many other measures are appropriate only if the threat of loss is sufficient to justify the cost of the extra protection.

Any system should reflect certain attributes to provide a fundamental level of security. These characteristics may be manifested in whole or in part by several types of security measures: administrative, physical, and technical. These attributes are briefly explained below.

1. *Identification.* All users, data, programs, transactions, outputs, and other system elements and resources should be uniquely and adequately identified. Such identification is necessary for the other security attributes to be present.
2. *Authorization.* There must be mechanisms to authorize (i.e., approve) the access of users, programs, terminals, and transactions to system resources, such as transactions and data.
3. *Access Control.* Technical, physical, and administrative mechanisms are needed to control access within the system in accordance with the authorization process.
4. *Controllability.* The system must be designed and constructed in such a way that its various components (e.g., transaction modules, programs, operating system interfaces, and data base) can fully control the data or capabilities they share with each other.
5. *Integrity.* The system must perform its designated functions, and *only* those functions, correctly, consistently, within time constraints, and exactly

according to specifications. This dictate implies integrity requirements for data, programs, and the processing capability itself.

6. *Recoverability.* The system must be designed and operated in such a manner as to enable timely recovery from loss of data or processing capability due to the entire range of minor (e.g., power fluctuation) to catastrophic (e.g., fire) threats.

7. *Auditability.* Activity within the system and at its interfaces must be identifiable and accountable.

The decisions to be made about security requirements should answer the following questions:

1. What should the requirement be?
2. Where should the control be placed?
3. What action should be taken?

Design

Once specific functional requirements have been defined in terms of *what* must be done to meet security requirements, the next step is to include these in design decisions.

1. *Transaction origination* requirements should be specified to govern the origination, approval, and processing of source documents, the preparation of data processing input transaction and associated error prevention, detection, and correction procedures.

2. *Data processing transaction entry* requirements should be specified to govern both remote terminal and batch data entry, data validation, transaction or batch proofing and balancing, error identification and reporting, and error correction and re-entry.

3. *Data communications* security design should be specified to govern the accuracy and completeness of data communications, including message accountability, data protection, hardware and software, security and privacy, error identification, and reporting.

4. *Computer processing* security design should be specified to govern the accuracy, correctness, and completeness of transaction processing, including transaction validation against masterfiles, error identification, and reporting.

5. *Data storage and retrieval* security design should be specified to ensure masterfile data accuracy and completeness, correct transaction/masterfile cutoff, data security and privacy, error handling, and backup, recovery, and retention. Note that file integrity controls reflect the growing use of general-purpose file handling and data base software, and an attendant trend to view processing procedures as independent of data files.

6. *Output, processing* security design should be specified to govern manual balancing and reconciliation of data processing input and output (both within the data processing input/output control section at user locations), distribution of data processing output, control over negotiable documents (both within data processing and user areas), and output data retention.

Measurement

Any potential design should be subject to extensive scrutiny and evaluation in accordance with measurement criteria for security and integrity. The measurement criteria should be expressed in terms of:

1. *Completeness*: Are all the vulnerabilities or risks covered? Is the requirement itself being met?
2. *Consistency*: What percentage of the time are the risk or externally imposed requirements being met? What is the probability of failure?
3. *Strength*: How strong or impervious is a specific safeguard? Even though a

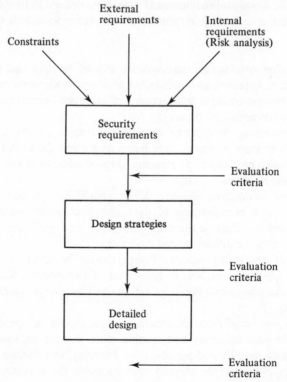

Figure 5-1.   Role of security requirements in the design process.

methodology for evaluating system security has not yet been developed, some analogy to the 'safe ratings' used in traditional industrial or military security can be postulated.

4. *Cost*: What is the incremental cost of a given or proposed safeguard? Costs can be measured in absolute terms and in increments over or under the baseline security measures. Costs of development and implementation must be carefully distinguished from on-going maintenance and evaluation costs. In addition, second-order costs of transition (e.g. education and workforce disruption) must be separately identified.

5. *Compatibility*: To what extent do the specific security requirements and their implementation conflict with or support the basic objectives and concepts of the system under consideration? It is naive to assume that all objectives will be consistent with each other or that varying specific designs will either be consistent or meet the basic requirements equally. Therefore, the measurements must provide a rational assessment of these variances.

6. *Flexibility*: The requirement to allow for changes in law or technology must be itself a primary requirement. The measurement must attempt to understand and rate flexibility and to allow performance of the necessary trade-off analyses (Figure 5-1).

ACCOUNTING AND SECURITY CONTROLS

Over the years organizations have taken advantage of the computer's processing capabilities and have converted manual operations to automated systems. In the process of converting, EDP systems frequently eliminate certain manual procedures, including related control techniques. Consequently, many manually segregated diversified functions have been concentrated in a single, centralized data processing entity. Even in an automated environment, control objectives and processing cycle requirements have remained characteristically the same. In fact, the objectives and essential characteristics of controls do not change with the method of data processing. In actuality, the requirements for security controls increase dramatically as an organization converts from a batch data processing environment to an on-line and/or data base processing environment.

Control Objectives

Such application systems should be specified, designed, and developed according to a basic set of control objectives. Examples include:

1. Computer data processing should produce accurate, complete, and valid information on a timely basis.
2. All transactions should be tracked, independently verified, and processed accurately, completely, and securely.

3. All data base maintenance (updating) should be performed accurately, completely, and properly, and only in an authorized manner.
4. Adequate and appropriate management/audit trails should exist to ensure data accessibility and cross-referencing.

DP Processing Cycle

As control objectives do not change with methods of data processing, neither do the basic data processing components (input, processing, and output). Each component in turn has certain control objectives and techniques which depend on the application systems function (e.g. Process Accounts Receivable) and the system's processing attributes (e.g. batch versus on-line). Regardless of system function or attributes, controls are necessary to assure the accurate, complete, secure, and valid processing of data.

Control Issues

Each system, regardless of functional objective (e.g. payroll versus inventory control) or system design (batch versus real-time), should utilize controls which, under given circumstances, provide for adequate assurance of the accuracy, completeness, security, and validity of data processed. Additionally, many control objectives, techniques, and procedures are applicable to both conventional and advanced systems. One strong distinction can be drawn: the design and level of security required for advanced systems will necessitate longer and careful study to fit controls to a more complex environment. Conventional systems are frequently identified as batch oriented. Their simplicity of design, however, does not eliminate the need for adequate data processing controls nor resolve pertinent issues of security. Any measurable progress in designing data processing controls can easily be recognized by referencing the techniques and procedures relating to data input controls, processing controls, and output controls.

Input Controls

Data input frequently is the weakest link in the computer processing chain of events. Therefore, adequate controls should be established to ensure the accuracy, completeness, and authorization of input. Furthermore, they should:

1. Prevent and detect errors at the point of preparation.
2. Prohibit submission of additional, unauthorized data.
3. Provide the ability to determine that all data reach the computers accurately and completely.
4. Promote accurate, complete, and authorized data entry.

Processing (Programmed) Controls

Regardless of the design and the processing environment, conventional systems should still have some method of ensuring the accuracy, completeness, and validity of processing. Minimal control standards/issues would be that:

1. Control procedures should ensure that only valid data are used; thus, file authorization checking is necessary.
2. All input data are accounted for and all transactions are verified.
3. Controls are in place to ensure accuracy and completeness of data during updating (e.g., run-to-run totaling, sequence checking, and record identification/matching).
4. Reports are made of all input and updating exceptions.

Output Controls

Output controls should ensure that information produced through computerized record-keeping is complete and accurate. In this phase, control issues requiring attention would include:

1. Data to support balancing and reconciliation processes.
2. Proper handling and distribution of output (only deliver to authorized persons).
3. Appropriate document accountability procedures (handling of checks).
4. Timely reporting, correction, and resubmission of processing detected errors.

The control objectives for data processed in on-line systems do not change (e.g. accuracy and completeness of input, provision(s) for adequate audit trails, and authorized input data); however, control design techniques present a different set of issues to be considered. This difference is directly related to the extension of the system to terminal input and output devices. Appropriate hardware and/or software techniques as well as direct physical security measures, therefore, must be incorporated to maintain integrity of data and to prevent unauthorized users from compromising the data contained within an on-line system.

System Design Considerations

There is an optimum point in time to consider controls. For example:

1. Controls to check, test, or verify data should be planned and developed during the initial design of the system and compared against controls existing in the system being replaced.

2. Both manual and computer system controls should be considered. Controls should be automated as much as possible. Manual controls should be limited to those situations where automated controls are not feasible, or where automated controls may be subverted.
3. Controls should originate as close as possible to the source of the action or information.
4. Controls should be simple but adequate to accomplish their objectives.
5. Requirements for editing programs should be dictated by the total systems requirements.
6. User and data processing departments should document and feed back control weaknesses to system maintainers. It may be desirable to require that a trouble report be prepared of all control check failures for review by the user and others involved. In addition to identifying system weaknesses, this practice may point to chronic mistakes by the user or data processing departments.
7. Designers and users should give consideration to the discretionary employment, within a control group, of control tolerances, error suspense files, and other methods that identify/isolate the error, but allow processing to continue.

TECHNIQUES TO ASSURE RELIABLE AND SECURE CODE

In order to achieve desired software security and control, it is not enough to specify disciplined design controls in an application. In addition, a disciplined and rigorous engineering approach must be taken to the software development process. *Ad hoc* development should give way to disciplined programming methodologies with systematic steps that can easily be followed. Software development is an evolutionary step-by-step process, starting from a loosely defined concept and evolving to a complete and maintainable implementation.

In the early 1970s, when the software problem was first recognized, much of the software engineering community (as this branch of computer science is called) focused on the techniques of structured programming, modularization, and top-down design. Many of these notions have more recently become more systematic and rigorous, covering all phases of software development.

Structured Programming

The early formulation of structured programming, also called 'GOTO-less programming', focused on the use of only certain programming language control structures which may be appropriately nested to produce a very readable program. These control structures are usually taken to be:

1. Sequences of two or more operations.

2. Conditional branch to one of two operations and return (IF X THEN a ELSE b).
3. Repetition of an operation while a condition is true (DO WHILE).

Other formulations using CASE statements and DO UNTIL are equally structured.

Structured programming has several benefits, for instance:

1. Fewer errors in the programming process.
2. Programs that are nearly self-documenting.
3. Programs that can be more easily read, modified, and maintained.
4. Elimination of traditional programming pitfalls.

However, it only attacks the actual coding phase of software development and does little to assist in the rest of software development. Structure and discipline are needed for the other aspects of the life cycle.

Modularization

Modularization refers to the process of decomposing a problem into a series of simpler subproblems until a level is reached where a solution can be attempted. Modularity is a fundamental underlying principle of structured software development; it is a key factor in controlling the complexity of software. In modular decomposition, each software module is developed in such a way that other modules only know the functional characteristics of the module and the module interface but know nothing about the actual detailed structure, i.e., code, and data structures of the module. Such a modular structure is particularly beneficial to software development, especially on large-scale projects. Once the modular structure has been established, different programmers may work independently on different modules.

Modularity is also beneficial for program modifications. Since only the behavior of the module is known externally (what it is supposed to do but not how), a program may be optimized, for example, by replacing modules with other modules which are functionally equivalent, but which run more efficiently.

The most common modularization strategies that have been suggested are top-down, bottom-up, outside-in, and inside-out. These approaches refer to the direction of the steps taken in the software development process.

1. In the top-down approach, decisions are made first which concern the highest level functions of the software, and these decisions are successively refined until one reaches the level at which the functions can execute on his particular machine.
2. In the bottom-up approach, the steps in software development proceed from

the level of existing resources (e.g. programming language and host machine) toward the required problem solution.

3. In the outside-in approach, the direction is from the outside of the system (what the user sees) toward the inside (the implementation). This strategy is similar to the top-down approach.

4. In the inside-out approach, the direction goes from the implementation to what the user sees.

The top-down approach is the most 'popular' and has received much attention in the literature. It establishes a good framework for software development and provides several advantages in improved understanding and communication among software developers. However, experience has shown that none of the approaches should be applied blindly to the absolute exclusion of the other approaches.

Design Tools

The design phase in the software development life cycle suffers from many of the same problems and constraints as the requirements phase. Errors which are introduced during design are also very expensive to correct when the system is in production. A coherent set of well-documented tools and techniques for the software designer has been lacking. It has been tempting to skimp on the design phase and begin 'writing code' to show tangible progress.

Software design today is still lacking a conceptual framework that is coherent, well-tested, and fully supported by languages and automated tools to make it effective. Over the last few years there has been an explosion of methods, techniques, and disciplines with grandiose claims of wide-ranging application. Some are being more systematically used and are still evolving. Adequate support tools are still lagging behind the spectrum of techniques which are in the early stages of application.

Several design methods will be highlighted in this section (and references included in the bibliography for further study). This brief description will provide the programming manager or software developer a flavor for the method, including its strengths and weaknesses. The design methods to be discussed are:

1. Michael Jackson Methodology

The Jackson Methodology was developed in the early and mid 1970s by Michael Jackson to provide a methodology for producing structured programs. It is based on two important principles:

a. deriving program structure from data structure, and
b. notions of Structured Programming.

The basis of the program design is the data which the program is to process. The major steps of the methodology are:

a. specify the data structures;
b. form the program structure from the data structure;
c. specify the program structure in a pseudo-code (schematic logic); and
d. code.

Two notational conventions from the core of the methodology are:

a. a graphic notation for diagramming the data and program structures; and
b. pseudo-code (schematic logic) derived from the diagrams.

The two advantages of the Jackson Methodology are its ability to handle:

a. structure clashes—when data structures are incompatible with each other; and
b. backtracking problem—when a decision cannot be made at the point where it is required but only after seeing more data.

The benefits of the methodology are that it depends little on the designer's insight; it is readily teachable, simple to understand, and relatively easy to implement from the pseudo-code into many programming languages. The major weakness of the methodology is that it is file structure oriented rather than function oriented, thereby limiting its applicability.

2. Structured Analysis and Design Technique (SADT)

SADT was developed by SofTech and has been in use since 1973. The basis of SADT is a diagramming technique and a top-down methodology for producing descriptions of systems using this graphic language. It relies heavily on the principle of functional decomposition to identify the key components of a system and their interrelationships. The graphic language is rigorous and imposes discipline on both the design process and the design itself. It is used to represent the data structures of the system, their interrelationships, and their relationship to the system functions. SADT also has systematic techniques for reviewing the design as it proceeds.

SADT is an abstract approach and currently is not automated. While the Jackson methodology is oriented toward program design and is based on data structures of the program, SADT is oriented toward system design and is based on the functions that the system is to provide. Its claimed benefits include:

1. Design notation provides explicit documentation useful for both peer review and for the implementation.

2. Documentation provides good basis for subsequent enhancement and maintenance.
3. Notational rigor enables effective project management control.

One of the major disadvantages of SADT is in the design creation. It has been criticized for doing little to reduce the skills required of the designer, who must be heavily experienced and creative.

3. Structured/Composite Design

The Structured Design Methodology was developed by Larry Constantine at IBM; a fellow researcher at IBM, Glenford Myers, developed the related techniques of Composite Design. Structured Design is based on the principle of functional decomposition. Its primary concern is *not* with design creation; rather it is with evaluation of the design against a set of criteria. The set of criteria is concerned with the relationships between modules (coupling) and the strength or intramodule unity (cohesion). In addition to these qualitative criteria, Structured Design focuses on a particular approach for producing a 'good' design composed of 'good' modules. Composite Design also uses the evaluative criteria of coupling and strength but is less formal than Structured Design.

Structured Design utilizes two graphic languages:

a.   a notation for specifying data flows (bubble charts); and
b.   a notation for specifying the structure of modules (structure charts).

The key strengths of Structured Design (and to a somewhat lesser degree the informal Composite Design) are in:

a.   establishment of criteria for qualitatively evaluating a design;
b.   ensuring correctness of a design at an early stage; and
c.   ensuring the maintainability of the final product.

Structured Design weaknesses include its inability to handle the design of data structures (it emphasizes data flow only) and its need for talented system designers in order for the methodology to produce useful results.

4. Warnier–Orr Methodology

This methodology was developed by Warnier in France and extended by Orr in the U.S. It is used in three different but related forms:

a.   Logical Construction of Programs (LCP);
b.   Logical Construction of Systems (LCS); and
c.   Structured Systems Design.

All forms of the methodology deal only with design. LCP deals with program design, and LCS deals with organizing the data of a system and the programs containing the data into a coherent system. Structured Systems Design is a methodology for developing logically correct hierarchical structured systems.

The Warnier–Orr Methodology, like the Jackson Methodology, derives the design structure from the data structure. This methodology has a rigorous theoretical foundation and relies heavily on ideas from set theory. The basic steps of the LCP (the other approaches are similar in principle) are to identify and document the data structure, to generate a flowchart, and then to generate pseudo-code. The technique assumes that a hierarchical relationship exists within the data to provide the required data structure.

The claimed benefits of the Warnier–Orr Methodology are:

a. improved productivity on medium-scale projects;
b. reduction in debugging and testing;
c. ease of maintenance; and
d. explicit recognition of the role of data bases and data base management systems.

The major disadvantage is a very practical one for anyone wanting to use the methodology—most of the documentation is in French. The only published work in English is of very poor quality and difficult to comprehend. Another weakness of the methodology is that it is unable to handle problems in which the data are not structured hierarchically.

Implementation Tools

Most of the software engineering research activity has focused on structuring the most error-prone phases of software development—requirements and design. Little has been done to further structure the implementation phase, other than the fundamental techniques of structured programming. Structured versions exist for most implementation languages in widespread use; e.g., FORTRAN, COBOL, PL/I, and even some assembly languages. Preprocessors and other language support software control and enforce particular coding styles and assure that the program is structured. It is still possible to write a bad program, albeit a structured one.

Several more recently developed programming languages are designed to support the development of structured programs. One in particular, Pascal, is being used in commercial data processing, especially for systems software.

The implementation phase is one in which numerous standards have been attempted and have often been ignored and eliminated. Such standards as a routine must fit on one page, a routine must be less than 100 lines of code, or a routine may contain only five DO WHILE statements are somewhat arbitrary and not very useful. The fundamental concept of structured programming used by talented programmers and properly managed and controlled has the greatest impact on quality software development.

QUALITY ASSURANCE AND TESTING

The primary goal of quality assurance is to validate that the software accomplishes all the functions that it was required to accomplish for all inputs and all expected operating environments within acceptable performance constraints. Quality assurance should be carried out throughout the life cycle rather than only in the test and validation phase after the implementation is completed. Each phase in the life cycle should incorporate a validation activity that should be completed before going on to the next phase.

Quality Assurance

Quality assurance activities include:

1. In-depth reviews of the requirements, preliminary design, detailed design, and the implementation to identify and resolve problems, find errors, and determine conformity with established standards.
2. Review of user documentation (draft user's manuals, data preparation manuals, operator's manuals) during the early stages of design.
3. Simulation of the system to validate that the performance requirements, e.g. throughput, response time, can be met by the design.
4. Use of automated aids, where available, to check consistency and completeness of the requirements or the design.
5. Design inspections and structured walk-throughs during the early stages of development by one or more individuals other than the designer.

The independent reviews and inspections are an extremely effective method of eliminating design errors. The review team should consist of one to four individuals who should check for consistency, responsiveness to requirements, good design practices, and compliance with standards. The technique used during the review may be a manual walk-through of the design after reading the documentation or a highly formalized procedure with checklists and action item worklists. Although this detailed review may appear time-consuming, it is very effective in practice.

Testing

Software testing refers to methods for ensuring that the software performs according to its requirements. The traditional approach has been to exercise the software with test data and inspect the output. If the test results are incorrect, it indicates that the program contains errors. If, however, the test results are correct, the program still may not be correct since it may be incorrect for some other input. It is in general not feasible to test a program for all possible inputs. Although much software engineering research has focused on testing, little progress has been made toward developing an effective theory of testing.

The inadequacy of testing has led to research in proving program correctness, demonstrating by rigorous mathematical proof techniques that the software is consistent with its specification. Unlike testing which requires that the program be run with input test data, a proof of correctness is done *a priori* and demonstrates that the program is correct for all valid inputs. This technology offers promise but it is still in the research and development stage and not yet ready for practical application on large software projects.

Advances in Computer Security Management, Vol. 2
Edited by M. M. Wofsey
© 1983 John Wiley & Sons Ltd.

Chapter 6

DATA PROCESSING—RISK ASSESSMENT

Timothy J. Saltmarsh

Information Systems and Network, Inc.

Peter S. Browne
Burns International Security Services, Inc.

Computer security is a risk management activity that requires a wide variety of skills, techniques, analysis tools, and management attention. The ultimate goal of any given computer security measure is to reduce risk by either decreasing the probability of a security breach or reducing the loss should that breach actually occur.

RISK ASSESSMENT IN PERSPECTIVE

Risk assessment is a way of linking the level of exposure due to given threats to the level of protection that would defend against that particular threat. The process of assessment is evaluative in nature. It focuses not only on the threat population, and the loss potential due to those threats, but also on the controls currently in place and their effectiveness. The outcome is information suitable to allow the selection of appropriate additional controls.

History

Risk assessment is typically used in industries or functions of high risk, where the costs of a given loss would be disastrous. Thus, the nuclear, health, insurance, and public safety industries typically have looked to some form of risk assessment as a prudent management tool. As organizations become ever more dependent on the computer, data processing risks are perceived as being significant.

Early efforts to assess DP risk focused on natural disasters and the resulting requirement for contingency planning.[1] At the same time, IBM, in concert with users of its equipment, began developing the concept of analyzing data files for risk.[2] Potential losses due to data destruction, modification, or disclosure were to be calculated individually. Both the occurrence rate and the amount of loss could be estimated in orders of magnitude, e.g., once in 300 years, once in 30 years, and once in 3 years; and $1,000,000, $100,000, $10,000, respectively. This approach has been followed by a number of commercial organizations and is used in an important National Bureau of Standards guidelines document.[3] Another early approach focused on the computer application, and has attempted to show a statistical distribution of risk.[4] Yet another approach recognizes the fact that many risks cannot be quantified accurately, especially where empirical data are lacking.[5]

Nature of Risk

Most of the methodologies that address risk explicitly consider the following equation:

$$r = p \times e,$$

where risk (r) is the product of threat probability or occurrence rate (p) and the single-time loss (e) that occurs upon activation of the threat.

Typically, threats tend to cause losses in a predictable way. A statistical correlation exists between the frequency of occurrence and the amount of loss. Risks which occur very frequently tend to cause minor loss, and those that are rare tend to be catastrophic.

Consider the distribution of threat frequency and loss combinations. Fires, for example, are known to follow the pattern depicted in Figure 6-1. At point A, the threat may be categorized as a 'minor fire', i.e., one in which the level of loss is low but the frequency of occurrence is high. Point B might reflect a level of loss of some significance to the organization, occurring at a moderate frequency. At point C, the losses are catastrophic, but the event would occur infrequently. While

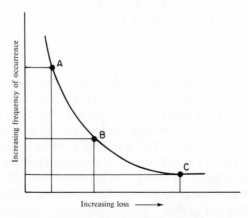

Figure 6-1.   Hypothetical distribution of frequency–loss combinations.

the underlying pattern will change its shape for differing kinds of threats, the management issue is to deal with the threat in a prudent manner.

Risk/Cost Trade-offs

The trade-offs between security and efficiency are well-known to professionals in the security field. Likewise, trade-offs exist between the costs of control and the benefits as expressed in risk reduction. As the expenditures for controls increase, the incremental benefits, in either a decrease in loss or a reduction in the probability of threat occurrence, will decrease. The optimum point is to spend money on controls only up to the crossover point between the cost of controls and the level of protection. Figure 6-2 illustrates this concept.

The total cost of controls is the sum of the costs for controls plus the sum of the expected losses that would occur at that given expenditure rate. For example, if the probability of an electrical interruption were 20 times per year, and the cost per interruption were $5,000 per occurrence, then the actual loss exposure would be $100,000 per year. If the cost of providing 80% electrical redundancy through an UPS system were $50,00 per year (amortized), and this redundancy would reduce outages to 4 per year at $5,000 each, then the total cost of electrical security would be

$50,000 (UPS costs)
+$20,000 (cost of 4 outages per year) =
$70,000 per year,

which compares favorably with the $100,000 unprotected cost.

ESSENTIALS OF RISK ASSESSMENT

What, then, is the systematic and well-defined process termed computer security risk assessment? Such a process can be described in terms of its components or tasks. In a contract for the National Bureau of Standards, two expert

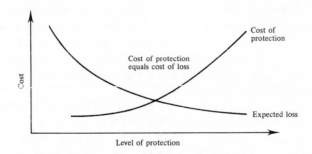

Figure 6-2. Level of security versus cost.

organizations identified six essential elements of a computer security risk assessment methodology:[6]

1. A statement of the scope and purpose of the risk assessment.
2. An analysis of resources which are of value to the organization being studied and which may be susceptible to loss.
3. An analysis of threats whose occurrence could cause loss.
4. An analysis of vulnerabilities in security controls which might increase the frequency of threat occurrences and/or the impact of such occurrences.
5. An analysis of overall risks which quantitatively and qualitatively measures the possible losses to the organization being studied.
6. An analysis of security control measures which, if implemented, would act as safeguards in reducing threat occurrences and/or the impact of such occurrences.

Each of these computer security elements is described in the following sections.

Risk Assessment Initiation

The first step of a computer security risk assessment is to organize the study effort. This process includes establishing the risk assessment team, drafting the risk assessment charter, and developing the risk assessment project plan and schedule.

The risk assessment team should be assembled from representatives of all the organizational areas affected by or participating in the risk assessment. Representatives should be considered from the following areas: DP operations, DP systems programming, DP applications programming, applications systems users, and security (both DP, if such a function has been established, and physical). The team can consist of anywhere from one to fifteen individuals depending upon the scope and objectives of the study. A team of two to six individuals is usually sufficient to conduct most DP risk assessments, however.

The risk assessment charter is a document usually drawn up by the management level which commissioned the risk assessment study. It notifies all organizational areas likely to be interviewed by the risk assessment team of: (1) what the purpose of the study is, (2) who is involved in the study (i.e. who is on or in charge of the team), (3) why their involvement may be necessary, and (4) what is expected of them. Likely recipients of the charter notification include all DP units, building or facility engineering and maintenance personnel, security personnel, application systems users, and corporate counsel.

The risk assessment project plan and schedule should be the first document prepared by the newly established risk assessment team. It need not be more than a few pages long and should be submitted for approval to the management official(s) responsible for commissioning the risk assessment study. In this way, the team can be assured that their understanding of the problem is the same as management's. The project plan should detail the scope of the study, the objectives of the study, and the cost plan. The project schedule should show the scheduled start date, the scheduled completion date, and project milestones (e.g. deliverables and presentations).

The amount of time spent on the risk assessment study depends upon a number of factors, including the intended scope of each of the risk assessment tasks and the overall level of experience of the team in conducting risk assessments. A rough estimate of the amount of time which might be spent on the DP risk assessment is from 20 to 60 person-days plus 2 person-days for each application system examined.

DP Tangible Assets Analysis

The tangible assets analysis is the first data collection task of the risk assessment study. The purpose of this task is to identify and quantify the value of all relevant data processing assets, e.g., equipment, facilities, personnel, and supplies.

The first step of the DP tangible assets analysis is to determine the scope of the analysis. The scope of the assets analysis refers to the types of assets which will be included in the risk assessment study. The following types of assets should be included unless their inclusion would not support the previously determined risk assessment purpose:

1. Physical facilities (e.g. building, electrical power distribution systems, raised flooring).
2. Environmental support equipment (e.g., air-conditioning and humidity control systems, heating control systems).
3. DP supplies (e.g. data cards, preprinted forms).
4. Office assets (e.g. chairs, desks, typewriters).
5. Personnel assets (e.g. system programmers, data entry clerks).

Information necessary for the inventory includes: a listing of the types of assets (i.e. facility, equipment, supplies, office, and personnel) on which information will be collected; a listing of the items within each category type; the number of each item on hand; a notation of whether each item is leased or owned; identifying characteristics of each item (e.g. manufacturer and model number); and the location of each asset item. The location of each asset should be indicated by what is termed 'exposure zones'.

Assets should be grouped together into exposure zones so that later in the risk assessment the assets can be mapped against threats to obtain loss information. Because certain threats (e.g. fire and water leakage) may destroy or damage assets in one area but not those in another, each threat will have to be examined against each area. From four to six exposure zones should be established as a workable number. Zone boundaries should be established based on the location of the DP assets. Areas separated by fire walls, hallways, and floors should be separate exposure zones.

After a complete inventory of DP tangible assets has been taken, replacement costs should be derived for each item (actually, both are usually done con-currently rather than consecutively). Asset replacement costs can come from a variety of sources. Facility replacement costs can be derived from interviews with DP, building facility, and engineering personnel and through inspection of blueprints, cost tables, cost specifications, and building construction cost manuals. Equipment and supply replacement costs can be derived from interviews with DP, procurement, and vendor personnel and through inspection of purchase orders and invoices. Personnel replacement cost estimates can be obtained through interviews with DP management, personnel management, organization management, and personnel recruiters (a.k.a., 'headhunters').

Replacement time estimates should also be determined for each item in the DP tangible asset inventory. These estimates will be used later in the risk assessment when the effects of delay caused by threats will be examined. The replacement time estimates can usually be obtained from the same sources as the replacement cost estimates.

Application Systems Analysis

The second data collection step of the risk assessment is the analysis of the DP application systems processed on the computer system(s) being studied. The purpose of the applications analysis is to determine the business losses which could occur due to threat effects on software and data.

The first step of the applications analysis is to determine the scope of this portion of the risk assessment. Rarely will an organization have the time and effort to perform an analysis of potential losses for each application system. Indeed, it is usually not even necessary to include all of the application systems in the analysis to gain an appreciation of the significant losses that could occur due to threats. Clearly, some systems are more important to the business functions of the organization than others. Thus, to set the scope of the applications analysis is to determine which are the most important. Important systems can usually be identified by one or both of two qualities, criticality and sensitivity.

Criticality refers to the organization's dependence upon the timely processing of an application system. For example, a payroll system might be considered to be very critical just before the payroll date. (This example introduces another concept; that is, an application system's level of criticality may increase or decrease at certain times of the day, week, month, or year.) If the system's processing is delayed and payroll is missed, employee disgruntlement will certainly result. Other responses could be union actions such as strikes, fines, slowdowns, and lawsuits.

Applications should be categorized by their relative degree of criticality. This breakdown will assist in the selection of those application systems which should be examined in greater detail.

Application systems require security consideration because they could cause losses to the organization not only through delays in processing but also through the disclosure or modification of software and data as well. This susceptibility is referred to as the 'sensitivity' of the application system. Sensitivity is the second criterion which should be examined when determining which applications warrant further attention in the risk assessment.

Application systems may be sensitive for any of a variety of reasons. An application system could contain information (in the program or data or both) which if disclosed could cause financial loss or embarrassment to the organization or an individual, or could have an impact on national security. Information types typically found in sensitive applications include personal, proprietary, financial, and national security information.

Once the scope of the applications analysis has been determined, potential losses should be estimated for each application system selected for further analysis. Loss information can usually be obtained by interviewing system users and DP management, programming, and operations personnel. Information to be gathered from these interviews falls into four types: delay, destruction, modification, and disclosure. Each of these loss components is discussed in the following paragraphs.

The effects of delays in processing an application system depend on a number of criticality factors, including the organizational dependence on the timely processing of the system, the system's role in fulfilling intraorganizational or governmental reporting requirements, the level of backup and recovery available for the system, and the frequency of processing.

Destruction of data and software is the second loss component. Like delay, it relates directly to the criticality of the system. The two major cost components of data and software destruction are (1) the delay caused by the destruction and (2) the cost to reconstruct lost data and software. The effects of destruction of data and software depend on a number of criticality factors, including the method of reconstruction, the amount of time necessary to reconstruct, and the level of backup and recovery available for the system.

Disclosure of data or software is the third type of event which can cause losses to the organization. The type and extent of losses due to information disclosure relate directly to the sensitivity of the system. Thus, to evaluate possible losses due to disclosure, sensitivity factors should be examined, including whether any information on the system has commercial value to an outsider, what would be the immediate effects of disclosure on an individual or the organization, and whether any legal sanctions against unauthorized disclosure are available.

Modification of data and software is the fourth and final application system loss type. Like disclosure, the type and extent of losses due to modification directly relate to the level of sensitivity of the system. Sensitivity factors to be examined in determining potential losses here include the effects and extent of data entry errors, the effects and extent of application program errors, and the incentive and possible method of modification for personal gain.

Threat Analysis

The next task to be conducted in a risk assessment is the evaluation of threats. The purpose of the threat analysis is to identify those threats which have affected or could affect the facility and computer system(s) under study. Later in the risk assessment, this threat information will be put together with the loss information developed in the DP tangible assets analysis and the application systems analyses to derive annual expected losses.

The first step of the threat analysis is to determine the scope of this task. Here, 'scope' refers to the types of threats which will be considered in the study. Usually, the scope of the threat analysis is comprehensive, in that all threats are included. Some organizations may wish to commission a risk assessment study which considers only one class of threats (e.g. intentional acts). In this case, the scope would be restricted or limited. The discussion that follows is for a comprehensive risk assessment covering all threat types.

Once the scope of the threat analysis has been determined, threats which could cause losses to the organization due to their effects on the computer system(s) under study should be identified. Threats can be categorized into three groups:

1. *Natural Hazards.* This class of threats covers those events or occurrences, such as floods or earthquakes, that could impair or degrade (sometimes totally) the ability of a specific computer facility to provide required services.
2. *Accidental Acts.* This class of threats covers those events or occurrences which arise not from malicious intent or a natural force, but from human errors and equipment failures.
3. *Intentional Acts.* This class of threats covers those events or occurrences which arise from a deliberate, malicious intent to destroy, divert, or modify data processing assets or the assets controlled by the data processing systems.

Once the threats that could cause losses to the organization have been identified, an estimated frequency of occurrence should be made for each threat. These frequencies of occurrence rates vary from site to site due to geography, organizational characteristics, and hardware and software characteristics.

Information on threat frequencies and effects can come from the following sources:

1. *In-House Records.* Most organizations collect data on a number of threats. Typically, these threats are the accidental act and intentional act threats. Occasionally, an organization will also keep records on natural hazard occurrences.
2. *Employee Knowledge.* In most risk assessments, the DP person who has been at the organization the longest is interviewed for threat occurrence

rates. This person is usually helpful in remembering such events as natural hazards, strikes, and sabotage, which tend to occur only rarely, may not be recorded in an event journal, and are long remembered by those who experienced their effects. DP management and operations personnel should be able to provide information on all accidental and intentional acts. Facility and engineering personnel may be able to provide information on water leakage, air conditioning failure, power outage, and power disturbance occurrences.

3. *Local Sources.* The risk assessment team should locate and contact the regional offices of the National Weather Service and the National Oceanic and Atmospheric Administration (NOAA) for data or estimates on natural hazard threats. The local power company should be contacted for power outage and power disturbance information. The local police department may be able to provide some information on intentional act occurrences in the area of the facility being studied. The local fire department (if the facility is in or near a large metropolitan area) may be able to provide information on the frequency of computer room fires.

4. *Other Sources.* If the previously mentioned sources lack threat occurrence rates or if they provide insufficient information, two other sources remain. The first is the academic community. In any threat area, usually a number of individuals in the academic community maintain and frequently update information on their threat area-of-study. Locating them may prove to be a problem. The second source is computer security consulting organizations. Most of those consultants who conduct risk assessments also maintain extensive records based upon the experience of their clients and their interaction with all of the aforementioned sources.

Vulnerability Analysis

The next task of the risk assessment is the identification of existing vulnerabilities in security controls of the computer system(s) under study. Vulnerabilities can be defined as weaknesses existing in a system that expose an organization to exploitation by threats. The purpose of the vulnerability analysis is to identify and categorize these vulnerabilities so that recommendations can be made to reduce the risks of the threats identified earlier.

Existing vulnerabilities may allow threats to occur more frequently or with a greater impact, and may reduce the ability of the organization to recover from threat occurrences. Vulnerabilities can be categorized into three major types: administrative, technical, and physical. Within each of these types are several subcategories of vulnerability types.

1. *Administrative Vulnerabilities.* These vulnerabilities result from lapses in the overall control of the following elements.

a. *Security Management.* An effective DP security program must be well-planned, balanced, and visible. To assure these qualities, organizational and DP management must provide guidance and support for the DP security activities. Security management measures include the establishment of responsibility for protecting DP assets and the allocation of necessary resources to the computer security functions.

b. *Personnel Security.* An important component of a successful DP computer security program is control over the personnel who access, operate, or otherwise use the DP assets. Personnel security measures include pre-employment background checks commensurate with the sensitivity level of the information processed, and a removal policy for personnel found committing security breaches.

c. *Procedural Controls.* The documentation of DP security policies, standards, and guidelines into official organizational procedures is often the most overlooked, yet one of the most important elements of an effective DP security program. Procedures are necessary to ensure a consistent, well-defined, and visible DP security program. Procedural controls include procedures of the design, procurement, installation, maintenance, and evaluation of every DP security control.

d. *Contingency Planning.* An effective DP security program covers not only the normal operations of the DP system, but also all possible operating and nonoperating states. Thus, the security program must plan for all possible 'contingencies'. Contingency planning controls include equipment backup and recovery planning, software backup and recovery planning, and tape rotation scheduling.

2. *Technical Vulnerabilities.* These vulnerabilities result from lapses in overall control of the following elements.

a. *Hardware.* An effective computer security program must assure that only authorized personnel are allowed to conduct only predetermined actions on system hardware. Hardware controls include the use of a system monitoring console, encryption, and TEMPEST-protected hardware.

b. *Operating System.* The DP security program must provide integrity and auditability control over the programs which manage the resources of the computer system. Operating system controls include a prohibition against system programmers entering the data center and an authorization policy on system modification.

c. *Application Systems.* An effective DP security program should ensure the availability, auditability, integrity, and reliability of programs executed on the computer system. Application system controls include data entry edits, an authorization policy over system modifications, and an authorization policy over system development.

d. *Communications.* As the role of communications in data processing grows, the role of security in communications also increases. Communication control measures include device identification, user/device authorization tables, and secured data lines.

e. *Data Base Management System.* Data available to multiple users and stored in a data base management system require special controls to ensure their integrity. Data base management controls include data base access controls and system recovery provisions to facilitate data base reconstruction.

3. *Physical Vulnerabilities.* Physical vulnerabilities result from lapses in the overall control of the following elements.

a. *Access Control.* The DP security program should ensure that only authorized personnel are permitted entry to the facility site, facility building, and DP areas. Access control measures include CRT monitoring, guard patrols, and door/window locks.

b. *Environmental Controls.* An effective DP security program must ensure the efficiency and effectiveness of the equipment which provides the controlled environment necessary for DP operations. Environmental control measures include air-conditioner redundancy, humidity/temperature monitoring, and environmental control systems maintenance provisions.

c. *Hazard Protection.* The computer security program must provide controls which help prevent, detect, or recover from natural hazard, accidental act, and intentional act calamities. Hazard protection measures include fire extinguishers, water alarms, and a prohibition against eating and drinking in the data center.

The first step of the vulnerability analysis is to identify those vulnerabilities which exist in each of the control categories previously described. This identification of controls can be conducted through the use of facility inspections; interviews with DP, security, and facility engineering and maintenance personnel; and questionnaires to be completed by the same personnel who are to be interviewed. Available in the identification of vulnerabilities are several checklists that should be consulted.[7]

Once vulnerabilities have been identified, the potential impact or 'severity' of each vulnerability should be identified. Identifying the especially serious vulnerabilities allows the organization to concentrate its resources on those areas of special concern before rectifying less serious matters. One method to categorize vulnerabilities is to label them as: management decision, critical, serious, important, or minor.

1. *Management Decision.* Rectification of these problems would require an especially high cost or lengthy implementation. Further analysis by organizational management may be necessary before action is taken.

2. *Critical.* These vulnerabilities threaten vital business operations and should be corrected immediately.

3. *Serious*. These vulnerabilities, while not threatening vital business operations, could cause severe losses. Thus, they should be corrected as soon as possible, and within a year at the outside.
4. *Important*. These vulnerabilities could cause direct losses to the organization, but should be corrected only after critical and serious vulnerabilities have been addressed.
5. *Minor*. These vulnerabilities, while probably not causing direct and measurable losses to the organization, could have negative effects, such as embarrassment to an individual or the organization, or loss of business reputation. These vulnerabilities should be corrected but are not pressing matters.

The findings of the vulnerability analysis will be utilized in the control selection/cost–benefit analysis, which follows the next step of the risk assessment—the loss exposure analysis.

Loss Exposure Analysis

The next step of the risk assessment is to determine the expected annual impact on organizational assets of each threat identified in the threat analysis. These assets were identified in the DP tangible assets analysis and the application systems analysis.

The first step of the loss exposure analysis is to determine the estimated single-time loss for each threat identified in the threat analysis. Losses from a threat occurrence can result from delay, destruction, modification, disclosure, or any combination thereof.

In determining the single-time losses, each threat should first be examined against each exposure zone. If it is determined that a threat would cause destruction losses in an exposure zone, the percentage of tangible assets, data, and software destroyed should be derived or estimated. The tangible assets analysis and destruction portion of the application systems analysis should then be consulted to determine the exact destruction loss. If it is determined that occurrence of the threat being considered would result in data or software disclosure, the disclosure portion of the application systems analysis should be referred to for the exact loss. If the occurrence of a threat would result in data or software modifications, the modification portion of the application systems analysis should be referred to for the exact loss.

For each of the three loss categories (destruction, modification, and disclosure), it should be determined whether any processing delays would occur as a secondary result of the threat occurrence. If delay would occur, the length of the delay on each application system should be estimated and the delay portion of the application systems analysis examined for the exact losses.

Once the destruction, modification, disclosure, and delay losses to each exposure zone from a threat have been determined, they should be added for all the exposure zones to derive the facility single-time loss for that threat.

The final step of the annual loss exposure analysis is the combination of threat occurrence rates from the threat analysis with the recently derived single-time losses to derive the annual loss exposure (ALE). The annual loss exposure represents the expected losses due to a specific threat's occurrence in an average year. Quite simply, the ALE is the product of the single-time loss and the occurrence rate. For example, if the annual occurrence rate for a major fire in the Input/Output exposure zone is 0.05 and the single-time loss is $300,000, the annual loss exposure would be 0.05 × $300,000, or $15,000.

Control Selection/Cost–Benefit Analysis

The final step of the risk assessment is to identify those controls which would, in a cost-effective manner, reduce the risks identified in the loss exposure analysis.

The first step of the control selection/cost–benefit analysis is the identification of controls which could reduce the vulnerabilities identified in the vulnerability analysis. Security controls to be identified can accomplish either or both of the following:

1. A reduction in the occurrence rate of a threat or set of threats.
2. A reduction in the effects of a threat once it has occurred.

Once controls have been identified for each vulnerability identified earlier, the cost of those controls should be determined. Two cost components exist for any control, the one-time cost of purchase and installation, and the yearly cost of maintenance. The one-time purchase cost should be divided by the expected lifetime of the control and added to the yearly cost to determine an annual prorated cost of the control. This figure is the 'cost' portion of the cost-benefit analysis.

As mentioned previously, controls can provide benefits to the organization by reducing the occurrence rate of a threat and/or by reducing the single-time loss of threat occurrence. These reductions should be estimated and used to produce a new annual loss exposure, the 'loss exposure after control implementation'. The difference between this new annual loss exposure and the original loss exposure is the 'benefit' of the control.

If the benefit of a control is higher than its costs, management should consider implementing the control. If the cost of a control is higher than its benefit, then the control should probably not be implemented. Instead, a search should be made for another control to reduce the vulnerability.

SELECTING A DP RISK ASSESSMENT METHODOLOGY

The preceding paragraphs described one general approach to computer security risk assessment, one that utilizes the risk assessment methodology elements found by the NBS study to be 'the necessary components needed to meet the basic objectives of conducting a computer risk assessment'.[8]

Many computer security risk assessment methodologies are available. Some incorporate the elements and general format presented earlier; some do not. When selecting a risk assessment methodology for use, an organization should determine whether these elements are desirable. The following considerations should also be examined.

1. *Cost*. Can the risk assessment methodology under consideration be utilized with the resources available for the study?
2. *Complexity*. Can the risk assessment methodology be conducted by the risk assessment team? Can the risk assessment process be understood by the management individuals who commissioned the study? Can the risk assessment results be understood by management?
3. *Depth of Coverage*. Does the risk assessment methodology under consideration present the required or desired level of detail and documentation?
4. *Adaptability*. Does the risk assessment methodology under consideration present the 'best-fit' methodology for the organization? In other words, is it compatible with the organization's structure, hardware/software configurations, and likely threats?

ALTERNATIVE DP RISK ASSESSMENT METHODOLOGIES

There are many discrete approaches toward measuring and evaluation risk in a DP environment. Many organizations have developed their own, and the number of academic or proprietary methodologies grows each week. This growth may reflect the relative immaturity of the field as well as the difficulty in deriving credible data.

All methodologies, however, can be grouped into the following three categories:

1. Quantitative methods use statistically valid techniques to discern both loss exposures and threat occurrence rates. Formulae, ranges of values, and table lookup methods help provide the algorithmic base for deriving risk values.
2. Qualitative methods express risks in terms of descriptive variables such as 'high, medium, or low'. They are based on the assumption that certain kinds of threat or loss data cannot be expressed in terms of dollars or discrete events, and that in many cases, precise information is impossible to obtain.
3. Hybrid methods use elements of both approaches, combining appropriate techniques in an eclectic manner.

Examples of each approach are described in the following paragraphs.

Computer Resource Controls

The risk assessment methodology of Computer Resource Controls is a statistical approach utilizing a systematic, quantitative, and qualitative examination of data processing assets, applications, vulnerabilities, and threats. It is performed to establish an expected level of risk from certain adverse events. This risk assessment is an organized approach to evaluating threats that may cause losses in the form of delays, destruction of data processing and communications assets, loss of system integrity, and other losses through modifications of data or software. The purpose of the risk assessment is to help establish priorities in order to install cost-effective countermeasures to reduce the probability of certain threats or to aid in recovery from a loss. It also aids in measuring the tolerance level to certain other risks.

The component tasks of the Computer Resource Controls risk assessment are as follows:

1. Regulatory Review. Existing laws and regulations are reviewed to determine the baseline of relevant guidance which would affect the assessment.
2. Value Analysis. This task identifies what is to be protected and quantifies the value of the following types of relevant data processing assets:

   a. Tangible Assets Analysis—derives data regarding costs for damaged or destroyed physical assets.
   b. Applications Analysis—derives data regarding costs for disclosure, modification, destruction, and delayed processing for applications systems assets.

3. Threat and Vulnerability Analysis. Threats to the system and vulnerabilities of the system are identified.
4. Threat Occurrence Probability Calculation. This task derives the threat occurrence probabilities and rates based upon the relevant data obtained during the threat and vulnerability analysis.
5. Single-Time Losses Calculation. This calculation quantifies the total single-time loss that would result from the occurrence of each of the threats.
6. Risk Exposure Analysis. Levels of risk are derived by mapping the single-time losses against the threat occurrence probabilities.
7. Countermeasure Selection and Cost. This task examines alternative counter-measures and their associated costs.
8. Cost/Benefit Analysis. This task analyzes the cost-effectiveness of counter-measures with the objectives of:

   a. Relating identified alternative controls to levels of risk reduction.
   b. Forming the basis for selecting cost-effective solutions from the possible control alternatives.

Advantages

1. The Computer Resource Controls methodology is complete with respect to the forthcoming NBS standard.
2. Every effort is made toward arriving at the most precise data possible.

Disadvantages

1. Since precise data are sought, this methodology can often be time consuming.
2. A certain level of analyst sophistication is required to exercise this methodology.

IBM/NBS Method

The IBM/NBS risk analysis methodology was originally developed by Robert M. Courtney, Jr, of IBM Corporation, and adapted and expanded by the National Bureau of Standards. It requires the quantification of information regarding:

1. The damage which can result from an event of an unfavorable nature.
2. The likelihood of the occurrence of such an event.

This information results in the calculation of an annual loss exposure (ALE), provides a method of quantifying the impact of potential threats on an organization, and provides a basis for the cost-effective selection of protective measures.

The three variables used in the calculations for the IBM/NBS approach are:

1. Dollar impact of an event (i).
2. Frequency of occurrence (f).
3. Annual loss exposure (ALE).

The component tasks of the IBM/NBS risk analysis are as follows:

1. Preliminary Security Examination. This start-up phase for the analysis results in the production of the following lists that facilitate the analysis:
   a. List of replacement costs for all assets.
   b. List of all threats to which the assets are vulnerable. The identification of these threats requires an understanding of the vulnerabilities and the possibilities for damage to the organizations being analyzed.
   c. List of all the organization's existing security measures.
2. Risk Analysis. Completion of this component provides a complete overview of the organization's assets, threats, and corresponding loss exposures from all sources.
   a. Damage or loss to an organization manifests itself as a loss of one or more of the following conditions: data integrity, data confidentiality, and data processing availability.
   b. The appropriate impact, frequency, and ALE are calculated for each data file.
3. Selection of Safeguards. This task provides management with a cost-effective basis for the selection of alternative safeguards. The cost of each safeguard is considered in three different ways:

a. In relation to the ALE reduction it brings about.
b. The total cost of combined measures in relation to the net ALE reduction.
c. The additional ALE reduction provided by each measure compared to its share of the total cost.

Advantages

1. Since only estimates in orders of magnitude, dollar loss, and frequency of occurrence, are given, little time is needed to perform the various data collection efforts.
2. The methodology is *complete*, in that it meets all the requirements of the forthcoming NBS standard.

Disadvantages

1. Insofar as orders of magnitude are utilized, little credence can be placed in the far ends of the scales; in other words, a great difference exists between $100,000 and $1,000,000, for example.
2. The analysis is supposed to take place at the level of the data file, often making this effort a time-consuming one.

CITIBANK Method

The CITIBANK approach to risk analysis involves:

a. Determining the likelihood of occurrence for each type of potential exposure.
b. Assessing the impact of each exposure type with risk containment features presently in place, stated in qualitative and, if possible, quantitative terms.

This approach deals mainly with qualitative terms because it was felt that the error magnitudes of the expected loss figures are so large that quantitative approaches alone are of little use.

Potential exposures are divided into the following major categories:

a. Equipment failure.
b. People related factors (internal and external).
c. Utilities breakdowns (supporting and public).
d. Natural disasters.
e. Neighboring hazards.

Within each category, the exposure is broken down into different types, the possible impacts of those exposures and possible containment measures. Then, for each type of exposure, the likelihood of occurrence is determined as very low, low, medium-occasional, high, and very high, and the rationale for the assignment of the 'likelihood' is determined with reference to applicable containment measures.

In addition, for each exposure type, the qualitative exposure (no risk, minor impact, clear and measurable negative impact, and potential continuing impact) and, if possible, the quantitative exposure per day or per occurrence (in millions of dollars) should be determined.

Based on this analysis, a report is prepared describing the operation, the major causes of operational risk, and planned actions to reduce risk. Once approved by management, these actions are then implemented, and contingency plans are developed based on the risk analysis.

Advantages

1. Minimal level of effort is required to complete the tasks.
2. Results are available within days of project initiation.
3. Involvement by users, facility personnel, and management is required.

Disadvantages

1. Results are inexact at best, if not merely guesses.
2. Investment in safeguards and development of contingency plans are based on a shaky foundation.
3. Exercise of the methodology will vary from site to site (due to the inexact nature of the methodology itself) so much that results cannot be compared.

Jerry Fitzgerald and Associates Method

The Fitzgerald methodology is a statistically based 'threat scenario' technique for risk assessment. This approach involves a brainstorming effort by a central team (Delphi technique). The team is composed of a user, a data processor, and an auditor. Threat data are weighted and ranked (Churchman Ackoff Processes) in order to determine what threats demand special safeguard attention.

Advantages

1. Is statistically based.
2. Involves various levels of an organization.
3. Can be 'quick and dirty'.
4. Is inexpensive.

Disadvantages

1. Demands much guesswork.
2. Obtains results through compromise and not consensus.

3. Is susceptible to 'garbage in, garbage out'.
4. Disregards an asset analysis.
5. Does not utilize a measure of risk.

Fuzzy-Metrics/SECURATE Method

This methodology employs linguistic values to describe the risks, cost, and benefits associated with a specific DP facility. The selection of the linguistic descriptors and subjective meanings are left to the individual. The method utilizes a program in APL to perform the review process.

The analysis process is based upon a model of a computer installation as a set of triples composed of objects, threats, and security features. Objects are defined as the resources of a system, threats are activities which allow unauthorized access to an object or chance events which may jeopardize an object, and features are protective measures which present some degree of resistance to a threat.

SECURATE uses security rating functions based on fuzzy set theory to provide security ratings for an installation as a whole and as sections. Each linguistic variable is a fuzzy set whose members are real numbers in the interval (0, 1). Each individual object is identified against a specific threat and feature resistance, evaluated using fuzzy-metrics variables. These variables are entered in the computer and processed against the system hierarchy, which has been previously programmed into the computer, to produce a security evaluation rating. This process can be used to provide an overall system rating (entire set of triples), an individual subjection rating (only triples for a specified subsection), a sectional rating (a rating for each subsection of the top specified level of the hierarchy), or a worst subsection rating (same as sectional rating but also highlights the subsection with the lowest rating).

Advantages

1. Allows quantification and manipulation of subjective descriptions.
2. Is automated, so as to simplify the calculation and portrayal of results.
3. Allows modeling of differing risks and safeguards.

Disadvantages

1. The approach is not statistically valid in that the input linguistic values are subject to differing interpretation.
2. The methodology is incomplete, in that it ignores vulnerabilities.
3. The analytical process may not result in consistent interpretation of results.

Relative-Impact Measure (RIM) Method

The Relative-Impact Measure of Vulnerability (RIM) is a methodology developed to assess the relative expected impact of system integrity violations on a computer system (i.e. the computer hardware and software, the computer facility, and the environment in which processing is performed). The most significant aspect of the calculated RIM is that it is a relative measure; it has meaning only when it is compared with another RIM value. In addition, the methodology relies on human knowledge and insight, and users are expected to have a general knowledge of computer systems, the organization's own system, its applications, and internal procedures and values.

The RIM methodology is specifically directed at intentional unauthorized acts perpetrated by people, and is concerned with system susceptibilities rather than actualities. Calculating the RIM value involves:

1. Determining characteristics of potential perpetrators.
2. Determining characteristics of potential targets, and assets.
3. Determining characteristics of potential system flaws (i.e. technical vulnerabilities).
4. Combining this information to obtain the RIM value.

The information is obtained by examining the organization under analysis and assigning values (either absolute or relative through a token-distribution procedure) to various established classes of perpetrators, targets, and flaws.

The RIM value can be represented as

$$RIM = q(P, F, T),$$

where the function is basically a summation of a product. The product of the various measures of the perpetrator, flaw, and target characteristics is used to calculate the RIM value for each incident. The summation of all these products then represents the RIM value of all perpetrator–target classes, using all flaws linking each perpetrator–target class. The RIM can then be used to facilitate comparisons between computer systems operating in a common environment, e.g., comparisons between a computer system and itself as modified in some manner.

Advantages

1. RIM was designed to facilitate comparisons between computer systems or the same system as modified.
2. It specifically addresses intentional unauthorized acts.
3. The token distribution system is statistically valid.
4. The RIM method does not require technical expertise in data collection and calculation.

Disadvantages

1. RIM is incomplete in that it does not address the value of comparable safeguards.

2. RIM is only useful in a relative sense. It can only be compared with other RIM values.

Scalar Techniques

The Computer Resource Controls system and other risk assessment methodologies often use a scale or range of values for the portrayal of losses or threats. Index values or symbols can then be substituted for a description of the ranges or scale. For example, an 'A' can stand for a loss of between $101 and $1,000, a 'B' for $1,001 to $10,000, and so forth. The index values can then be manipulated or combined in some fashion.

The approach does not involve a complete method, but it is useful in portraying complex losses or threats where more precise values are unknown. The essential criterion is that the ranges of values be objectively quantified and then used in a consistent manner so as to avoid ambiguity.

Churchman Ackoff Process

As a computational variant, the Churchman Ackoff process supports various risk analysis methodologies by providing a scheme for evaluating the relationships between threat and vulnerabilities in a particular environment. This process ranks threats in terms of their relative importance (either magnitude and/or probability of occurrence) and the susceptibility to a particular vulnerability. This priority ranking is based upon numerous interviews with key personnel (Delphi technique) and results in the identification of a number of threats which have a high potential for harming an organization's data processing resources.

Bayesian Decision Model

As a computational variant, the Bayesian Decision Model is a theoretical, mathematical model for cost and risk estimation. The application of this theoretical approach requires a good working knowledge of Bayesian statistics and probability theory. The model consists of a series of structured submodels, with each submodel corresponding to a particular type of threat. Each submodel, in turn, consists of two components: a probability function for the number of threats, and a probability function for the cost per threat exposure. The determination of the probability functions requires knowledge of historical information and prior probability distributions.

The components of the Bayesian Decision Model are

1. Frequency of Exposures
2. Cost of Exposure
3. Total System Cost of Exposure.

Fault Tree Analysis

As a computational variant, Fault Tree Analysis can be used to support the risk analysis process by identifying the multiple causes of a threat, and thus determining the probable source cause of a threat. Fault tree analysis can also be applied to safeguard analysis. By utilizing the fault tree process, the most effective safeguard configuration will be identified. Although no methodology currently utilizes this approach in the analysis of threats and safeguards, it shows great promise in the area of threat analysis and safeguard selection.

Failure Mode Analysis

As a statistical tool Failure Mode Analysis is the application of the Fault Tree Analysis in the identification and evaluation of human frailty potential. Like the Fault Tree Analysis, Failure Mode Analysis can support the risk analysis process by identifying the human element involved in data processing threats, vulnerabilities, and safeguards. The Failure Mode school believes that all potential actions and processes (e.g., threats and vulnerabilities) have a human element, and that unless these elements are identified and evaluated, the probable source of an action or process has not been formed.

DP RISK ASSESSMENT TRENDS

So far, this chapter has examined the need for computer security risk assessment, the components of a computer security risk assessment methodology, considerations in selecting a computer security risk assessment methodology, and some of the more widely used methodologies—in other words, the state-of-the-art of DP risk assessment as it stands today. Although forecasting is a hazardous business, it might be useful to use the remaining paragraphs of this chapter to examine what the DP risk assessment of tomorrow might look like. Three trends seem clear.

First, risk assessment will continue to grow as a management tool. It will not, however, replace management's role in the decision-making process. It is important to understand this difference. Risk assessment is a tool and should not be used to replace sound management judgment. It should, instead, be used as one of the sources that management draws on when seeking guidance on computer security matters. The trend is clear that this source will continue to be used in the years to come.

The continued and expanded role of risk assessment in the federal segment of government is assured with the publication of the Office of Management and Budget's (OMB) Circular No. A-71, TM-1.[9] This document requires that DP risk assessments be conducted periodically at every federal agency. Many local and state government agencies are now following the federal government's lead and conducting risk assessments of their computer facilities.

In the private sector, the banking industry has led the way to risk assessment becoming a standard DP management decision-making tool. Many other private corporations are now following the banking industry's lead by conducting risk assessments. Some private industries are now even establishing permanent risk assessment sections.

A second noticeable trend in DP risk assessment is that improvements will be made to risk assessment methodologies by streamlining their processes. This streamlining will be necessary if the first trend—growth of risk assessment as a management tool—is to come about because most of the comprehensive risk assessments have been done by large, high-risk businesses and government agencies. The risk assessment methodologies which evolved from these studies are, for the most part, relatively complex, costly, and labor-intensive, as they were designed for large computer systems. Before these methodologies can be used by smaller organizations, they will have to be streamlined so that the process used is easily understood, less costly, and less labor-intensive, and has more easily understood results.

The third trend is that the risk assessment process of the future will be automated. This trend is actually one of the ways the second trend (streamlining the DP risk assessment methodology) will be accomplished. With the introduction of Pansophic's automated risk assessment methodology, PANRISK, this trend has already begun. Other organizations have announced plans to market automated DP risk assessment methodologies, and at least one federal agency has begun automating its methodology. The reason behind this trend is clear; portions of the risk assessment process lend themselves readily to automation. The loss exposure analysis and the cost-benefit analysis, for example, require 'number crunching', which can be done much more easily, in much more detail, and with greater accuracy on a computer than by manual methods.

REFERENCES

1. Brown, W. F., Greenlee, M. B., and Jacobson, R. V.: *AMR's Guide to Computer and Software Security.* New York, AMR International, 1971.
2. Courtney, R. H., Jr.: *Security Risk Assessment in Electronic Data Processing Systems.* Poughkeepskie, N.Y., IBM Corporation, August 1976.
3. Reed, S. K.: *Automatic Data Processing Risk Assessment*, FIPS Pub 65. Washington, D.C., U.S. Department of Commerce, National Bureau of Standards, March 1977.
4. Browne, P. S.: Computer Security, a Risk Management Approach. *In Readings for the EDP Speciality.* FLMI Insurance Education Program, Life Office Management Association, 1976.
5. Hoffman, L. J., and Michelman, E. H.: *SECURATE: A Security Evaluation and Analysis System Using Fuzzy Metrics.* Berkeley, California, University of California, September 1977.
6. Computer Resource Controls, Inc. and Computer Sciences Corporation: *Special Report on the Identification and Description of Necessary Factors for Risk Assessment.* October 1980.
7. Fitzgerald, J.: *Internal Controls for Computerized Systems.* San Leandro, California, E. M. Underwood, 1978.
8. Computer Resource Controls, Inc. and Computer Science Corporation: Special

Report on the Identification and Description of Necessary Factors for Risk Assessment. October 1980.
9. Executive Office of the President, Office of Management and Budget: *Security of Federal Automated Information Systems*, Circular No. A-71, TM-1. July 1978.

ADDITIONAL READINGS

Martin, J.: *Security, Accuracy, and Privacy in Computer Systems*, Englewood Cliffs, N.J., Prentice-Hall, 1973, pp. 492–580.

American Federation of Information Processing Societies (AFIPS): *Security: Checklist for Computer Center Self-Audits*. Arlington, Va., American Federation of Information Processing Societies, 1979.

U.S. Army: *Security, Automated Systems Security*, AR 380-380. 14 October 1977, pp. H-1–H-17.

Krause, L. I.: *SAFE: Security Audit and Field Evaluation for Computer Facilities and Information Systems*. Englewood Cliffs, N.J.: Prentice-Hall, 1980).

Advances in Computer Security Management, Vol. 2
Edited by M. M. Wofsey
© 1983 John Wiley & Sons Ltd.

Chapter 7

PHYSICAL AND PERSONNEL SECURITY CONSIDERATIONS FOR DATA PROCESSING SYSTEMS

James R. Wade

The Scott and Fetzer Company

Absolute security of most business data processing systems is neither cost-effective nor technically attainable using today's state-of-the-art. Any data processing system currently in general business use can be penetrated, in time, if a technically knowledgeable penetrator can gain unrestricted access to the system. These facts, however, should not discourage the security professional from developing security programs for data processing systems to reduce the risks to an acceptable level. On the contrary, the multifarious vulnerabilities associated with a data processing operation should challenge the security manager to develop a data processing security program that is both comprehensive in scope and complex in application.

Overview

The security of a data processing system must be addressed from its various interdependent organizational and operational elements. These mutually supporting security elements should be designed and coordinated to complement and supplement each other using a total systems approach. With this approach, the data processing system will have security-in-depth in order to achieve the objectives of:

1. Limiting access to the data processing system to only authorized persons.
2. Increasing the risk that the penetrator is caught.
3. Detecting any attempts to penetrate the system.
4. Providing an audit trail to answer the interrogations of who, what, where, when, and how.
5. Developing adequate hazard protection and environmental safeguards to sustain the integrity and support the reliability of the data processing system.

As a minimum, the security elements which should be included in the total systems approach in providing the desired level of protection are:

1. Administrative.
2. Technical.
3. Physical.

Each of these security elements must be analyzed in respect to the strengths and weaknesses of the others to determine the overall security posture of the data processing system. Even though the purpose of this chapter is to discuss the physical and personnel security considerations of protecting a data processing system, other sections of this volume will prove invaluable in analyzing the other elements of the total systems approach outlined.

PHYSICAL SECURITY CONSIDERATIONS

Inasmuch as data processing systems are tempting targets for sabotage, fraud, larceny, malicious mischief, and other wrongdoing, it is essential that physical security be a major consideration in the overall security program. The physical security for a data processing system and facility includes all aspects of protection against physical threats.

Facility Location and Design

It is impossible to overemphasize the importance of considering physical security in selecting the location and designing a data processing facility. A great number of vulnerabilities can be avoided if the site selection as well as the design and construction of the facility are analyzed from the security perspective prior to installing the data processing system.

Locating the Facility

In choosing the location of the building which will house the data processing facility, it is necessary to evaluate all local factors likely to have an effect on its security and operational efficiency. Local factors which should be evaluated when selecting a data processing site location include both those that are natural and those that are man-made.

Natural factors should be assessed in selecting a site location to determine their likely effect on the data processing operation. These natural factors include:

1. Windstorms (e.g. tornados, hurricanes, tropical storms, snow and ice storms) are a threat to data processing systems located in geographic areas where these natural phenomena occur. Although a particular storm may not inflict damage directly upon the facility, the storm could interrupt power and

other utilities as well as disrupt transportation and support services. Storms also create hazardous conditions which could prohibit data processing personnel from reporting to work.

2. Cataclysmic events (e.g. earthquakes and volcanos) should be evaluated for proposed sites to determine their probability of occurrence. For obvious reasons, data processing facilities should not be located either on or in proximity to earthquake fault lines and potentially active volcanos.

3. Flooding is one of the more common causes of damage to data processing facilities. Johnstown, Pennsylvania, was subjected to flooding in July 1977 after several inches of rain fell in a short period of time causing a river to overflow into the town. At least four data processing systems that had been housed in buildings on first floors or in basements were severely damaged or destroyed.

Data processing sites which are likely to be adversely affected by one or more natural factors of a local area should be avoided if at all possible. Frequently, however, other considerations dictate that a data processing facility be located in a less than favorable area. In these situations, the impact of the occurrence of one or more locally prevalent natural factors may be reduced by implementing appropriate countermeasures.

For example, if the data processing facility is to be located in a flood-prone area, the computer hardware and support equipment should be located above the maximum level of natural water courses. Although this location will not guarantee that the system may be operative during flooding conditions due to the system's dependence on external sources of power, communications, personnel, and support services (which are all very vulnerable to disruption during a flood), it does reduce the likelihood that the system will be totally destroyed by a flood. A formally developed and tested backup, recovery, and contingency plan and an out-of-area recovery site would be an absolute requirement for business survival in this example.

If the data processing site is located in an area that is susceptible to windstorms or other cataclysmic occurrences, the facility construction should be designed to protect against structural failures caused by the effect of the relevant natural hazards. In this situation as in the previous one, the impact of such a disastrous event cannot be totally avoided because of the probable interruption of external sources of system support; therefore, plans of action should be developed and periodically tested to cover any anticipated problem.

A myriad of man-made factors could adversely affect the operation and security of a data processing system. During the site selection process, as many appropriate man-made factors as possible should be analyzed to evaluate their probable impact on the system. Man-made factors which could adversely impact a data processing facility include:

1. Hazardous processes (e.g. restaurants, nuclear energy plants, laboratories,

flammable storage) in the proximity of a data processing facility could have a disastrous effect on the security of the operation, especially when a data processing system is located in a multi-tenant building. If the computer equipment is installed in an area above a restaurant or some other flammable process, a fire starting in an adjacent hazardous area could quickly spread, with its ruinous effects, into the data processing facility.

In a situation where the hazardous process is located in a space above the computer equipment, the change in relative location may reduce the direct impact of the fire; however, the data processing system will be vulnerable to the water used to extinguish a fire.

The ramifications of locating a data processing site adjacent to or near a nuclear energy plant should be obvious since the near-tragedy at Three Mile Island in 1979. Less obvious may be the societal issues. These issues may result in civil action (ranging from picketing to rioting) being directed at the nuclear facility. If the data processing facility is located in the general proximity of a nuclear energy plant or similar process, civil action directed at the hazardous process could, at the least, make it difficult for the data processing employees to get to work and, at the worst, spill over into the data processing facility.

2. Electromagnetic interference (EMI) from sources such as radar transmitters, manufacturing equipment, and electrostatic discharges may interrupt the processing as well as cause damage to the computer hardware. Locating the data processing center near facilities which generate relatively high-powered radio frequency signals (e.g. radio and television stations, radar and microwave installations) or other sources of EMI (e.g. high voltage substations and power lines, large relay contactors) should be avoided.

3. Hazardous transportation areas (e.g. airports, railroad tracks) should be avoided when selecting a site for a data processing facility. The direct and indirect impact of an accident involving some form of hazardous transportation may be devastating to a data processing facility located in the area.

Designing the Facility

In terms of the previous discussion, few locations are ideal for a data processing facility; therefore, the facility must be designed to offset as many of the site-specific risks as possible. Generally, the data processing facility should be in a building constructed of non-combustible materials. Preferably, the building should house only the data processing operations and miscellaneous support services. All other company operations could be located in other buildings in the general vicinity. If the data processing facility is located in a multi-tenant office building, the company should occupy the entire floor on which the facility is located as well as the floor above and below the data center. Additionally, for leased space, a stipulation in the lease agreement should exclude the introduction of any hazardous process anywhere in the building.

The computer equipment, media storage, and support areas should derive a level of security from being placed in the inner core of the building; that is, the data processing facility should be physically surrounded on all sides, above and below, by non-hazardous processes under the direct control of the company. Further, the data processing equipment storage areas and the support service areas should be separated from all adjoining areas by fire-resistant floors, roof, and partitions that extend from the structural floor to the underside of the structural floor or roof above. The fire-resistance classification of the partitions must be no less than either 1 hour or the fire hazard rating of adjacent areas, whichever is the greater. The local fire department can provide the specific code requirements for the minimum fire-resistant separation, and this policy should be followed.

Any penetrations through the fire-resistant partitions should be protected by appropriately rated fire doors, fire windows, and dampers. Any openings made for ducting, conduit, or pipe must be sealed around the penetrating object. The sealing materials must resist the passage of heat, flame, and smoke for a period of time equal to the rating of the partition.

The best way to limit the extent of damage or injury from a fire is to be able to contain it within a limited area and deal with it before it spreads. This capability requires that areas be separated from one another through some type of fire-rated barriers that will inhibit the spread of fire and allow it to be isolated within a single area. These barriers are especially important surrounding areas that have a normally high degree of exposure to fire (e.g. a computer room with its large amount of electrical equipment or an area that contains large quantities of flammables, such as paper storage rooms and tape library areas). The fire barriers can take the form of fire-rated doors, fire-rated walls that extend from the true floor to the true ceiling, and the treatment of wallboard with fire- and heat-resistant compounds. These types of barriers must be used in conjunction with one another for maximum effectiveness. For example, if the walls but not the doors are fire-rated, the fire isolation potential of the walls becomes irrelevant as the fire engulfs the doors that are not fire-rated and spreads throughout a facility.

If the data processing system is housed in a building or facility that is shared by other, non-data processing departments, offices, and operations, the data processing and support areas must be isolated from all other areas. Ideally, the computer equipment and associated mechanical/electrical areas should be physically located in the core of building surrounded by the system development, programming, operations, and other data processing administrative offices. Other company offices and non-hazardous operations should be positioned around the data processing areas for further isolation of the facility. Personnel traffic into the data processing areas should be controlled to admit only those personnel who are absolutely necessary.

The data processing areas which should be able to be secluded from all other areas include:

1. Computer equipment room.
2. Media libraries.

3. Data processing maintenance and operations.
4. Mechanical/electrical equipment rooms associated with the computer hardware.
5. Systems support and programming areas.

In addition, the data processing areas should be configured to restrict traffic between the individual areas. For example, a data processing user that visits an applications programmer in a programming area should not be able to gain unrestricted access to other data processing areas. Other physical security considerations which must be addressed during the design of the data processing facility as well as retrofitted to existing facilities will be discussed later in this chapter.

Access Control

Access control for the data processing facility begins with the barriers and lighting around the building and the various features existing within the building that are designed to protect other critical company assets. The purpose of this chapter is not to discuss physical security in general; but to consider how it applies specifically to the data processing facility. This approach does not mean, however, that the overall security of the building and grounds should be ignored when considering the totality of the physical security problem.

Purpose

The purpose of access control as part of the physical security protection for the data processing system is to control personnel gaining physical access to the facility during normal operating hours as well as during periods of non-occupancy. Access control during normal operating hours should be structured to admit and identify only authorized personnel and escorted visitors and to exclude all others. Besides non-data processing personnel, those who may not be authorized access to the data processing facility include former data processing employees; friends and relatives of current authorized employees; personnel who may either be on strike, on vacation, or laid off; and employees from a different location, department, or shift. Certain data processing groups, including administrative, programming, systems, and maintenance personnel, should not be granted unescorted access to the computer equipment and support areas at any time.

The purpose of access control for periods other than normal operations is to prevent surreptitious entry into the data processing facility regardless of the reason, to detect forceable entry by any means, and to restrict the access of normally authorized personnel to a minimum number who should be specifically authorized entrance during these times. A permanent record should be made of access exceptions made during normal operating hours and of all accesses during non-operating hours. Access control should be continuously monitored to identify security hardware problems and any attempts to defeat the system.

Design Considerations

One of the considerations when designing a physical security access control system for the data processing facility is that, regardless of the access control that exists in the other areas of the building, entry to data processing areas must be more restrictive than that for most other company areas. This rationale is based not only on the high dollar value of the assets contained in the area but on the fact that, for most companies, the data processing system is the caretaker and administrator as well as the processor of business and fiscal information that is used to control the company. Certain decision-making features (e.g., inventory ordering, check writing, funds transfer) are sensitive functions that in the past have been controlled in manual environments but are quickly becoming automated processes found on data processing systems; therefore, access to all aspects of an automated decision-making system should be vigorously controlled.

Access controls must be enforced throughout the data processing facility. Different levels of access may be designated to establish some specified areas that are more restrictive than others. For example, the media libraries should admit only the library personnel and exclude all others, including operators and programmers. In another example, access to the computer room should be restricted to equipment operators and to a limited number of data processing operations personnel. All other personnel possessing verified purposes for entry to the computer room must be escorted.

Another design consideration is that access control should become progressively more restrictive as a person moves from the perimeter of the facility to the computer room. The idea is to erect a series of barriers to personnel movement that become increasingly constrictive closer to the system, thereby limiting the normal physical access to the data processing areas to those personnel given specific authorization.

The access control system must be designed to impose a specified level of control without being unduly difficult to operate. A system that is too rigorous may be such a nuisance to authorized personnel that the work flow will be interrupted or the system bypassed and ignored. The system design must take into account the relative risk exposure to the data processing, the cost of implementing and operating the various access control mechanisms, and the potential interruption to the work processes caused by the access control system.

The final design consideration is to control exits from the facility as aggressively as entry to the facility. The purpose of controlling exits is to reduce the temptation to steal by those who are granted access. This feat is accomplished by convincing people that reasonable measures will be taken to ensure they are not carrying out company property. Another purpose of controlling exits is to complete the circle of control on visitors and other escorted personnel. If the system is properly designed to identify, check in, and escort all personnel not possessing specific authority for being in the data processing areas, the system should be designed to check out those personnel to verify their exit from the facility. If the escorted person was admitted to perform a particular job, the exit process can be used to verify the status of the work.

A warning should be issued at this point. The security professional should not attempt to make the data processing facility an impenetrable fortress—unless it is justified by the risk. Most data processing systems are designed to make as much information available to as many people as possible as quickly as possible; therefore, the access control system that is modeled after 'Fort Knox' is in general conflict with the operating premises of the data processing department. The trick is to implement as much security as can be reasonably expected given the risks to the system and the need for cost-justification.

The design considerations discussed in the preceding paragraphs are intended to develop an access control system that is fully integrated to achieve the previously stated objectives of:

1. Limiting access to the data processing system to authorized personnel.
2. Increasing the risk that the penetrator will be caught.
3. Detecting any attempts to penetrate the system.
4. Providing an audit trail to answer the interrogatives of who, what, where, when, and how.

Many access control techniques and methods may be implemented based on an analysis of the risks to the data processing system. The problem is that many of the available techniques and methods will not necessarily fulfill the previously listed objectives if implemented either singly or in combination with other measures. The security professional must continuously test the access control system to ensure that it meets the stated objectives in a cost-effective and efficient manner. Basically, the access control system will consist of some type of positive physical control constraint and a means of monitoring this constraint.

Positive Constraints

The purpose of the positive physical control constraint is to fulfill the first two objectives of an access control system. The first objective, limiting access to the data processing system to authorized persons, will be accomplished by an access control system that discriminates between those who are authorized access and those who are not allowed access privileges.

Discrimination by the system is based on one or more of the following techniques:

1. Personal key. This approach is based on some unique, personally identifiable characteristic which answers the question, 'Who is he?' The type of

technologies which attempt to control access using a personal key are hand geometry, fingerprint, visual recognition, and voice.

2. Password key. This technique answers the challenge, 'What does he know?' to discriminate between authorized and unauthorized personnel. Although the normal form of a password key has in the past been some type of memorized combination, future technologies may key on a set of facts known only to a specific person.

3. Physical key. The question, 'What does he have?' is the basis of the physical key, which normally takes the form of a key, badge, card, or token.

The second objective of the access control system is to increase the risk of a penetrator being caught. Accomplishing this objective usually involves using more than one of the techniques of discriminating between the authorized and the unauthorized. The intent of using more than one technique is twofold. First, multiple positive constraints should significantly delay the penetrator to increase the odds of his being detected. Second, if a combination of techniques is used, it becomes more difficult for a felon to bypass the access control system. This practice also should further increase the delay period and increase the chance that the criminal will be detected before he penetrates the system.

Technological advances are making an impact in the positive constraint mechanisms implemented for physical security. It is not the purpose of this chapter to attempt an exhaustive discussion of every technology used for access control; however, those technologies that are frequently in use for access control are discussed in the following paragraphs.

Key Locks

The most common of all positive constraints is the key lock. A master and sub-master key system is the minimal level of security for a key and lock system. Various sets of sub-master keys should be created to allow employees possessing a key to enter only one particular data processing area (e.g., computer room, media library, or terminal room). Appropriate supervisory personnel could be issued a master key that would allow them to access multiple areas within the data processing facility.

Aggressive positive key controls must be instituted to develop as much security as possible for a key and lock system. Each key should be stamped with a control number for identification and with the phrase 'do not duplicate' to discourage illegal duplicates from being made. Control numbers, which uniquely identify each key, should be registered to the employee who has been entrusted with a key. It is important to flag the personnel file for employees with keys. The flagged personnel file should alert the administrative function to recover the key if an entrusted employee is terminated.

The key and lock system should have changeable lock cylinders to allow locks and keys to be changed periodically in an effort to discourage unauthorized duplication of keys. Changeable lock cylinders also permit an adequate hold on security to be maintained when keys are lost or stolen.

Several problems are inherent to using a key-operated lock as the access control mechanism. First is the problem of key control. In spite of the measures that are normally taken in terms of *ONLY* authorized persons, some keys will be lost, stolen, and duplicated. Generally, the more keys there are to control, the weaker the system becomes. Another aspect of the key system is that the technology does not normally cause a significant delay to the skilled criminal; therefore, most key and lock systems are not a substantial deterrent to penetration.

Some high-security lock systems manufactured are of quality material and use controlled key stock. Many of the weaknesses of key locks have been thwarted by the high-security lock; however, since the key is critical in the operation of a high-security lock just as it is in the operation of all other key and lock systems, an effective key control system must be devised and implemented. Another consideration in using a high-security lock system may be the cost. These systems are not necessarily inexpensive. The security professional should perform a cost/benefit analysis reflecting the price of the system as well as the costs for maintaining and administering the high-security lock system. This analysis should be compared with the cost/benefit analysis performed for alternative positive constraint techniques to select the most cost-effective system.

It would be unfair for the key and lock to be rejected unequivocally as a positive constraint for access control. Key systems that are properly designed, aggressively administered, and augmented by other techniques of discriminating between authorized and unauthorized personnel may be effective. However, users of this method of access control should be warned against becoming slack in their surveillance because of the weaknesses that usually develop in implementing this type of system.

Keyless Locks

Whereas the key lock systems use a physical key technique to attempt to discriminate between authorized and unauthorized personnel and to delay those who are unauthorized from gaining entry, the keyless lock systems use the password key technique to control access. Keyless lock systems can be either mechanical or electrical. Some systems use both mechanical and electrical functions to control a door. Regardless of the method used, keyless systems are operated by manipulating the proper combination.

The combination for most keyless locks is changeable; therefore, the combination that operates the lock may be periodically changed in an attempt to ensure that only authorized personnel are granted access to the data processing facility. One major problem inherent in any system using a combination for a key is that of controlling the combination. This problem, in some respects, may be more difficult than controlling keys because of the relative ease of compromising a combination; therefore, a keyless lock should not be implemented as the only means for limiting access.

Card Systems

Another type of system which uses a physical object to control access is the card access control system. This type of system has proliferated in recent times. Card systems are designed to use several different applications of magnetic technology, e.g. magnetic stripe cards, magnetically encoded cards, magnetic-pulse generating cards, and proximity cards. They all basically do the same thing; that is, through their introduction into or passage through a reading device, the controlled door will be unlocked.

A card access control system can be combined with a personnel badge identification system. Besides using such personal identifiers as physical description, photograph, and fingerprint to identify employees, the badges can be color-coded to indicate access authority to specify data processing areas. For instance, personnel with green badges could be given access to only the computer room, blue badges could be allowed access to only the media library, yellow badges could be granted access to the programming area, while red badges could be authorized in all data processing areas. Color-coding the personnel badge identification system facilitates the rapid identification of personnel in critical data processing operational areas.

Two fundamental problems are involved with using card access type systems. First, just as with all other physical key systems, access is granted or denied based upon whether the person seeking entrance possesses the proper device. Therefore, in reality, the system does not positively identify an individual but the card. Consequently, unless some other control technique is used in conjunction with a card system, or other physical key system, little true security has been gained.

The second problem that is frequently present in card systems is tailgating into the facility. The way this works is that one person possessing an authorized badge will open a door and then anyone following that person will just follow through the open door. The countermeasure most usually put forward to stop this problem is to tell everyone possessing an authorized badge to challenge anyone they do not recognize as authorized in the area. This practice may work in small facilities with few personnel; however, in large facilities occupied by a large number of people in diverse offices, it usually is not effective.

The countermeasure for these problems is to implement other access control techniques with the card system, construct mantraps, use turnstyles, or use some combination of these methods. Unfortunately, too many facilities are protected by a single system or technology which has weaknesses that are not offset by some other technique. This approach results in a false sense of security.

Radio labeling

A relatively new application of short-range radio labeling has been developed for access control. This system uses a small code-transmitting device called a token that continually emits a low-powered coded signal that is detected when the token-bearing person approaches a controlled door. The code transmitted by the token is electronically assessed by the system and, if the code is authorized access, an electrically operated lock is released allowing the token-bearing person to enter. Since the code-transmitting token can be worn on the person's clothing like an access badge, the controlled door can be unlocked without the person having to handle the access control device. This hands-free operation tends to enhance the convenience of the system as well as the security of the facility by discouraging the propping open of doors.

This access system can detect unauthorized personnel tailgating because of an absence of a token or a token emitting a code not authorized in the area. Upon detecting tailgating, the system can sound an alarm to draw attention to the penetration. If this system is used in conjunction with a mantrap, the system could apprehend the penetrator by allowing tailgating through the first door but then locking both the inner and outer doors until the security force arrives.

Another advantage of this system is that the battery-powered tokens will operate for only 24 hours unless returned to their special charging unit; therefore, the token must be surrendered prior to departure from the facility so that it can be placed in the charger. This system of battery-powered tokens could easily be instituted using a badge exchange operation. The authorized employees would be issued a uniquely identifiable badge (e.g., picture, personal data, fingerprint) which would be exchanged for an authorized charged token upon arrival for work and then exchanged back upon departure. If the employee should forget to exchange his badge and token, the charge on the token would drain in less than 24 hours, rendering it useless. The security force would also be able to determine who had been issued a token for access to the facility by auditing the badges and tokens.

Monitoring

During the following discussion security professionals must keep in mind that monitoring techniques are not an effective deterrent to unauthorized access if implemented alone. Positive physical control constraints are not totally effective if they are not monitored; therefore, the access control system must combine both positive physical control constraints and monitoring to provide an adequate level of security for the data processing facility.

The purpose of monitoring the positive physical control constraint is to fulfill the last two of the four objectives of an access control system. The third objective, detecting any attempts to penetrate the system, may be accomplished by continuously monitoring all control points, such as entrance and exit doors and windows. This aspect of monitoring may be accomplished by implementing one or more of the following techniques.

Personal Recognition

The most common of all monitoring techniques is personal recognition. Receptionist and guards are frequently given the task of recognizing authorized people entering a facility and sounding an alarm if an unauthorized person attempts to penetrate the system. The greatest problem with a personal recognition system detecting all attempts to penetrate the system is human failure; that is, the monitoring person could think that he recognizes a person as being authorized when in fact the person was seeking to penetrate the area. Personal recognition systems in combination with positive access constraints can be effective in small areas if everyone in the facility is charged with the responsibility of challenging and reporting *all* unauthorized personnel found in the area.

Personal recognition systems using receptionists or other non-guard personnel are not normally effective in monitoring access points to detect attempts to gain unauthorized entrance to the data processing facility. Untrained personnel are generally not aggressive enough to challenge people who may not be authorized access, nor can they given sufficient attention to the monitoring function while performing all the other duties assigned to them. Therefore, using non-guard personnel alone to perform the monitoring function tends to make the area vulnerable to penetration.

A well-trained and highly motivated guard can be very effective in monitoring the positive physical control constraints and detecting attempts to bypass the system. The guard should wear a uniform and be clearly visible as a psychological deterrent. The guard's instructions should require that he challenge all personnel entering the data processing facility to determine those who have authorized access. Further, the guard should identify and log in all visitors as well as ensuring that all visitors are escorted while in the area.

Alarm Systems

Another monitoring technique which may be implemented to detect attempts to gain unauthorized access is an alarm system. Such a system can be designed to monitor all control points, including entrance and exit doors, windows, and gates. The system should be designed to set off an alarm whenever access is gained through some unauthorized means or when one or more of the positive physical controls have been violated. For example, most facilities have exits to be used only for emergencies, which should operate an alarm if they are opened.

It is imperative that an alarm system be monitored at the facility and off site at a central alarm station if it is being used to detect all unauthorized entrance attempts during periods of occupancy and non-occupancy. During normal operating hours, the alarm system should be continuously monitored locally by someone who will respond to violations of the system. The central alarm station could be given the monitoring responsibilities during minimum manning situations (e.g. second or third shifts) as well as during periods of non-occupancy.

Alarm systems used as a monitoring technique must be implemented in conjunction with some type of response if the system is to be effective. Once people find out that no one responds to a violation of the system, they will either ignore the security system or habitually bypass the positive physical control constraint.

Closed-Circuit Television

A closed-circuit television system can be implemented as an effective monitoring technique to detect unauthorized access attempts. The most effective implementation of closed-circuit television in detecting unauthorized access attempts at primary entrances is through the use of an entrance mantrap equipped with a split-screen closed-circuit television system. The person seeking entrance to the data processing facility would be permitted to enter the mantrap as both the entry and exit doors are locked. The entering person would be required to place his personal identification badge in a television viewer while standing in front of another television camera. A split-screen monitor displays a picture of the badge and the entering person for comparison. If the person in the mantrap is authorized access to the facility, the entrance door is released permitting entry. However, if the person is not allowed access, the person would be detained in the mantrap until apprehension of the attempted penetrator is accomplished. The mantrap can also be equipped with detectors to screen for explosives, metal items, and magnetic devices to prevent their unauthorized introduction into the data processing facility.

Closed-circuit television cameras can be placed at all data processing facility entrances and exits. Since the closed-circuit television system must be designed to operate at all times, the lighting at the camera locations is extremely critical. For situations that are vulnerable owing to minimal lighting, low light cameras are available to permit surveillance.

The last objective of monitoring the positive physical control constraint is to provide an audit trail to answer the interrogatives of who, what, when, where, and how of accesses to the data processing facility. Except for the most sensitive facilities, the volume of traffic in the data processing areas dictates that a record be made of access exceptions rather than of every normal access. During low traffic periods (e.g. second and third shifts), all accesses into the data processing facility could be recorded. The audit trail of accesses should be viewed and all exceptions investigated. The audit trail may be recorded by implementing one or more of the following techniques.

Access Register

As a minimum, the receptionist or guard should maintain a manual register to record the following information about persons entering the data processing facility at each entrance:

1. Name (printed).

2. Date (in and out—if appropriate).
3. Time (in and out).
4. Purpose (reason for entering the area).

If only exceptions are noted during normal operating hours, the access register would record visitors to the data processing facility. A register which reflects visitors should also record the name of the person or department visited as well as the name of the person who escorted the visitor. During low traffic periods, access at every entrance to the data processing facility should be recorded.

The access register must be frequently reviewed to determine any unauthorized activity that should be investigated. All unauthorized activity must be aggressively resolved, with sufficient publicity given to punitive action to place people on notice that such activities will not be tolerated.

System Access Log

Many of the automated access control systems (e.g. card, token) generate a system access log as a record of system activity. Some of these systems can optionally record the access exceptions as well as all accesses into the data processing facility. Regardless of whether only exceptions or all accesses are recorded, it is critical to investigate every violation of the system in a timely manner.

Video Tape

Closed-circuit television systems can be connected to video tape recorders to make a record of the monitored areas. Special long-playing surveillance tape recorders permit overnight and weekend recording. A video tape marked with a date and a time stamp is particularly effective in prosecuting trespassers and other law violators.

Access Control Summary

The total systems approach must be used to develop and implement an access control system for a data processing facility if the system is to be effective. It should be apparent from the previous discussion that access control is more than just a lock and key or even a card access system. The access control of critical data processing areas must be carefully designed to reduce the risks of penetration to an acceptable level by:

1. Limiting access to the data processing system to authorized persons.
2. Increasing the risk that the penetrator will be caught.
3. Detecting any attempts to penetrate the system.

4. Providing an audit trail to answer the interrogative of who, what, where, when, and how.

An access control system consisting of some combination of positive physical control constraints and monitoring techniques will provide an effective level of access control for the data processing facility.

Hazard Protection

An important aspect in any data processing security program is protecting the system from a wide range of hazards which may adversely affect the operation and continuity of the data processing system; therefore, the security program should consider the ruinous effects of fire, water, and other hazards. Even though every data processing security program should address and provide some degree of hazard protection, the level of protection will be dictated by factors such as the dollar value of equipment, facility, and supplies; operational requirements for uninterrupted system availability; and the uniqueness of critical system hardware, software, configuration, and facility. The impact that these factors may have on a particular business or operation should influence the resources committed to ensure that an adequate level of protection is provided. Inasmuch as the protection from the effects of wind, earthquake, flooding, and other natural phenomena was addressed in a previous section, this section primarily focuses on the protective measures for fire and water hazards.

Fire Protection

Before the discussion on protecting the data processing system from fire, it seems advisable to alert the security professional that the majority of fires which have adversely affected the computer room began in some other location and spread into the data processing areas. It is incumbent on the security professional to develop the fire protection measures for the data processing system by starting with the most remote parts of the facility, working through the peripheral areas adjacent to the data processing areas, and arriving at the computer room itself.

Housekeeping

Good housekeeping and the overall cleanliness of data processing areas are absolutely vital in reducing the risk from fires. The truth is many data processing areas are cluttered with a profusion of documentation, media, printouts, and paper stock. All unnecessary paper and media must be stored in fire-protected storage areas with only one operating day's supply of paper kept in the computer room. Paper products and media that must be kept in the computer room for operational reasons should be stored in fire-rated containers.

One area in the computer room which must be given special housekeeping attention is the space under the raised floor. This area is frequently littered with trash and contaminated with dust, resulting in a very combustible situation. Care should be taken while cleaning this area to avoid contaminating the rest of the computer room. Additional care must be taken if smoke detectors under the raised floor could be adversely affected by stirring up dust.

The introduction of flammables into data processing areas is strongly discouraged. All too often, flammable cleaning material is brought into data processing areas by either maintenance or janitorial personnel and is left in the area. If flammables must be kept in the computer room for frequent usage, they must be stored in a special container designed for flammable material.

Equipment

All equipment used in the computer room should be constructed of non-flammable material. Furniture such as desks, tables, and chairs should be constructed of metal to avoid adding to the fire risk of the computer room.

Trash cans and other waste receptacles used in the computer room must be made of non-flammable materials and equipped with either self-closing or fire-suppressing covers. Plastic trash can liners should not be used in the computer room because of their susceptibility to catching on fire. Trash should not be allowed to accumulate in receptacles in any data processing areas, especially not in the computer room.

Fire Extinguishers

The first line of defense against fire in data processing areas is provided by portable fire extinguishers for use in extinguishing fires while they are still in a controllable stage. Even though computer room fires are infrequent, every effort must be made to put them out so that the fire cannot spread and the system can have only a minimum interruption of service.

In addition to the other fire protection systems and equipment, each data processing area must be equipped with appropriate portable fire extinguishers to use on small fires and to assist in personnel evacuation. Data processing areas where ordinary flammables (e.g. paper, wood, plastics) may be found in quantity must be provided with pressurized, plain water, Class A portable fire extinguishers. These extinguishers should have a minimum rating of 2A, available within 75 feet of travel to any part of the area, and must be conspicuously marked for easy location and identification. All electronic equipment areas should be equipped with Class C portable extinguishers (CO_2 or Halon) with a minimum rating of 10B/C. They also must be conspicuously marked for easy location and must be available within 50 feet to travel to any part of the area.

All fire extinguishers must be conspicuously marked to aid emergency personnel in locating them during the general confusion accompanying most emergencies. One way to provide conspicuous markings at the physical location of each extinguisher is to paint a large circle (approximately 12 inches in diameter) directly over the extinguisher on the wall and close to the ceiling. If an extinguisher is mounted on a post, paint a stripe (approximately 6 inches wide) all the way around the post near the ceiling to help locate extinguishers even in an area filled with equipment. The fire extinguisher mounting area on the wall or post should also be painted to facilitate locating the extinguishers in an emergency.

Since at least two different types of fire extinguishers are needed in data processing equipment areas, each extinguisher must be clearly identified to avoid inadvertent use on the wrong type of fire. It would be catastrophic to use a water fire extinguisher (Class A) on an electrical fire; therefore, all extinguishers must show a clear indication of the type of fire for which they are to be used. One way of marking the proper use for each extinguisher is to color-code both the extinguisher and all associated markings (e.g. red could be used to indicate the Class C extinguishers while yellow could be used to indicate the Class A extinguishers). Additionally, the type of fire should be marked on each extinguisher in large print using non-technical terms. Label both the extinguisher and the wall above the extinguisher with a descriptive term describing the type of fire (e.g. USE ON ELECTRICAL FIRES ONLY; USE ON PAPER, WOOD, PLASTIC FIRES ONLY).

Fire Alarms

The fire alarm system in the data processing areas should be fully integrated with all other building fire alarm systems to provide maximum protection of critical data processing assets. Fire alarms consist of both manual pull stations and those which are automatically triggered by some type of detector. All alarms should annunciate not only in the immediate vicinity and at either the local fire department or a central station supervisory service, but also at the guard desk and in the computer room. Personnel in the computer room must be aware of any alarm, whether fire, smoke, or water flow, in any of the data processing peripheral areas. The advanced warning provided by the alarm sounding in the computer room would allow the data processing operations personnel to take actions (e.g. shutting down the system gracefully, covering the hardware with plastic covers) that could lessen the adverse impact of the smoke or water spreading into the computer room. The building or facility guards must be alerted to a fire so that they can provide direction to fire fighting personnel and ensure the continued security of the area.

Smoke Detectors

Prompt detection is a requirement in minimizing smoke and fire damage in data processing areas. Many data processing organizations assign data processing personnel the responsibility of detecting smoke and then sounding the appropriate alarm. Unfortunately, the overall effectiveness of this type of detection system is questionable, from both the standpoint of human error and the difficulty of individuals performing a multiplicity of functions effectively. Consideration should be given to installing products-of-combustion detectors to detect fires during their incipient stage, especially in data processing and peripheral areas, when a significant hazard of fire exists.

Detectors should trigger both an audible and a visual alarm signal in the computer room, in other data processing areas, at guard stations, and at the appropriate fire department. All detectors should be marked on a facility floor map to pinpoint the exact location of the detector which is sounding. This map permits personnel to locate the source of the alarm and take appropriate action quickly.

Emergency Power-Off

Emergency power-off controls should be installed in the computer room to disconnect the electrical service from all computer room electrical equipment except lighting and emergency equipment. Controls for disconnecting power for emergency purposes must be in addition to any emergency shutdown controls for individual items of computer equipment.

Emergency power-off controls should be installed at locations readily accessible to personnel during emergencies, such as adjacent to computer room exits. Each emergency power-off control should be covered to prevent inadvertent or accidental operation. Additionally, these controls must be conspicuously marked and prominently labeled to aid in their location and use for emergencies.

Smoke Exhaust

Data processing equipment areas should be equipped with a smoke exhaust capability which could be manually activated by fire fighting personnel. Exhaust equipment must be under the direct control of professional fire fighting personnel who may utilize this capability primarily for removing the contaminating smoke from the computer room in order to reduce the damage to the data processing system and to accelerate the clean-up process.

Automatic Sprinklers

Water is the most cost-effective fire extinguishing agent available for combatting Class A (e.g. paper, wood, plastics) fires. Once the electrical service has been removed from the computer and other electrical equipment, a fire in the computer room is primarily a Class A fire. Therefore, the most effective way (for the investment) to extinguish fires in the computer room is with an automatic water sprinkler system.

Typically, water sprinkler systems consist of pipes located in the ceiling and filled with water, which is released when the heat from a fire melts a fusible metal link that opens a valve in a sprinkler head. The water discharged from the sprinkler system cools the source of the fire until it is extinguished. Implementing a typical automatic water sprinkler system in a computer room has several obvious disadvantages. First, a fire would normally be in an advanced stage before the temperature at the ceiling which contained the sprinkler heads reached the required temperature (160°F or higher) to melt the fusible link to release the water. The heat from such a fire would likely damage computer hardware and media located in the vicinity of the fire. Another disadvantage with the typical automatic water sprinkler system is that once the fusible link has melted, water will continue to discharge until the water supply to the system is turned off. If the system is not monitored, water being discharged from one or more sprinkler heads could drown the system before the water is shut off. Last, contaminated water could be accidentally discharged into the computer equipment owing to a leaking pipe, defective sprinkler head, or some other problem.

Inasmuch as water is the most cost-effective fire protection system, a properly engineered automatic water sprinkler system can offset most of the afore-mentioned problems. The use of a dry pipe system counters many of the concerns about having water pipes over electrical equipment. This system is, as the name suggests, void of water until a fire causes the water supply to be released and charge the sprinkler lines, which discharge through a head when the fusible link has been melted by the fire. If this system is connected to a smoke detection system, the water supply could be controlled by requiring that two or more detectors must detect products of combustion.

When the water is released into the dry-pipe sprinkler system, a water-flow sensor could cause all electrical energy to be removed from the computer room to eliminate the chances of water being discharged on energized electrical equipment. This water-flow sensor could also trigger the alarm in the immediate vicinity and at the appropriate fire department. The requirement that two or more detectors must sound the alarm prior to activation of the system provides an operational delay for human intervention in case of false alarms or for minor fires that can be smothered using portable extinguishers.

One other problem with a water sprinkler system concerns the clean-up once water has been discharged. If the facility has been properly designed, the computer room floor will have adequate drainage to evacuate the discharged water. Also, if the smoke exhaust fans are reversible, the fans could be used to draw in fresh air to expedite the drying process. Besides the obvious problems of draining the facility and drying the equipment is the problem of contaminated water. Since most sprinkler systems sit inactive for long periods of time, the pipes and valves may become corroded so that conductive sediment would pollute the water being discharged, possibly causing shorts in the electronic circuits of the computer hardware.

A pre-action, dry-pipe system where the system is initially charged with some pressurized gas will tend to counter the corrosion problem. The fact that the pipes are pressurized with gas will prevent contamination and keep water out of the pipe until a fire both triggers a detector and melts a fusible link. This type of system can provide a delay to permit human intervention for responding to false alarms or minor fires that can be handled with a portable fire extinguisher. Another advantage is that the power supplied to the computer room can be removed from the equipment before the water discharge occurs.

Automatic Flooding Systems

Halogenated fire extinguishing agent systems, commonly called Halon, may be utilized in addition to all other previously discussed fire protection measures for critical data processing systems. Halon is a colorless, odorless, heavier-than-air gas stored under pressure as a liquid that is discharged by a system designed to develop a concentration of approximately 7% in a specified area. Unlike water systems which extinguish fire by lowering the temperature below that necessary to sustain combustion, Halon in proper concentrations has a chemical action on the combustion process to put Class A (e.g. wood, cloth, paper, rubber), Class B (e.g. combustible liquids, flammable gases), and Class C (e.g. electrical equipment) fires. If the Halon gas is released into the air at a slow rate or in less than required concentrations, the gas may become less effective in extinguishing fires and, if exposed to moisture, could be harmful to humans and equipment.

Properly designed Halon systems are effective in quickly extinguishing deep-seated fires with little resulting effects to the data processing system (except for any damages caused by the fire itself). Halon systems should be installed according to the National Fire Protection Association Standard Number 12A.

In spite of the apparent effectiveness of Halon systems in solving the fire protection problem for data processing areas, Halon systems are very expensive to install and maintain. Another problem with most Halon systems is that usually only one opportunity exists for the gas to extinguish the fire unless backup containers of Halon are available for a second attempt. Once the Halon has been discharged, the fire extinguishing capability of the equipment is gone until the system is recharged.

Water

Inasmuch as electronic data processing equipment requires a dry environment in which to operate, any water entering the computer room may damage the hardware and supporting equipment. Additionally electrical shock may endanger the lives of computer room personnel. Water from other than flooding may leak in through the computer room ceiling from a leaking roof, seepage due to puddling on a flat roof, or an overhead water pipe. Water also may come into the computer room from a peripheral area (resulting in water accumulating on the floor) or a leaking air conditioning system. An additional source of water damage may be the accidental activation of a water sprinkler system.

Many of the threats from water may be countered during the design and construction of the data processing facility. The true ceiling and walls in the computer room must be devoid of penetrations through which water may leak. All water pipes and sewer lines should be routed around the computer room to avoid installing any unnecessary pipes over the computer equipment. All water shutoff valves should be conspicuously marked and accessible so that they can be readily located and turned off during a water emergency.

The computer room should be equipped with waterproof covers to be placed over de-energized computer equipment should water inadvertently leak into the area. These covers should be stored where they can be quickly located and spread over the equipment during a water emergency.

A water drainage system should be installed in the computer room floor to evacuate any water that has leaked into the area. Water detectors should be installed to activate whenever water starts accumulating on the computer room floor. The detectors should be strategically placed in areas of the floor where water could puddle (e.g. near floor drains or air conditioner condensation drains).

Environmental Safeguards

The proper maintenance of the controlled environment within the computer room is essential for the most efficient operation of the data processing system. The environment that must be controlled includes the system power; heating, ventilating, and air conditioning (HVAC); as well as humidity.

Power

Power fluctuations and interruptions can cause malfunctions in the data processing equipment and data loss or alteration. The power supplied to the data processing equipment must meet or exceed the manufacturer's specifications if the system is not to be upset by every transient or sag on the power supply.

Emergency or backup power sources can be obtained and installed for critical data processing operations. These systems can range from a battery system to an on-site emergency diesel generator. The extent of any emergency power source depends on the criticality of the data processing system and a cost/benefit analysis.

The power used by the data processing equipment should be electrically isolated and totally dedicated. Power conditioners and isolation transformers are available to reduce the impact of power fluctuations on the system. The power in the computer room should be totally dedicated to that area and separate from all other power consumers in the area.

Power should be supplied to the data processing system from at least two feeders. These feeders should originate at separate power stations or substations and should terminate at a transfer switch used to select the feeder source.

HVAC

The temperature and humidity in the computer room should be kept within the limits specified by the computer equipment manufacturer. Generally, the optimum operating temperature is 72°F and 45% humidity. Due to the computer equipment's dependence on a constant supply of controlled air, a separate air conditioning system is needed for the computer room.

The adequacy of the air conditioning system is of concern to the security professional because the absence of the proper supply of conditioned air will deny the availability of the system as much as will any catastrophic event. The air conditioning hardware itself must be secured at the same level as the computer room and areas of the data processing facility.

If the criticality of the system is such that a backup power supply exists, consideration should be given to redundancy in the air conditioning system, that is, extra air conditioning capacity which could be used when and if parts of the air conditioning system were not operating. Additionally, if a backup power supply is available, the air conditioning system must be supplied with power from the backup source when required.

Other Concerns

Other concerns which may adversely impact the environment of the data processing system should be addressed when developing a comprehensive security program. Smoking is a fire hazard. Additionally, the smoke itself as well as the resulting debris may contaminate an environment which must be kept as clean as possible. Eating in the computer room may attract rodents which may chew through essential cabling, and drinking there may result in liquids being spilled into critical data processing equipment. Static electricity can cause data processing equipment to malfunction as well as cause personnel to experience discomfort.

PERSONNEL SECURITY CONSIDERATIONS

The proliferation of computers into almost all areas of daily life combined with the fact that many governmental and business functions are totally dependent on data processing systems has generated concern about the overall security of these automated systems. This concern has been the impetus behind the significant effort being expended in the areas of technical security (e.g. encryption, secure software, access control, and hardware security) and physical security, as discussed in the preceding paragraphs. Unfortunately the axion, 'the system is only as secure as the weakest link', is as true today as ever before. The weakest link in the security of any system is still the people who have access, either direct or indirect, to the system; however, this area of personnel security is one of the most difficult to address.

Management at all levels has failed to acknowledge the problem of personnel security in data processing for several reasons. First, management is fearful of being liable for legal action if they question and examine their employees' integrity and reliability. Many managers are concerned that they may somehow break a law or violate an employee's privacy by inquiring about an individual's background; therefore, managers are reticent to admit that their employees could be involved in unethical activities.

Another reason for inadequate emphasis on personnel security is management's unfounded notion that most of the computer security problems are caused by 'outsiders' rather than by employees. This attitude results in unreasonable trust in a person just because he is an employee.

The last reason that causes some managers to overlook the threat from data processing employees comes from management's emphasis on education and technical expertise. These managers frequently feel that the relatively high levels of education and technical expertise possessed by many data processing personnel place this group of employees above suspicion of wrongdoing.

Personnel security is but one aspect of the administrative security element which must be considered in the total system approach to protecting the data processing system. As one part of the total data processing security program, personnel security must be designed and implemented to complement and supplement the other data processing security elements.

Policy

Critical to the discussion of personnel security is the absolute requirement for a clear and concise policy statement of the organization's position of securing company assets. The absence of a personnel security policy annunciated from the highest to the lowest levels of management tends to create a poor control environment which exposes the organization to acts of defalcation and non-compliance with the Foreign Corrupt Practices Act of 1977.

An organizational security policy must address several issues. One of those issues has to do with the organization's attitude toward honesty. A policy such as the following must be emphasized and supported by all levels of management.

1. All company employees are required to adhere to the standards of honesty and highest integrity even if the law seems permissive or when peer pressure, local customs, morals, or traditions suggest that exceptions are endorsed or tolerated.
2. The company expects all employees to conduct business with an ethic that transcends the one typical in the marketplace today.

These statements of policy must be made available and enunciated during the pre-employment interviewing, in the hiring process, and also during the duration of employment. During the pre-employment interview, the prospective employee should be asked to read the statement and then sign a declaration that he has read and understood the policy. If an applicant is hired, the security policy should be reiterated. While employed with the organization, an individual should be given training in applying the policy to his particular job.

Pre-Employment Screening

Although pre-employment screening provides only a point-in-time indication of a prospective employee's past, this screening process may reveal individuals who have personality weaknesses that may disqualify them from a position of trust and responsibility. All too often, data processing personnel positions are not identified as being critical so they do not require any type of a background check. Some level of pre-employment screening should be required for every data processing employee, including operators and media librarians. A more comprehensive background investigation may be required for such critical data processing employees as a systems programmer, lead operator, or operations manager.

Separation of Duties

The basic criteria that must be firmly established and strictly enforced to obtain separation of duties are that no person should have knowledge of, be exposed to, or participate in any data processing function outside of defined areas of responsibility. For example, the following functions should be separated from each other:

1. Data processing operations.
2. Media library.
3. Data control and scheduling.
4. Systems analysis and programming.
5. Applications analysis and programming.
6. System users.

Separation of duties can be implemented by doing two things: (1) erecting physical barriers between the functions and (2) establishing procedures. The physical area of each data processing and user function should be protected from all the other functions. Thus, functional separation must be enforced by controls which permit access to only those personnel who work in a given area. Everyone else must be properly identified and escorted. The methods for accomplishing this requirement were covered in the discussion of physical security considerations.

Second, procedures must be established to reinforce the physical separation, for example:

1. Programmers shall not operate the computer.
2. Operators shall neither write nor submit programs.
3. Operators shall not enter the media library.
4. Media librarians shall not mount media.
5. Schedulers shall not be given the job control language necessary to execute jobs.

6. Users shall not run jobs unless they have been properly scheduled.
7. Programmers shall not possess data processing media.

Many of these procedures may cause the data processing personnel to complain; however, if the duties of data processing functions are to be separated, these kinds of procedures must be implemented and enforced.

Time on the Job

The amount of time a data processing employee spends on the job should be strictly controlled. Many managers rate an employee by the number of hours the employee spends at the data processing facility; that is, the more hours an employee spends on the job, the better the employee. Employees who frequently work overtime or who seldom take time off may be involved in defalcation.

Managers should periodically review who is working overtime and why. If a data processing employee habitually works beyond the normally scheduled hours, the manager should require the employee to have permission from his supervisor prior to working the extra hours.

Beware of the data processing employee who frequently takes a computer terminal home at night. Even though the employee may state that he is using the terminal on an authorized project, he could be using the terminal for unauthorized purposes. Strict controls should be established on remote terminals as well as on the dial-up lines used for access to the data processing system.

Policies and controls should be established to ensure that all employees take their earned vacation. Employees who take little or no vacation may be involved in some unauthorized or illegal activity. Managers should ensure that all data processing employees take their vacations, holidays, and all other authorized time off.

Collusion

The 'two-person rule' should be enforced throughout the data processing facility because strict compliance would mean that two or more employees would have to collude to perpetrate an illegal or unauthorized act. The odds of several people being involved in a conspiracy for very long without discovery are much greater than for an individual employee. One employee should not have the knowledge or the access to execute the entire processing cycle; in that manner, wrongdoing could be done only in collusion with other employees.

In summary, the data processing security program must be developed using a total systems approach. Besides the considerations of physical and personnel security discussed in this chapter, equally important areas include software security, communications security, and contingency planning. This total systems approach will aid the security professional in identifying threats to the system as well as vulnerabilities within the system, and it will also help in implementing countermeasures to reduce the risk to an acceptable level.

Advances in Computer Security Management, Vol. 2
Edited by M. M. Wofsey
© 1983 John Wiley & Sons Ltd.

Chapter 8

HARDWARE AND SOFTWARE SECURITY

Charles L. Cave

Cave Associates

The widespread use of digital computers in the 1950s within the Defense Department brought a corresponding need for protection of data stored and processed in these computers. The Department of Defense has issued several policy statements and/or directives concerning ADP security within the past 13 years. The thrust of these documents, that is, the basic policy, is established in 'Security Requirements for Automatic Data Processing (ADP) Systems'.[1] These security requirements also apply to government contractors to the Department of Defense, as described in the Industrial Security Manual for Safeguarding Classified Information.[2] A number of federal laws and agency regulations contain security requirements for federal non-DOD ADP systems. Laws and regulations containing ADP security requirements include the following:

1. The Privacy Act of 1974 (P.L.89-306, Dec. 31, 1974). This document requires federal agencies that maintain identifiable personal information about individuals to

> establish adequate administrative, technical and physical safeguards
> to ensure the security and confidentiality of records and to protect
> against any anticipated threats or hazards to their security or integrity
> which could result in substantial harm to any individual on whom
> information is maintained. . . .

2. Transmittal Memorandum Number 1, OMB Circular A-71 (July 27, 1978).[3] The subject of the memorandum is security of Federal Automated Information Systems. It establishes requirements for each agency of the federal government to implement a computer security program and defines a minimum set of controls to be incorporated into such security programs. It assigns to the head of each agency the responsibility for providing physical, administrative, and technical safeguards required to protect personnel, privacy, or other 'sensitive data' not subject to National Security Regulations as well as national security data. Sensitive data are data which require a degree of protection owing to the risk and magnitude of loss

or harm which could result from inadvertent or deliberate disclosure, alteration, or destruction of the data, e.g. personnel data and privacy data.

No standard security requirements or personnel clearance levels exist in the private sector. However, as in government agencies, secure systems are needed for the protection of assets and resources, regulatory compliance, maintenance of management control, and safety and integrity. In the private sector some attempts to develop levels of sensitivity can be compared with the DOD security classification levels. These levels apply to information that has corporate sensitivity, personnel data, or any other elements that are subject to some type of loss. Additional information on the need for trusted computer intersystems in government and industry can be found in reference.[4]

The remainder of this chapter is devoted to discussions on hardware/software security objectives, current hardware/software implementation in government and industry, and discussions of current security-related development activities and trends in hardware and software security.

HARDWARE/SOFTWARE SECURITY OBJECTIVES

The Ideal System

The ideal totally secure computer system would include those hardware/software features that would provide the necessary levels of security protection without additional overhead or loss of functional capabilities. This ideal system should provide at least the following security protection:

1. Separation of user data and system resources.
2. Protection of user's data from other system users.
3. Assurance that remote terminal users can access only data or resources for which they have authorization.
4. Assurance that messages or remote terminal requests cannot be misrouted because of hardware or software malfunctions.
5. The ability to define levels of sensitivity or security classification to the element or individual field of a data base.
6. Permission for users of the data base to access only those elements or files for which they have authorization or a need-to-know.
7. Sufficient software audit trail capability for appropriate personnel to assess loss due to security incident.
8. Sufficient software/hardware monitoring tools to allow security officers to detect potential systems misuse or security violation.
9. Hardware/software reliability to the degree that system malfunction will not cause a security violation.

Desired Hardware/Software Features

A combination of hardware and software features is essential to provide protection for material stored or processed in a secure resource-sharing ADP system. The presence of these features will not guarantee a totally secure system; however, in combination with other provisions such as procedures, communications, and emanations security, it will be satisfactory for most installations. Although no one has developed a proven model of the required hardware/software features in a secure system, several attempts have been made to list those required features. The most often referred to list of desired hardware/software features is contained in the Department of Defense *ADP Security Manual*.[5] The majority of the features described here are taken from this reference.

Desired Hardware Features

The primary purpose of hardware features in terms of security protection is to assure that the hardware is performing the way it was intended and to place bounds on data and instructions. Desired hardware features for a secure ADP system include but are not limited to the following:

1. The execution state of a processor should include one or more 'protection state variables' which determine the interpretation of instructions executed by the processor. A good example is a master mode and a user mode of operation in which the hardware feature would not permit a user to operate in master mode.
2. The system should be able to control access of locations in memory, for example, to restrict users from accessing memory locations reserved for the operating system (O/S).
3. The operation of certain instructions should depend on the protection state of the processor; for example, instructions which perform input or output operations would execute only when in master mode.
4. All possible operation codes, with all possible execution options, should produce known responses by the computer.
5. All registers should be capable of protecting their contents by error detection or redundancy checks.
6. Any register which can be loaded by the O/S should also be storable by it, so that the O/S can check its current contents against its presumed contents.
7. Error detection should be performed on each fetch cycle of an instruction and its operant.
8. Error detection and memory bounds checking should be performed on transfers of data between memory and storage devices or terminals.
9. Automatic programmed interrupt should function to control system and operator malfunction.
10. The identity of remote terminals for input or output should be a feature of hardware in combination with the operating system.
11. Read, write, and execute rights of the user should be verified in each fetch cycle of an instruction and its operant.

Desired Software Features

A secure ADP system ideally should not have less functionality or more over-head than commercially available non-secure ADP systems. These requirements make it more difficult to implement software features required to develop and implement a secure system. However, we can develop a list of desired software features that would, if implemented, provide an acceptable level of security. These features would include but not be limited to the following:

1. The user and master modes of ADP system operations should be separated so that a program in a user mode is prevented from performing control functions.
2. The operating system (O/S) should contain controls which provide the user with all material to which he is authorized access but no more.
3. The O/S should control all transfers between memory and on-line storage devices, between the central computer facility equipment and any remote device, or between on-line storage devices.
4. The O/S should control all operations associated with allocating ADP system resources, memory protection, system interrupt, and shifting between user and master protection modes.
5. The O/S should control access to programs and utilities which are authorized to perform maintenance functions on the O/S, including any of its elements and files.
6. The O/S should control all user programs so that access to material is made via an access control and identification system which associates the user and his terminal, in the ADP system, with the material being accessed.
7. The O/S should provide for security safeguards to cover unscheduled system shutdown (abort) and subsequent restart, as well as scheduled system shutdown and operational start-up.
8. The O/S or other system software should ensure that classified or sensitive material or critical elements of the system do not remain as accessible residue in memory or in on-line storage devices.
9. All classified or sensitive material accessible by or within the ADP system should be identified as to its security classification and access or dissemina-tion limitation, and all output of the ADP system should be appropriately marked.
10. The file management system should have the capability to classify the data base to the data element level and control access to that same level. It should also have to be capable of limiting changes to the data base to those individuals who are authorized to do so.
11. The system software should maintain an audit log or file history of use of the ADP system to permit a regular security review of system activity. The log should record security-related transactions, including each access to a classified file and the nature of the access. Each classified file successfully

accessed during each 'job' or 'interactive session' should also be recorded in the audit log.

12. Security monitoring software tools should be made available to the ADP security offices to perform at least the following functions:
    a. On-line surveillance of system activities in order to detect possible security violations.
    b. Analysis of audit log to obtain statistics of usage as well as potential loss of data due to known security violation.
13. Reliable test and diagnostic software should be available to assure the reliability of the ADP system.

Procedural Requirements

The other chapters in this text deal with aspects of procedural security, communications security, personnel security, and related issues. However, it is essential to have a complete set of operational procedures to augment the hardware/software features required to implement a secure ADP system. These procedures, which encompass both the development of the software system and the day-to-day operations and maintenance of the ADP system, can be grouped into the following categories:

1. *Hardware Configuration Control.* These procedures deal with control of the hardware configuration from the vendor's facility to the final user configuration.
2. *Hardware Maintenance and Testing.* These procedures should include rules for verification and record of access to equipment, documentation of changes, and parts control.
3. *Software Development.* Procedures should be developed for software design, implementation, and testing to assure the integrity of the system and to prevent deliberate attempts to plant software trapdoors in the system.
4. *Software Release Control.* Procedures should be developed to control the implementation of new software releases and change or modification of current releases.
5. *System Software Storage and Control.* Documented procedures should be developed for storage and dissemination of master copies of software releases to minimize inadvertent or intentional compromise of the software system.
6. *Application and Other Software.* Procedures should also be developed for development, implementation, testing, release, and control for other software such as applications, diagnostic, and security-related software.
7. *Operational Procedures.* Detailed procedures should describe each step in any ADP processing cycle. These procedures should at least include provisions for handling: special output marking, security incident reporting, and back-up procedures for system failure.

CURRENT HARDWARE/SOFTWARE IMPLEMENTATIONS

The majority of the commercially available ADP systems that are currently installed in government and industry do not contain the hardware/software features required to provide a reasonably secure ADP system. Those ADP installations that have a security requirement or process classified or sensitive data have resorted to what is termed the 'band-aid' approach, which refers to fixing or patching the systems software to correct known vulnerabilities. Several methods are now being employed to detect these operating system vulnerabilities. The first step in the process is to review system documentation to determine whether the system contains any security protection features. Second, a risk analysis can be performed on the ADP system. Risk analysis is the systematic quantification of system security capabilities, vulnerabilities, probable threats, and estimates of potential loss. Another method is to conduct a Security Test and Evaluation (ST&E). This method involves the documentation of security requirements that the system must meet according to the sensitivity of the data being processed. The next step in the ST&E is to evaluate the hardware/software and operating procedures to verify their capability to meet the stated security requirements.

A method of testing the security protection features of an ADP system that was used extensively 5 to 10 years ago was the Tiger-Team approach. A team of experts in the various security disciplines had as their task to try to penetrate the system. Sometimes this operation was accomplished covertly, other times with the knowledge of the ADP personnel. This approach is not being used extensively in current ST&E.

A variety of hardware/software features is being implemented in government and industry ADP installations that have a requirement to process classified or sensitive information. The hardware features are normally used to provide reliability and predictability for the hardware functions of the ADP systems. The software features are used to control user access and protection of user data and system resources.

Some installations use a combination of hardware, software, and/or firmware primarily for user access control, user identification, and protection of security-related software. The following are examples of current security protection features being implemented.

User Access Control and Identification

User access control and identification mechanisms are used to restrict access—to the ADP system and files resident in the system—to authorized individuals by assigning each user an identification and unique password to gain initial access to the system. The generation and dissemination of passwords vary from allowing the user to select his own to computer-generated passwords using complex algorithms. Most of the current commercially available operating systems have this capability as an option. For those second and third generation systems that were installed without security protection features, several different approaches have been used to improve system access control. Some of these approaches are discussed in the following paragraphs.

System Software Modification

One approach that has been used is to modify vendor-supplied system software to incorporate a user identification and password protection mechanisms. This protection is normally used at log-on for initial access to the system. These mechanisms are usually resident in both the operating systems and terminal handling software. The terminal handling software utilizes a terminal security matrix that contains a table of terminal ID's showing which terminals can access the system and the security level of that terminal.

Supplementing System Software

The most commonly used approach today for controlling system access is to use software packages supplied by the hardware manufacturer or system software houses. Several of these software products are available for the most used computer systems. Although these products exist for other computer mainframes, this discussion will focus on the features of three products available for IBM users since literature is more readily available for these packages. The two software products that have been in existence for a while and are the most used are IBM's Resource Access Control Facility (RACF) and ACF2 developed by the Cambridge Systems Group.

RACF provides the checking needed to assist an installation in controlling user access to applications, permanent DASD data sets, tape and DASD volumes, IMS/VS transactions and transaction groups, user-defined resources and resource groups. RACF will perform user identity verification when batch, IMS, and TSO users enter the system and check the authorization of users to DASD data sets and other protected resources based upon this verified identity.

ACF2 was designed as an extension to the IBM OS/VS-MVS Operating System to control access to the computer system and further to control access to data residing on the direct access storage and tape devices of the system. In ACF2 all data are protected by default, and the purpose of the ACF2 system extension is to control the sharing of the data. Non-hierarchical protection levels of READ, WRITE, ALLOCATE, and EXECUTE only are augmented by the concept of program paths. Program paths allow a user of the system to be qualified for more powerful access to data if he is using a specified program or a set of programs.

A new product on the market, developed by cga/allen Software Products Group, Inc., is entitled TOP SECRET and is intended for use with IBM MVS operating system. The first installations of TOP SECRET began in the fall of 1981. TOP SECRET is designed to protect most resources without the need for defining them to security. The same also applies to accessor ID's, those elements of security that identify a user to security. Only those users whose accessor ID's have been defined to TOP SECRET will be allowed to access the system. A positive definition is required first to access a system facility and second to access the resources. TOP SECRET SECURITY is activated when the system is being IPL'ed and becomes an integral part of the operating system thereafter. By directly using the Standard MVS Security Interface (SU-32), TOP SECRET accepts and validates all security checking requests issued by security drivers inherent in major O/S components.

The preceding brief descriptions of security-related software are intended to show some of the capabilities available. It is not an endorsement nor is it intended to slight other hardware manufacturers or software developers. Also the purpose was not to give a complete description, only a synopsis taken from available literature.

Hardware/Software Solutions

Several manufacturers and ADP users are incorporating security features in firmware to gain added protection and to avoid inadvertent or deliberate changes to the security mechanisms. Work is also being done to incorporate security functions in hardware. One interesting approach that was implemented in the middle seventies involved a combination of hardware and software. The application is a minicomputer operating in a remote batch and remote concentration of interactive terminals connected to two remote large-scale computers with different levels of security classification. The solution to this multi-level security problem was to develop an Electrically Alterable Read Only Memory (EAROM) that attached directly to the I/O bus of the computer and could be addressed the same as any other peripheral device. The EAROM was designed to store terminal and user authorizations as to which host they were allowed to access and their level of security access. The EAROM contained two segments of storage, one a mirror image of the other. The security information was stored in both segments; and when an access request was made to the EAROM, a hardware comparison was made between the two fields to avoid inadvertent misrouting due to hardware malfunction. A special software program was developed to load or change the EAROM contents: the security officer used a key lock and combination of toggle switches. The operating system was modified to incorporate security checks in all of the modules that involve user access. The dynamic buffer allocation module was also modified to separate the storage of information of different classification levels. This system was thoroughly tested and accredited and is still operating in a secure environment.

File Protection

In addition to system access controls, some ADP installations have the requirement to restrict access to certain files or portions of files. In the past, modifications have had to be made to the vendor-supplied Data Base Management Systems (DBMS) or additional overhead software added to provide the minimum security protection for file access control. The majority of the DBMSs currently available or being developed have some security provisions built in or available as options. Also several of the most used applications programs that depend upon data base transactions (e.g. a personnel system) also include security protection features. Most of the file management systems do not provide classification and access control to the data element level. However, the private sector seems to be more aware of the need for a secure DBMS.

Other Security Related Software

Efforts to provide security protection for ADP installations have resulted in the development of security software tools to aid the ADP system security officer in the performance of his duties. These software tools include but are not limited to the following:

1. Color change software.
2. Declassification of ADP storage media.
3. Security audit software.
4. Security monitoring tools.
5. Physical security access control and monitoring.
6. Risk assessment tools.

Color Change Software

Color change software is usually defined as that software required to purge ADP system storage media when changing from a classified or sensitive to an unclassified or non-sensitive operating environment. Some ADP installations have requirements to process data of different levels of sensitivity or as classified and unclassified. This color change software is used to erase all storage media, such as internal memory, disks, and drums, to prevent the access of memory residue by unauthorized personnel. It can also be used prior to processing classified or sensitive information to prevent the insertion of penetration type software, such as 'trapdoors.'

Declassification of ADP Storage Media

At certain times, classified or sensitive data stored on ADP storage media are no longer needed. When that time occurs, the media must be erased or declassified to prevent unauthorized disclosure. Magnetic tapes are usually erased by using degaussing equipment that removes all data from the tape by creating a magnetic field. However, software is normally used to declassify internal memory, disks, disk packs, and drums. Internal memory is purged by setting each addressable location alternately to all 'ones' and all 'zeros' for a specified time period until the state is changed a specified number of times. The period of time and the number of times that the state is changed depend on the sensitivity of the data being processed. The normal procedure for clearing disks, disk packs, and drums is to overwrite all storage locations a minimum of three times, once with the binary digit '1', once with binary digit '0', and once with a single numeric alphabetic, or special character.

Security Audit Software

Most ADP systems have the capability to create a log of system activity, to some extent, usually for accounting purposes. Logging for security purposes normally requires additional information, such as number of unsuccessful attempts to log on to the system, and accesses and changes to files. The vendor-supplied logging software usually has to be modified to obtain these data. The security officer needs additional software to analyze system usage and assess damage or loss due to detected security violation.

Security Monitoring Tools

Security monitoring tools are the software products that allow the security officer to monitor on-line system activity for potential security violations. Although attempts have been made to develop ADP systems security officer stations, using microprocessors, most attempts were not successful.

Physical Security Access Control and Monitoring

Physical and personnel security issues are discussed in other chapters in this volume; however, one application in those disciplines utilizes ADP hardware and software. Some ADP and other sensitive facilities are using computer-based security access control and monitoring systems to prevent unauthorized entry to the facility and limited access areas within the facility. These systems use individual personnel identification cards that must be inserted in badge readers to gain entrance to limited access areas. The badges or ID cards contain embedded codes concerning the individual's authorization to enter a specific area. The remote badge reader is connected to a central computer-controlled console that contains authorized access lists. If the code is verified, the computer activates an electric strike on the door on which the badge reader is attached and the door is opened. These systems can also be connected to closed-circuit television (CCTV) systems to monitor traffic in the secure area or to monitor alarmed doors. They can also be used to control other sensors, such as motion detectors and fire and smoke detectors. Several of these systems are available today and are working quite well.

Risk Assessment Tools

Risk assessment is also discussed elsewhere in this text. However, it may be in order to mention that several of the risk assessment methodologies in use today utilize software tools to assist in the performance of ADP system risk analysis.

Operating Procedures

In maintaining a secure ADP environment, it is essential that documented procedures be developed for utilizing the hardware/software. These procedures should include rules for:

1. Control of software development and releases.
2. Control of program testing and troubleshooting.
3. Storage and control of system software.
4. Labeling and control of computer output.
5. Security incident reporting.
6. Back-up procedures.

CURRENT ACTIVITIES AND TRENDS IN HARDWARE/SOFTWARE SECURITY DEVELOPMENT

During the seventies both the federal government and private sector showed an increased awareness in the requirement for computer security. Several computer security and privacy policy documents were promulgated. A recent survey[6] identified policy fragmentation across-the-board and lack of cost-effective, feasible implementing guidance. This lack of both cohesive guidance and commercially available secure operating systems has resulted in a regrouping by the security community. Meanwhile, computer security needs are continuing to be addressed by the 'band-aid' approach. However, this lack of significant advance in the computer security field may have generated development efforts that will produce vastly improved security systems for the eighties. Positive results of the seventies have been:

1. Increased security awareness in both government and industry.
2. Increased participation by computer manufacturers and systems organizations.
3. Establishment of computer security R&D efforts in both the federal government and the private sector.
4. A clearer understanding of computer security requirements and the vulnerabilities of current systems.
5. Significant increase in the number of security-oriented business organizations.

Among the research and development activities that began in the seventies, some of these efforts may produce significant results in the eighties.

DOD Computer Security Initiative

The Department of Defense (DOD) Computer Security Initiative[7] was established in 1978 by the Assistant Secretary of Defense for Communications, Command, and Control and Intelligence to achieve the widespread availability of 'trusted' ADP systems for use within DOD. Widespread availability implies the use of commercially developed trusted ADP systems whenever possible. A 'trusted' system is defined as one with sufficient hardware and software integrity measures to allow simultaneous processing of multiple levels of sensitive information. The computer security initiative is a technical consortium consisting of DOD and industry representatives. Some of the key objectives of the consortium are to:

1. Develop methodologies for formal specification and verification of both of the design and the implementation of a system.
2. Develop evaluation methodologies for system certification.
3. Design and implement trusted computer systems.

The computer security initiative program, in its third seminar,[8] reviewed the security R&D in the seventies and forecast the thrust for the eighties.

DOD R&D in 1970s

1. Operating system major emphasis, mostly software, some hardware.
2. Applications—minor focus until late 70s.

DOD R&D Thrusts in 70s

1. Operating system
   a. Kernelized secure operating system
   b. Kernelized VM370 system
   Driven by—
   a. What can be achieved in 3 to 5 years?
   b. What can be expected in 5 to 8 years?
   Intended as demonstration capabilities, not as competition with manufacturers.
2. Applications
   a. Security fitters between existing systems.
   b. Communications front-end systems—access protection to existing systems.
   c. Multiple single-level functions.

    d. Trusted multilevel systems
- special purpose—message handling
- general purpose—DBMS

3. Verification technology
    a. Evolved from efforts to build 'correct programs'.
    b. Several approaches evolving.

DOD R&D in 1980s

1. Operating systems
    a. Rely mainly on industry evolution
    b. Some specialized development
2. Applications
    a. Major emphasis by R&D and user community
3. Verification technology
    a. Major thrust beginning—ensure understanding of product integrity.

Technology Evolution in 80s

1. Hardware cheaper, more powerful
    a. Complex software functions moving into hardware.
2. Better understanding of operating systems
    a. What is needed, how to provide efficiently.
3. Assurance techniques improving rapidly.

Trusted Computer System Development

Several R&D efforts have been underway since the early to middle seventies:

1. Kernelized Secure Operating System (KSOS-11): Ford Aerospace and Computer Corporation.
2. Kernelized Secure Operating System (KSOS-6): Honeywell Corporation.
3. UCLA Data Secure UNIX: University of California at Los Angeles.
4. Kernelized VM-370 (KVM): System Development Corporation.

Detailed information concerning these projects is available from other sources, most of which are listed in reference 6. A brief description of these efforts and their current status follows. Before the specific efforts in the development of trusted systems and methodologies are discussed, Security Kernel should be defined. A Security Kernel is 'a mechanism within a computer system, comprised of hardware and software, that controls the access of users (and processes executing on their behalf) to repositories of information resident in or connected to the system'.

Bell Laboratories developed an operating system called UNIX between 1971 and 1975. UNIX is a general-purpose time-sharing computer system designed to provide a good environment for a user to develop and operate information processing and computation systems. UNIX is a trade/service mark of Western Electric. In 1976 UCLA and the Mitre Corporation began development of secure UNIX prototypes. In 1978 Ford Aerospace began an effort to implement a Kernelized Secure Operating System (KSOS-11), 'Secure UNIX'. KSOS-11, implemented on a Digital Equipment PDP-11 series computer, is in varying stages of testing at Alpha and Beta test sites.

Some of the problems encountered to date have been:

1. A substantial slowdown of system performance.
2. Maintenance of consistency between the multiple independent representatives of a system component.
3. Multiple language support.

In 1976 System Development Corporation (SDC) began development of a 'kernelized' version of IBM VM370 Operating System (KVM). Some of the design goals of KVM were:

1. Provide certifiable secure version of IBM VM370 O/S.
2. Guarantee separation of virtual machines provided by VM370.
3. Verifiably protect against compromise.
4. Enforce controlled sharing consistent with DOD policy.

The KVM was designed to operate on IBM 138, 145, 158, 168, 3031, 3032, 4331, and 4341 as well as on IBM look-a-like AMDAHL, ITEL, and Nanodata VMX. KVM supports most IBM operating systems, CMS, and most IBM-SHARE applications programs. KVM/370 Security Kernel is interrupt-driven and controls:

1. All real I/O.
2. All paging and spooling I/O.
3. Allocation of: DASD pages, storage pages, DASD spooling cylinders, and I/O devices.

KVM/370 is being tested at Alpha and Beta test sites.

Honeywell Corporation is developing a Trusted Computing Base (TCB) called the Secure Communication Processor (SCOMP) on the Honeywell Level 6 Minicomputer. SCOMP is a combined hardware/software implementation. The SCOMP implementation is based on a commercial Level 6 minicomputer. The Level 6 is enhanced with a Security Protection Modules (SPM), several new processor instructions, security kernel software, trusted process and a SCOMP Kernel Interface Package (SKIP). The SPM is the system component which plugs into the Level 6 bus between system elements and provides mediation for: central processor unit (CPU) references to memory: CPU references to I/O devices and I/O device references to memory. The active elements (CPU to I/O device), on behalf of a process, request access to objects by a virtual address. Physically the SPM consists of two motherboard-daughterboard pairs and a smaller daughterboard mounted on the central processor. The daughterboard, called the Virtual Memory Interface Unit (VMIU), provides mediation for processor to memory references without the delay associated with accessing the SPM through the bus. The VMIU contains a cache for up to 256 descriptors for use in mediation of CPU memory request. The SCOMP software consists of a Security Kernel (KSOS-6), Trusted Software and a SKIP. The Security Kernel is a basic operating system which enforces the security rules. The Trusted Software consists of user functions which reside outside the Kernel but perform security related tasks and must be verified similar to the Kernel. The SKIP provides the user application interface. SKIP includes process control, hierarchical multilevel file system and user I/O capability. SCOMP is currently being tested.

Other efforts currently in progress to develop Trusted Computer Systems are:

1. Digital Equipment Corporation—Research in security enhanced systems, kernelized systems, network security protocols, end-to-end encryption.
2. IBM Corporation—Security and protection of data in the IBM System/38.
3. TYMSHARE, Inc.—GNOSIS, a secure capability based 370 operating system.

Methodology Development

In addition to the hardware/software development previously discussed, other efforts currently in progress deal with methodologies for design, specification, implementation, and verification of software. Two such projects, which will be described briefly, are a Formal Development Methodology (FDM), developed by SDC, and a Hierarchical Development Methodology (HDM), developed by SRI International.

Formal Development Methodology (FDM)

FDM enforces rigorous connections between successive stages of development. It is used as follows:

1. The correctness requirements for the software are modeled.
2. A top-level design specification is written and verified to be consistent with the model.
3. The design specification is repeatedly refined to include more detail until a program design specification is derived.

4. The intermediate design specifications and the program design specifications are verified as the refinement process is carried out.
5. An implementation is coded from the program design specification, and this implementation is verified to be consistent with the program design specification.

By verifying that specifications are consistent with the model, design errors are detected immediately rather than during implementation verification.

Hierarchical Development Methodology (HDM)

HDM is an integrated collection of languages, tools, concepts, and guidelines to aid in developing and verifying large real-world software systems. Among the characteristics of HDM are:

1. Orientation toward real-world solutions to real-world problems.
2. A formal basis.
3. Comprehensive quality.
4. A research vehicle.
5. Support for design and code verification.

Organized Efforts in Computer Security Evaluation

One of the bright spots of the eighties is the government's recent announcement of the establishment of a Computer Security Technical Evaluation Center (CSTEC). This center will be placed under an existing DOD agency and be responsible for technical evaluation of computer system security.

This responsibility will include the conduct of 'Trusted Computer System' evaluation of those systems produced under the previously discussed computer security initiative. Key functions of the SCTEC are:

1. Provide technical assistance to DOD components on computer security matters.
2. Propose, coordinate, establish, and maintain technical protection criteria.
3. Maintain evaluated products list of those systems that have been evaluated and certified.
4. Conduct seminars and workshops on computer security.
5. Develop a computer security program for DOD research and development.

Other Developments Expected in the 80s

In addition to the DOD computer security efforts described previously, increased participation by industry is expected to take place in the eighties. Identification of the need for trusted ADP systems in the private sector will expand the market area for hardware/software suppliers. Security-related events that should take place during the 1980s are:

1. Increased activity by hardware manufacturers to include hardware/software security features in commercial ADP systems.
2. Increased effort by software houses to develop security-related software.
3. Increased use of software encryption techniques for program and file protection.
4. Increased security awareness in government and industry, and development of standard security requirement definitions that will apply to both environments.

In summary, the Department of Defense has had a need for secure ADP systems for over 20 years. Awareness of security and privacy requirements has increased, and a documented need for more secure ADP systems in the private sector appeared during the 1970s. Research and Development efforts to develop secure operating systems and design methodologies proliferated. The DOD Computer Security Initiative Program is now demonstrating the feasibility of designing and implementing trusted computer systems that can provide high levels of protection to data, programs, and processing in certain constrained operational environments. Both awareness of computer security needs and activity in development of secure ADP systems should heighten during the 1980s, with perhaps a significant step toward developing the ideal secure ADP system.

REFERENCES

1. DOD Directive 5200.28, *Security Requirements for Automatic Data Processing (ADP) Systems*. December 18, 1972.
2. DOD 5220.22-M, *Industrial Security Manual for Safeguarding Classified Information*. July 1981.
3. Transmittal Memorandum Number 1, OMB Circular A-71, *Security of Federal Automated Information Systems*. July 17, 1978.
4. Turin, R.: *Trusted Computer Systems, Needs and Incentives for Use in Government and the Private Sector*. June 1981.
5. DOD 5200.28-M, *ADP Security Manual*, January 1973.
6. Epperly, E.: Trends in DOD Directives: Survey of Federal Computer Security Policies. *In Selected Papers and Presentations from the U.S. Army Third Automation Security Workshop*. Williamsburg, Virginia, December 8–10, 1980.
7. *Proceedings of the Second Seminar on the DOD Computer Security Initiative Program*. National Bureau of Standards, Gaithersburg, Maryland, January 15–17, 1980.
8. *Proceedings of the Third Seminar on the DOD Computer Security Initiative Program*. National Bureau of Standards, Gaithersburg, Maryland, November 18–20, 1980.

Advances in Computer Security Management, Vol. 2
Edited by M. M. Wofsey
© 1983 John Wiley & Sons Ltd.

Chapter 9

VULNERABILITIES OF DATA TELECOMMUNICATIONS SYSTEMS

William C. Grayson

Bedford Group International

Professional data managers who are sufficiently concerned about computer security are likely to initiate or consider initiating protective actions for systems elements they perceive to be most vulnerable to credible threats. These threats are most commonly profiled as mature, tenured personnel in the employ of their organizations for several years. They victimize their employers through embezzlement or unauthorized personal use of data processing resources. In many cases, tightly woven computer security schemes offer strong defenses against potential attacks on the system and its hardware and software components, which may be widely dispersed geographically. Under most circumstances, data managers have high levels of confidence in the security programs that they have developed to counter these internal threats.

As the evolution of the information age continues to unfold, increasing numbers of corporate bodies will find themselves relying upon the telecommunications connectivity to support word and data processing functions, distributed data systems, electronic funds transfer, electronic mail systems, and other automated processes. Traditional paper documents in sealed envelope mail are giving way to data and information flows over telecommunications networks organized and operated by outside suppliers. These suppliers, which are providing telecommunications service to subscribers, are identified generically as 'common carriers'. They include well-known telephone companies with established corporate histories as well as newly formed companies specializing in network service to the business community.

From a data security viewpoint, common carriers are usually not included as components when data managers define and describe their automated systems. Since system connectivity is generally not an asset of the data manager but is instead leased from the common carrier, it is easy to overlook its importance when assessing threats and vulnerabilities to the overall system. Data managers satisfied with the progress they have made in neutralizing internal threats should turn next to evaluating whether a window in their fortress may have been left open and unprotected.

The open window may likely be the telecommunications linkage among processors and terminals throughout the system. If it is reasonable to postulate threats to data and information in process or storage, it follows that threats may be extended to unauthorized access through wiretapping, induction, or passive electronic interception of data flows.

One of the results of an effective computer security program may be to force the unauthorized perpetrator to seek alternative means of satisfying information requirements now denied him by the strengthened security program. Since a principal product of eavesdropping is information, the data overheard may become, in addition to the actual data, a tool for committing further computer crimes. Data flows contain passwords, account numbers, fiscal and bookkeeping data, for example, plus an insight into the software and languages used. The opportunity to study data communications may provide the temptation to use the knowledge obtained for personal gain.

If a potential interceptor considers eavesdropping on the telecommunications of any organization, only three factors are present in any decision to do so:

1. *An information requirement.* Is information available to the eavesdroper through interception as perhaps the only remaining source following implementation of an otherwise strong security program? Is information required by the eavesdropper to support other attacks against the system? (The computer security programs of some organizations begin and end with concealing passwords from public view and restricting access to operating areas. A perpetrator bent on unauthorized access can recover passwords and logon procedures by intercepting and reading unprotected data transmissions.)

2. *The technical capability.* Does the threat have the ability to determine and isolate specific circuits and channels to which the common carrier has assigned the subscriber's data? Does the capability also include knowledge of such specifications as bandwidths, bit rates, and transmission formats?

3. *The inclination to spend resources and assume risks.* As will be demonstrated later, the expenses required to intercept and process someone else's data may be viewed relatively as expensive or modest, depending on individualized cost/benefit factors. Naturally, the more sophisticated the data being transmitted, the greater the investment in processing hardware, software, and analysis personnel.

Wiretapping on the victim's premises is many times less expensive than passive electronic interception from within the public networks operated by common carriers. However, where bribes or other inducements become necessary to subvert the carrier's employees, wiretapping may also become very expensive. The latter is also a high-risk undertaking. All 50 states and the federal government have enacted criminal statutes making wiretapping an offense punishable by fines and/or imprisonment. In the corporate world, disastrous public embarrassment and loss of goodwill could follow indictment for wiretapping as well.

Passive electronic interception requires neither breaking and entering nor making physical connections to telecommunications circuitry. It is at the same time much less risky but much more expensive.

TRANSMISSION TECHNOLOGIES

All of the common carriers offering commercial telecommunications services employ one or more of the three basic technologies: cable, terrestrial microwave, or communications satellite. Where any two or all three of these are available to the carrier, they may be used in combination, depending on network routing or other technical considerations. Media selection is a carrier function where a choice is possible, although clients may request specific routing for certain leased services. The largest carrier, the American Telephone and Telegraph Corporation, maintains a network operations center at Bedminster, New Jersey, which is largely automated. Since the choice of traffic routing may be automated to take advantage of less busy trunks, AT&T personnel may, at any given time, be unaware of the specific trunks in use by individual subscribers to the public switched network.

It is generally not possible to trace end-to-end routing with identification of cable, microwave, or satellite links. Identical routings are unlikely to occur on successive days or at different hours of the business day in large public switched networks.

Quite the opposite may be true of the smaller carriers. The most recent entries into this newly deregulated industry may be divided into two groups:

1. Value Added Network (VAN) carriers, which own no transmission facilities themselves. They are organized as network nodal points from which they receive a client's data for entry into the transmission channels of another carrier from which the channels are leased. Unlike the automated switching which occurs in the public network, leased channels tend to be static in nature and may follow the same routing for long periods of time.
2. Recently organized companies which own transmission facilities but favor terrestrial microwave and/or satellite transmission over cable for both long-distance and local use. Within some of these carrier companies, cable use may be minimal and localized.

Businesses attracted by lower charges for long-distance telecommunications service may now be leasing from carriers whose transmission path between given points may be consistently predictable in terms of geography and transmission technology. Each transmission technology has peculiar vulnerabilities to unauthorized interception. While the selection of a carrier will almost certainly be made on a cost basis, managers who opt for reduced operating costs may also be buying an unwanted increase in eavesdropping vulnerability.

TELECOMMUNICATIONS CABLE

Into this category fall all of the usual cable types in use today: twisted pairs (of wires), coaxial cable, and optical fibers carrying modulated light. Whether used for local distribution within buildings or cities or in long-distance toll circuits strung on telephone poles, buried in the ground, or lying on the seabed, all cables are subject to wiretapping. Taps may be made on the cables themselves or within any pieces of equipment to which the cables are connected, such as junction boxes, switches, or distribution frames in telephone company buildings or 'wire closets' at the customer's place of business.

No protection against wiretapping is provided if the cable is buried or if it is underground cable in a sealed, pressurized conduit. Telephone companies use pressurization linked to an alarm system to identify and isolate broken cables. A knowledgeable technician can drill into a pressurized sheath at two points, perhaps 12 inches apart. The selected foot-long section can be sealed off with commonly available sealing compounds to restore the pressurization. The cable could then be opened up to make the tap. A brief alarm may sound at the telephone company's maintenance plant but is likely to be ignored if it does not repeat.

Undersea cable is similarly vulnerable to tapping. While the ocean depths are vast and cable laying companies have fleets of highly sophisticated vessels to locate and raise the cables, so many are apparently accidentally raised by commercial fishermen that one telephone company advertises in coastal newspapers that they will provide free cable charts so that trawlers and dredgers can avoid raising them.

Most office buildings have a wire closet in a public area on each storey. Inside these closets, which should always be locked but often are not, is a distribution frame that fans out all of the pairs of wire serving each individual telephone or 'hard-wired' piece of data equipment on that floor of the building. Frequently, telephone repairmen have pencilled-in extension numbers next to terminal points on the frame for future reference. If penetrated by a would-be eavesdropper, a tap may be placed in the wire closet unknown to the users, the telephone company, or the building management. Responsibility for the security of wire closets is rarely a subject of discussion among these groups. Building security inspections normally do not include wire closets, and the inspectors are usually not trained to recognize unauthorized equipment elements or evidence of tampering with telephone company equipment. A cleverly placed tap may enjoy a very long life before detection (if any) and removal.

The most recent development in cable technology is fiber optic cable carrying modulated light. Its advantage as a finer, lighter strand of glass replacing thicker, heavier, more expensive metals (usually copper) is obvious. Since they are non-electric, optical fibers are not affected by other sources of electricity in close proximity. Equally, they are not vulnerable to inductive coupling wherein a sensor may be placed on or next to the cable to pick up radiations. To the wiretapper, optical fiber cable represents a formidable challenge. Alligator clips, which work on metallic wire, will not pick up a signal being carried on fiber cables.

An intrusion into the fiber will probably cause a signal reflection back in the direction of the sending station. One likely and immediate effect would be a recognizable and unacceptable degradation of the data flow followed by a system shutdown and fault isolation. Government and industry research into the inherent security of fiber optics is continuing. At the present time, secret government data are not transmitted over optical fiber cables without encryption—an indication of its unsettled susceptibility to tapping. Optical fiber cables must, in any case, be joined to the usual junction boxes, switches, repeaters, and other elements, which may themselves be attacked for wiretapping purposes.

TERRESTRIAL MICROWAVE

Representing another modern innovation to avoid the cost of investing in expensive metal cable, and then installing and maintaining them on poles or underground, is terrestrial microwave radio transmission of telecommunications (Figure 9.1). Telephone companies can multiplex up to 14,000 channels into one microwave transmission. A microwave 'beam' is transmitted (at between 4 and 12 gigahertz) to a receiver within line of sight for relay to the next point, and so on, to establish across-town or transcontinental linkage. Terrestrial microwave transmission is especially advantageous in difficult terrain or harsh climates where cables have inherent susceptibilities. A characteristic of microwave transmission enhancing its popularity with telephone companies is its concentration into beams of energy which lend themselves to highly directional aiming. By coupling this feature with their reflective properties, telephone companies can point a microwave beam at a passive reflector on a mountaintop for reception on the other side, not in line of sight of the transmitter. In these passive relays, no power is required at the mountaintop site and the structure is virtually maintenance free.

These highly attractive features have led telephone companies to rely on microwave transmission for over 70% of toll applications. For local distribution, intracity cable was the norm until the 1981 decision by the Federal Communications Commission which permits competition for local distribution markets. As a

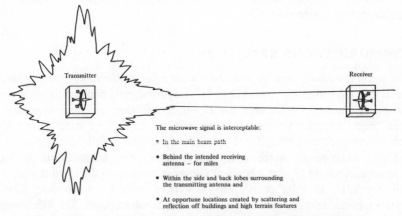

Figure 9-1.   Terrestrial microwave radiation pattern (overhead view).

result of the 1981 decision, any carrier can now file with the FCC to sell local distribution over a microwave network. Rooftop microwave dishes are proliferating in metropolitan areas as business information and data have emerged from underground, so to speak, and entered the radio spectrum.

The use of microwave systems instead of cables represents an opportunity for price competitiveness with which to penetrate established marketplaces. When considering vulnerabilities to eavesdropping, however, microwave systems in local distribution or long-distance toll environments have special drawbacks.

At the transmitting antenna, a focused beam of electromagnetic energy is aimed in line of sight at an intended receiving antenna perhaps 25 or more miles away, depending on respective elevations. Although the beams are highly directional, they spread nonetheless before reaching the receiver so that not all of the transmitted energy is collected at the distant end. An unintended receiver with the proper antenna can intercept the transmission at any point in the beam corridor or behind the intended receiving antenna.

Surrounding the transmitting antenna, also within line of sight for miles, will be side and back 'lobes' of electromagnetic energy containing all of the signal elements to be found in the main beam. Using the same intercept antenna as before, the unintended receiver can passively intercept the signal from these lobes and recover transmitted data. The highly reflective properties of the microwave transmission, moreover, will bounce off downtown buildings or surrounding high terrain features causing a scattering effect. The interceptor can therefore identify points from which a desired transmitter may be continuously monitored and then set up a fixed intercept site. In such a situation, detection of the passive eavesdropping activity is remote and may go on so long as the eavesdropper is inclined to continue.

Merely intercepting the microwave signal, however, does not satisfy the eavesdropper's information or data requirements. Within large telephone company microwave transmission systems, the unauthorized listener may have to deal with up to 14,000 simultaneously transmitted channels of information and data intricately multiplexed.

COMMUNICATIONS SATELLITES

A communications satellite is a microwave relay platform in space. A satellite containing a receiver and transmitter for relaying signals back to Earth is placed into geosynchronous orbit over the Equator such that its rotation around the globe keeps it relatively over the same point on Earth. The satellite receives its signal from a transmitting Earth station which has aimed its antenna at the satellite's location in space over the Equator. The transmission is highly directional in nature so that a beam of energy is focused on the satellite's location. This 'up link', as it is called, has associated with it surrounding lobes of electromagnetic energy, which are vulnerable to interception. The lobes contain the same information or data content that is found in the up link itself. Interception of the main beam, however, is impractical. Theoretically, an airborne or spaceborne platform could be made to hover in the main beam for signal acquisition purposes. Long-term flying of this nature would soon be recognized for what it was. It is unlikely to become a credible threat, especially in light of the relative ease by which the 'down link' from the satellite can be intercepted (Figure 9-2).

Whereas the Earth station's transmission is a concentrated beam of signal energy aimed at the satellite in space, the relayed signal sent back down from the satellite is a wide-angle transmission. It is aimed not at a single receiving Earth station but rather at a broad receiving area in which many dispersed receiving Earth stations may be located. Because of the curvature of the Earth, the outline of the targeted geography takes on the shape of a footprint and the telecommunications industry has adopted 'footprint' to refer to the potential receiving area.

The footprints of today's communications satellites are vast. A typical receiving area covers most of the continental United States plus some adjacent ocean areas. Collection of satellite down link transmissions requires a dish-shaped antenna aimed accurately at the satellite. Since received signals coming from extraterrestrial space are weak, sophisticated amplifiers are needed to boost the signal before it can be demultiplexed and distributed to individual addresses. An

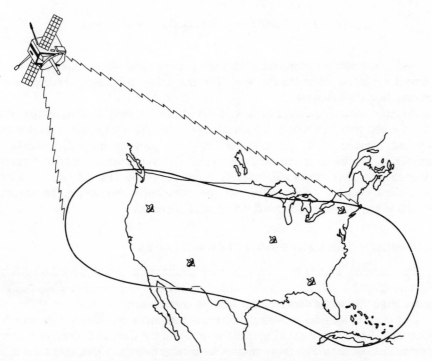

Figure 9-2.   Typical communications satellite downlink footprint.

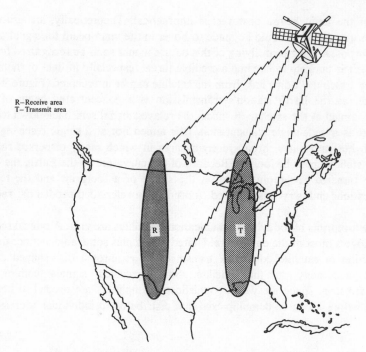

R—Receive area
T—Transmit area

Figure 9-3.   Satellite spot scanning beam (development).

eavesdropper bent on intercepting data being transmitted via satellite can situate himself anywhere within the footprint. The probability of his being detected is so remote as to approach zero.

Presently under development is a satellite 'spot scanning' technique that will sharply constrict potential reception areas on the Earth's surface (Figure 9-3). Desired because of its potential for improving security on traffic handling capacities, satellite spot scanning will curtail an eavesdropper's receiving areas dramatically. These areas will, however, reach from Canada to Mexico and may be several hundred miles wide, so the curtailment is relative. Moreover, detectability of eavesdroppers will not be at all increased.

COMBINED TRANSMISSION TECHNOLOGIES

Two industry leaders have brought forth schemes for combining transmission technologies that will attract telecommunications and data managers anxious to move large volumes of data long distances at lowest costs.

One concept includes moving data from a customer's premises to the carrier's Central Office by local cable or microwave. From the Central Office, the carrier combines these data with those of other local subscribers and transmits them in a multiplexed format via microwave to its regional Earth station. From the Earth station, the transmission is 'up linked' to a satellite and relayed back down to a distant regional Earth station. From there, the signal travels again by terrestrial microwave to another Central Office in a distant city for local distribution by cable or local microwave to the location of the addressee.

A similar concept developed by a rival carrier has some variations which eliminate the Central Office and regional Earth station features. Rooftop satellite antennas will handle data from customers' premises within that office building for direct transmission to and reception from a satellite. In either scheme, all transmitted data will be vulnerable to interception by unauthorized parties over all legs in the combined technologies. The satellite footprints in both concepts are very broad. Terrestrial microwave transmission patterns will make them vulnerable, especially in downtown, urban areas. Wiretapping, while admittedly more risky than passive electronic interception of microwave and satellite links, will continue to be a threat to local distribution cable in buildings, industrial parks, and urban areas.

DIAL-UPS VERSUS LEASED LINES

While once again business decisions to lease individual private lines or even whole switched networks will always be made on the basis of cost/benefit analyses, questions of eavesdropping vulnerability should hopefully arise before and not after operation has begun. In the discussion on transmission technologies, it was noted that large telephone companies, which rely on automated switching, normally cannot describe the exact transmission paths in terms of channel and route for data sent in the public switched network. This limitation would not necessarily be present when a business subscriber has leased a channel from the telephone company. The business subscriber will have specified a point of origin of the data, an addressee's location, and certain technical aspects of the intended transmissions. While the subscriber will not generally be aware of it in precise terms, the telephone company will assign the leased circuit to a pair of wires in a trunk cable or to a fixed channel to be sent over microwave or satellite. Over a long period of time, perhaps years if no changes are required, the private channel will be a static assignment in the multiplexed arrangement. Whereas neither the telephone company nor an eavesdropper could find—without considerable effort—a desired channel in the public network, both the telephone company and the eavesdropper can find and return easily to a private channel because of its static nature. Private lines, in this sense, are not private at all but have an even greater vulnerability to unauthorized interception.

SIGNALING

In any switched telecommunications system, signaling is needed to address traffic to an intended, selected recipient. Address signaling is the feature that an eavesdropper must exploit to acquire data transmitted in the public switched network. Since the advent of all-digit dialing and area codes, each telephone in the United States has become a unique, discrete telecommunications address, which is not duplicated anywhere in North America. The net effect on intercept vulnerabilities of this property is that an eavesdropper can automate his traffic identification function by providing a 'look-up' table to a computer used in eavesdropping. Following intercept and demultiplexing, the intercepted channels are scanned for the 10-digit addresses which precede all telephone calls and computer dial-ups. Programmed to ignore unwanted telephone numbers not in the list, the computer starts a tape recorder whenever a wanted address is noted. With such a technique, the inherent protective qualities of the public switched network become somewhat eroded. An option to automate search and traffic identification functions is still the eavesdropper's to make; the inclination to devote what may be expensive resources underlies all interception decisions.

A recent development in switching which is already being implemented in many parts of the United States separates the address signaling (10-digit telephone numbers) from the following data of information. The address information is routed over a data link to a signal transfer point containing a processor which sets up a link for the data or voice to follow separately. Intercept of the data link would tell an eavesdropper that his desired telephone address was indeed called up but he would not be able to access any of the data subsequently transmitted to that address. On the other hand, interception of the information channel without any address information to identify who is receiving the data would become excessively burdensome since huge quantities of data would have to be processed in the hope of finding a desired transmission. In the United States this development is known as Common Channel Interoffice Signaling (CCIS), and it represents an enhancement of the inherent protection of the public network from

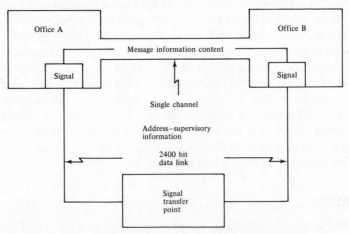

Figure 9-4.   Common channel interoffice signaling (CCIS).

eavesdropping. CCIS is not, however, currently planned for application to private networks leased by the government and larger corporations. Their special vulnerabilities will continue unchanged.

PROPRIETARY TRANSMISSION FACILITIES

Where economy dictates, a firm may buy its own microwave transmitting and receiving system and avoid paying a carrier to move its data. Decisions will naturally follow cost/benefit reasoning, and eavesdropping vulnerability will rarely be a consideration. Proprietary microwave systems have the same inherent vulnerabilities as the systems used by telephone companies. The signals are totally interceptible in line of sight and, because they carry a limited load of channels, are more easily exploited by the interceptor.

THE INTERCEPTION INVESTMENT

A leading manufacturer of telecommunications hardware, which is also one of the prominent common carriers, estimates that the equipment costs for intercepting the various telecommunications technologies would be approximately as follows:

1. *Wire.* A few cents worth of copper wire in a wire closet can strap two telephone terminals together in such a way that two telephones on different numbers will ring when only one is dialed. From the second 'wired-in' telephone, listening in on voice or data will be possible. 'Bugs' of various types can be planted at many points in data processing hardware or communications boxes to enable transmission to a recorder or eavesdropper's terminal. The investment may be under $100. Should the tap be placed on trunk cable carrying multiplexed, packetized, or otherwise interleaved traffic elements, the hardware investment may be as high as $500.

2. *Terrestrial Microwave.* $4000 will buy an antenna and receiver capable of collecting signals in the 4 to 12 GHz range. Additional equipment would be necessary for processing signals in complex multiplexed formats.

3. *Communications Satellite.* An investment of at least $25,000 would be necessary. As with terrestrial microwave, signals processing equipment would be needed in addition to the antenna and receiver group bought with the $25,000.

In each case an additional investment would be required for specialists to perform various signal acquisition and processing functions. The price can become relatively high but if the data to be intercepted are available only through intercepts and would be worth the investment, the only decision remaining revolves around the inclination to devote the resources. These costs are surely within the reach of governments, the larger corporations, organized crime, and even individuals or small conspiratorial groups who could muster the investment in pursuit of potentially large but ill-gotten gains.

PREVENTION

Just as the eavesdropper has but three questions to consider in any intercept decision, the data manager, too, must confront three areas in order to arrive at a decision on preventing (or terminating) the vulnerability of his organization's data to interception.

1. *Risk assessment.* To perform a meaningful risk assessment, the data manager and, it is hoped, his firm's telecommunications manager and director of security should review the total telecommunications environment. At a minimum, all facets of data sensitivity, circuit vulnerability, potential threats, and their expected capabilities and inclinations must be studied. Data sensitivity must also be expressed as being of a perishable versus a long-term nature, as applicable, since data that need protection for only a short period can be treated in ways not available for data that have long-term sensitivities.

2. *Liability.* Separate from assessing the risks of eavesdropping, the firm must determine the value of potential losses of data through interception. Procedures similar to establishing Annual Loss Expectancies in general computer system risk assessments are applicable here. The difference in the telecommunications context is that the firm normally has no control of the data it has provided to the common carrier for transmission. Where proprietary information, trade secrets, formulas, customer lists, and other private material are vital to profitability and survival but must nonetheless be transmitted, liabilities may be easy to quantify.

3. *Inclination to commit resources to protection.* Armed with an assessed risk as credible and likely in combination with high liability, management may determine that the situation is unacceptable and that corrective actions are necessary. The available corrective measures will almost certainly be expensive. If the vulnerability is a characteristic of the common carrier, and management demands that something be done to eliminate or reduce the vulnerability, a change in carriers can be made.

Should the threat be determined to be principally one of wiretapping, the defense may be frequent countermeasures sweeps by a reliable and qualified security firm together with a program of aggressive physical security controls and inspections. For many firms, however, protectable data are being transmitted over long-distance telecommunications circuits, and an acceptable level of protection may be obtainable only through encryption.

The inclination option now is in management's court. They can elect to devote the necessary resources to protection, probably at a sacrifice of something else that is important and desirable. Alternatively, management may opt to recognize the potential threat and assume the risk. In the latter case, the likelihood is that should the firm be victimized by an eavesdropper who had unrestricted access to the firm's data over a long period, detection of the act would be highly improbable and ruinous damage could be done before the problem was even suspected.

Advances in Computer Security Management, Vol. 2
Edited by M. M. Wofsey
© 1983 Computation Planning, Inc.

Chapter 10

MODERN COMPUTATIONAL CRYPTOGRAPHY

Herbert S. Bright

Computation Planning, Inc.

THE DP SECURITY PROBLEM

Security of data processing, viewed as a management problem, is growing in importance and in emphasis. It may be considered as having four major components, as described in the following paragraphs.

Physical Security

Management understanding of the requirements for physical security has improved substantially in recent years. This entire problem, ranging from building safety and workspace-access control to fire safety and electrical power assurance, is under good control in many large computing facilities.

Personnel Security

The populations of highly trained computer scientists and qualified system programmers are increasing rapidly. One unwelcome result of this progress is that a growing number of people are competent to plan and execute attacks on the integrity of even 'secure' systems.

Legal protection of individual rights and freedoms is broadening much faster than legal protection of organizations and legal remedies against computer-based malfeasance. This trend is making it more difficult for management to determine which individuals are worthy of trust.

Opportunities for both accidental and purposeful misuse of computer-based information seem to be growing along with system complexity and access convenience.

For these reasons, information security that is based primarily on correct performance by personnel is becoming more and more difficult to sustain at a high level. Information security measures should minimize dependence upon personnel security.

Systems—The Concept of Trusted Systems

'System Integrity' of the entire hardware/software complex is subsumed by all existing table-controlled information security techniques supported by IBM (from OS Password to RACF), and by access-control software provided for IBM systems by competitor software vendors. Present-day operating systems are enormously complex evolutionary products of 20 years of development. Their design and programming techniques are directed toward facile operation and maintenance rather than toward security.

All such software must be presumed to be less than perfect. It must then be possible to change it, either to correct errors or to add improvements or extensions. Therefore, it must be possible, at least for the software maintenance personnel, to bypass all information security software and hardware features (including addressing restrictions on read-write-execute) that have been built into a system for the purpose of protecting system integrity. If software maintenance personnel can bypass system security, then any appropriately skilled person (or, more likely, a colluding group of persons who collectively possess enough knowledge and skills) can invade a complex of system-and-application software. So much for traditional system security.

Recognition of the need for stronger controls has been growing for several years. Significant improvements in 370 system controls[1,2] have been developed. Security has helped to justify the high cost of adoption of executive systems that include such improvements. Unfortunately, many vulnerabilities remain in typical systems because of limitations imposed by the fundamental techniques that are used in their design and implementation.

In recent years much effort has been expended on developing system concepts[3,4,5] and elements[6,7] that are fundamentally less vulnerable to the whole spectrum of security weaknesses as defined by the military science community. These vulnerabilities range from denial of service to traffic analysis and statistical invasion of data bases and their use.[7] They include the traditional security concerns with errors, accidental or purposeful bypassing of access controls, and static or dynamic tampering with application and system programs.

As a result, it is possible to specify development of 'Trusted Systems'[8] that are intrinsically more secure than those now in general use. However, systems will continue to have certain vulnerabilities to physical invasion of systems and elements and to inadequate personnel performance, including malfeasance as well as the more common problem of errors and omissions.

Information in the Open

Information outside systems in removable file input/output media or in electrical or other readable form is protected only by 'correct performance of persons' unless it has been encrypted. It is not subject to protection even by the Trusted Systems of the future.

The HARD-NODE™ System Security Module

The recently patented HARD-NODE device and usage processes,[9] a physically protected slave computer and operating programs, may provide a definitive answer to both information security and system security. With this approach, the most sensitive information and the most sensitive processes are protected physically (are contained within a physically secure housing) whenever they are not protected cryptographically, by encryption or cryptographic authentication.

HARD-NODE provides protection against specific security exposures, ranging from dynamic patch and Trojan Horse[10] attacks on system and application software and operator intervention in program execution to third-party interception and modification of telecommunicated information.

For some of the exposures, use of Host System secure-kernel operating system software, mentioned above as Trusted Systems, is a desirable or even necessary adjunct to the basic System Security Module and its usage processes.

For others, use of a terminal-attachment device of the same general type, but of smaller (microcomputer) scale, is required in order to provide protection of telecommunicated information between locations in a system or network.

BASIC SECURITY LIMITATION OF CONTROL TABLE TECHNIQUES

The basic reason for the vulnerability to Password, RACF, and other access control software based on reference to control tables is that the information needed to bypass the controls must be resident in or accessible to the host system in the form used by the control processes.

Although such software may provide complex mechanisms for protecting the control-table information, those mechanisms (e.g. one-way encryption of passwords[11]) provide at best only nuisance-level difficulties to a competent penetrator.

In order to bypass table control, an invader need only acquire the control information, perhaps by such elementary techniques as browsing, and apply it directly. In the case of encrypted-password protection, as an example, a dynamic patch on the password-processing routine will bypass the encryption process and permit direct use of the encrypted table data.

More complicated processes, involving ricochet-reference to a multiplicity of tables, lower the probability of accidental penetration and increase the effort required for invasion, and thus discourage casual or mischievous attack. They do not raise the cost for invasion beyond feasible limits when high-value information is the target.

The widely held belief that 'the size and complexity of our operations protect us against security violations' should be recognized as obsolete in the modern business DP environment: larger and more complex operations provide more opportunity for hiding, or for failing to recognize, security faults. Complexity, in and of itself, *decreases* security.

CRYPTOGRAPHY VERSUS TABLE-CONTROLLED METHODS

Cryptographic protection of data by key-controlled transformation algorithms[12] is different from table-controlled access restriction in this fundamental way: with encryption/decryption ('cryption'), the control data (cryptographic key) required to make it feasible to inspect or modify the information being protected are implicit in that information itself.

The effort and cost to acquire the cryptographic key by an efficient analytical or other direct attack on the transforming algorithm (the 'cost to break') can be made astronomically high. It can be made to increase exponentially *without limit* at only linear increase in the cost of transformation.

With cryption by software, or by hardware that is in a CPU or is accessible to a CPU, a basic application design criterion is that control keys, unless crypted under higher-level key(s) that are protected from access, should be present in a system for the minimum possible time. This approach may be contrasted with control table methods, which require that the control information be present or accessible all the time. With regard to this important measure of security, control table methods correspond to worst-case cryptography.

One basic rule of thumb for planning cryptographic applications is that the cost-to-break should be larger, by some safety margin, than the value of the protected information. If one chooses a strong algorithm (e.g. the Data Encryption Standard Algorithm DEA,[13] QIK-CRYPT,[14] or, with suitably chosen keys, MIT-RSA)[15] and if key-management and system considerations are well planned and implemented, cost-to-break will be beyond most problem requirements. When very-large-volume data have low economic value, and when concern is primarily for privacy rather than integrity, in some cases it may be appropriate to choose very-low-usage-cost cryption techniques[16]

> *Remark*: A common misconception is that, except for military and diplomatic information, privacy-sensitive data typically is less important than integrity-sensitive data . . . especially with regard to its economic value. The privacy of some commercial data (e.g. trade secret information, financial planning data, product and marketing plans) has extremely high value. When considering information security requirements of an application, DP managers should carefully appraise the economic value of privacy as well as that of integrity.

KEYED CRYPTOGRAPHY CONCEPTS AND DEFINITIONS

The following paragraphs detail seven features of cryptography.

Key-Controlled Transformations

A cryptographic algorithm executes a particular mathematical transformation, which is different for each possible value of control key. Some algorithms[13,14] use

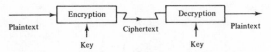

Figure 10-1.   Basic concept of keyed cryptography.

the same key for both encryption and decryption, and are called 'symmetric' or 'one-key'; others[15] use different but related keys for encryption and decryption, and are called 'asymmetric' or 'two-key'. For discussions of these considerations, see two recent survey papers by Simmons and by Popek and Kline,[17] and a later section of this chapter, One-Key Versus Two-Key Algorithms. Figure 10-1 is a schematic of the simplest cryptosystem that provides invertibility.

Determinism and Invertibility

In order to be useful for cryptographic transformation, an algorithm must be *deterministic*: for a given key and input datum, one and only one output datum must be produced.

If the algorithm and its usage mode permit inversion of the transformation to recover the original input data, the transformation is said to be *invertible*. MIT-RSA is invertible; DEA and QIK-CRYPT are invertible if input data are entered to the 'cryption' port for each, but not if input data are entered to the 'key' port. Thus, the symmetric algorithms can be used for one-way cryption (where recovery is required to be infeasible). They also can be used, with data into either port, for authentication processes where input data recovery is not required.

Garble Extension Concept

One characteristic of an ideal error-detecting or change-detecting procedure would be that any change, however small, in content of a particular information element, however large, would result in complete change of data[18] in an observable test field. This technique would make it easy to detect change of information content by visual inspection, and would provide maximum flexibility for computer-processed detection procedures; in order to observe the result of the test procedure, it would be necessary to examine only a small part of its output. In this ideal case, the length of the test field that would need to be examined is a function of the acceptable probability that any two randomly selected test fields that should be different would, by chance, actually turn out to be equal. If all binary values for the test fields are possible and of equal probability (i.e. if the data are truly random in nature), then the probability of chance equality of two different test fields is $p = 1/2^L$ where p is probability of test field equality and L is length of test field.

Expressed in a different way, the required length of test field for this ideal procedure would be

$$L = \log_2 \left(\frac{1}{p} \right)$$

For a procedure that operates on entire segments or blocks of information (a 'block procedure'), any change in content of an input information segment should cause complete change[18] of the output data segment.

For a procedure that operates unidirectionally on an input data stream, a change at a given point can (and for an ideal procedure should) change only the corresponding output that appears after the point at which the input data stream change occurred.

The section entitled Modern Strong Algorithms will show that these algorithms meet the requirements described previously to qualify as 'ideal procedures' for use in error and change detection.

Privacy

Privacy of information is defined as protection against *unauthorized inspection*. The original, and most widely recognized, application of cryptographic protection is for securing privacy of information that is in the open. After two millennia of more or less continuous development of privacy protection techniques for military and diplomatic information, and in recent years for commercial and identified-personal information, cryptographic transformation of data under control of a 'key' that can be kept secret still offers 'the only known technologically feasible method (for protecting information in the open)'.[19]

Cryptographic transformation ('encrypting') of information, competently performed, should and can convert 'Plaintext' or 'clear' information into a representation ('ciphertext' or 'cipher') in which its content has been made meaningless to human or machine. For privacy purposes, the cipher must be capable of being transformed ('decrypted') to recover exactly the original plaintext information. This technique requires use of an invertible transformation algorithm, as defined earlier in this section.

The nature of a cryptographic algorithm and of its use to protect privacy-sensitive information must assure that the cipher does not contain information that could compromise privacy. Such information includes redundant or cyclic patterns that could offer recognizable clues to plaintext content. If present, it could permit attack by the 'dictionary' technique or other statistical approaches. Even a strong algorithm such as DEA, if used in native or 'electronic code book'[20] block mode to encrypt 64-bit blocks of plaintext information having patterns that include repetitive elements of 64 bits or greater length, may be (and, if repetitive elements of 128 bits or greater length are present, must be) subject to statistical attack.

Avoidance of that privacy vulnerability requires a stream mode of usage of a block cryptor like DEA (e.g. 'cipher feedback' or 'cipher block chaining'),[20] or a stream cryptor such as QIK-CRYPT[14] used in single-cryption mode or in block (double-cryption) mode with substream or block lengths chosen to be long enough to assure absence of substream or block redundancy.

A cryptographic control key may range from a few decimal digits, suitable for remembering, to a length greater than any file or message that is to be transformed. Key length considerations are discussed in a later section.

'Key management' includes all aspects of generation and handling of cryptographic keys. Its most basic objective is to assure that key secrecy is maintained, namely that a private key is accessible only to properly authorized persons.

Privacy requires that only persons authorized to inspect encrypted data have access to the key that can decrypt the data. If privacy is not to have first-order dependence on system security, keys must never be retained in a system unless encrypted under an external key; in plaintext form, a key must be used in or accessible to a system for the shortest possible time.

Integrity

Data that must be protected against *undetected change*, whether the change is due to an accident ('error') or to unauthorized purposeful modification ('tampering), are said to require *integrity*.

Error or tamper detection may be performed with great effectiveness by modern, highly nonlinear cryptographic transformation algorithms that have the characteristic of 'garble extension' as defined earlier in this section. Use of these techniques can provide privacy protection as well, if that is permitted or required, but need not do so; integrity protection of information that is maintained in plaintext form can be provided by the technique of 'content-authentication'.

The techniques described in a subsequent section, Content Authentication, affords resistance to resequencing or substitution attack on integrity-sensitive information.

Accountability

Because the transformation for each key is distinct, cryption of a particular input datum under any other key produces different output data. If a cryption process produces an expected result, it may be assumed that both the correct key and the correct data were used.

Key-controlled cryptographic techniques can therefore be used to provide for *accountability*: assignment of a particular cryptographic control key to an individual or to an organization, for use in controlling cryption transformation for privacy or integrity of particular information, can be used to assign responsibility and authority to the assignee.

Authentication

Authentication is defined as a process for confirming that information is characterized by both integrity and accountability—that its content is not only unchanged from its presumably correct value, but that the value was confirmed by the responsible and authorized person or organization. A standardized date-time indication can and should be included with identifier data in an information segment that is to be authenticated, so that the authentication process confirms when, as well as by whom, the information was certified as correct.

Note that privacy is distinct from integrity and accountability. Therefore, authentication can be applied to information that is in either plaintext or ciphertext form.

The remarkable characteristic of modern cryptographic Strong Algorithms, which permits authentication of an information segment of any length to be performed reliably by use of only the final several bytes of cryption output, is discussed under the heading Garble Extension Performance.

SHANNON'S PROOF OF SECURITY; CHAITIN'S LIMIT ON RANDOMNESS

Many pre-1975 ideas, algorithms, products, and methods for cryptographic protection outside the military community have been shown to be weak or have become obsolete, if not worthless, with the advent of DEA and the beginnings of serious academic attention to related problems and ideas.

One truth has survived unchallenged for three decades: Shannon's proof of the cryptographic privacy-security of a Vernam system in which even a simple linear transformation is used to combine data with a truly random (unpredictable) key stream[12]

Chaitin showed that no truly random data stream can be represented by a finite amount of information.[12,21] It is possible, however, to approximate the Shannon premise closely enough[16,22] if key stream generation, extrapolation, and access are properly controlled, so that cost-to-break is made as high as required to deter unauthorized access.

Either strong cryptographic algorithms, used as quasirandom number generators of nonlinear type, or linear quasirandom number generators[22] having adequate cycle length and randomness, can be used to generate long key streams. If long key streams[16,22] having adequate cycle length and randomness are adequately protected against disclosure or extrapolation, and against being recreated from any information that can be discovered by an attacker; and if key streams have real or virtual length[16] greater than that of any file, then high security can be achieved by Shannon–Vernam indirect cryption.

STRONG ALGORITHM VERSUS LONG KEY; DIRECT VERSUS INDIRECT CRYPTION; KEY LENGTH

Cryptographic transformation (called 'insertion of equivocation' by Shannon) can be performed either by combining an adequately unpredictable key stream with data, as suggested by Vernam (referred to in NBS publications and in reference 16 as '*indirect encryption*') or by using a modern cryptographic Strong Algorithm to perform '*direct encryption*' of data under control of a presented key.

The choice between direct and indirect means for encryption/decryption ('cryption') should be made on the basis of data volume and speed requirements, and on whether Garble Extension is required; indirect cryption does not provide Garble Extension. By comparison with direct cryption, indirect cryption is faster but entails more effort and complexity in implementing applications and key management. Because it provides for detection of data error or change, direct cryption is recommended where data integrity is required.

The length of the cryptographic control key to be presented to a system should be great enough to discourage 'brute-force attack', the key-finding[23] stratagem of trying every possible key value under Known Plaintext Attack.[24] The number of trials required, hence the cost of such attack, increases exponentially with key length; for a binary key, the number of trials for assured key-finding is 2^L, where L is key length in bits. To avoid other vulnerabilities, data elements should be at least as long as, or should be padded to the length of, the presented key.

The basic rule of thumb for key length choice is that the cost of brute-force attack should be larger, by a safe margin, than the presumed value of the information being protected.

A common choice for retail credit-card and debit-card protection is 4 decimal digits, equivalent to a binary length of 13.3 bits, requiring 10^4 trials for brute-force attack. The presented key length used for the Data Encryption Standard Algorithm DEA is eight 7-bit bytes, giving a binary length of 56 active bits and an effective length (because of a mathematical symmetry characteristic of the cryption algorithm) of 55 bits. This length requires 2^{55} or about 10^{17} trials for brute force attack.

DEA key length has been the subject of a popular-press controversy since the September 1976 Workshop Conference at NBS. This length has been claimed to be inadequate for high-value data, in view of technology projections that might make 10^{17} trials too low in cost to provide the required safety margin. At present the fastest hardware implementations require about 5 microseconds to crypt a single 64-bit block. Performance claimed for one 'bulk encryption' device is 1.3 microseconds for one block.

At these speeds, a brute-force key-finding attack on DEA with its 55-effective-bit key length would require a few thousand years on a single device, or a day on a million-channel machine proposed by Hellman *et al.*[23] Unless and until DEA is shown to be vulnerable to more economical schemes, its key length appears to be adequate for many kinds of applications.

Yuval proposed[25] a DEA-attack technique which, if successful, would merely require pregenerating and pair-matching something in excess of 2^{32} random plaintext-cipher block pairs from about 10^{10} cryptions. Dictionary attack could then be performed on independent (namely created by DEA in ECB Mode) blocks of random cipher by accessing a trillion-bit file. Hardware for such an attack is economically more appealing than a million-channel Hellman machine; all required elements are available as announced-product end-user system components.

Many people, including this writer, have proposed that worries about long-term adequacy of DEA key length could be deferred for several years by modifying the Standard Algorithm to make active use of the 8 parity bits, which would extend effective key length to 63 bits and increase the cost of brute-force attack by a factor of 256.

In principle, double cryption under DEA could provide an effective key length of 110 bits at only a doubling a cryption cost; however, the basic DEA 64-bit fixed block length for data complicates cost-to-break arithmetic and requires that Usage Mode[20] be chosen and implemented with great care in order to concatenate data blocks to not less than 14 bytes in length.

A 128-bit presented key length was selected for one byte-stream or variable-block-length cryptor algorithm.[14,26] This design choice appears to meet all known key length requirements. For particular applications, many users of that algorithm choose presented key lengths that are shorter than 128 bits (and expand each presented key to 128 bits in the key management routines). A length of 64 bits is often chosen.

Care should be taken that effective key length is not shortened by choice of key representation. Restriction of presented keys to eight alphabetic-and-decimal characters results in an effective key length of 41.4 bits; eight alphabetics, 37.6 bits; eight numerics, 26.6 bits. Hexadecimal representation (two hex digits per byte, as used by NBS and IBM) permits all binary values to be entered or displayed, hence is covenient for cryptographic variables.

MODERN STRONG ALGORITHMS

Small Change, Large Effect

A strong block cryptor algorithm applied under the same key to two source data blocks that are different, however slightly, produces result data blocks that are completely different.[18] A strong stream cryptor algorithm applied under the same key to two source data streams that are different, however slightly, produces result data streams that are the same before, and completely different at and after, the point corresponding to the first difference between the two source data streams.

This effect is shown pictorially for the Feistel transformation in reference 27. Actual data from a cryption demonstration[28] using DES emulator software are shown in Table 10.1. Examples A19 and A20 show that DEA-encrypting, under

TABLE 10-1
Small change/large effect: Decryption of ciphers modified by 1-bit change

Example	Key	Data	Cipher (encrypted)	Cipher modified by 1-bit change	Decryption of modified cipher
A 1	1334577799BBCDFF1	0123456789ABCDEF	85E813540F0AB405	85E813540F0AB404	242FB5B08EED3339
A 2	1334577799BBCDFF1	5555555555555555	6F159B9AB784158C	6F159B9AB784158E	83C3F1A8A47211DE
A 3	1334577799BBCDFF1	FFFFFFFFFFFFFFFF	A6EC719BDC2D5F53	A6EC719BDC2D5F57	CA2A6FB8E8AF7204
A 4	1334577799BBCDFF1	FFFFFFFFFFFFFFFF	5A3DB304D64924FD	5A3DB304D64924F5	21970BCB59353F70
A 5	1010101010101010	FFFFFFFFFFFFFFFF	99742F7BC2D7005	99742F7BC2D7015	CFD505CFD29A3E6F
A 6	1010101010101010	FF00FF00FF00FF00	13FFF50892CA366A	13FFF50892CA364A	71D0EE2367DC6F30
A 7	1010101010101010	F7F63CD12A8605F1	0000000000000000	0000000000000040	5FBFBB6181B35B8C
A 8	975BCE2637DCA749	285BC74684BCD734	AB8D222A1E8B0887	AB8D222A1E8B0807	0C89D97E8C34D5E1
A 9	49BC26469EBA7304	0573BC52D6837492	B02B087B03484D84	B02B087B03484C84	1E009E25626F6A2A
A 10	0101010101010101	0000000000000000	8CA64DE9C1B123A7	8CA64DE9C1B121A7	D3BFE0EDB5CD6B8D
A 11	7F7F7F7F7F7F7F7F	0000000000000000	5EFA76B8A5A9EB37	5EFA76B8A5A9EF37	F27262F536640F7A
A 12	7F7F7F7F7F7F7F7F	1111111111111111	CEDA5902D980D525	CEDA5902D980DD25	C8132B12C1D06626
A 13	0101010101010101	AAAAAAAAAAAAAAAA	3AE716954DC04E25	3AE716954DC05E25	3827A678299D0BD9
A 14	0101010101010101	AAAAAAAAAAAAAAAB	17D8E9C374D14494	17D8E9C374D16494	F684C30B62C4A543
A 15	0101010101010180	AAAAAAAAAAAAAAAA	E91439E9838DCC9D	E91439E9838D8C9D	85F784F1D1B3C1C5
A 16	0101010101010101	5555555555555555	B109FD803EB2D05E	B109FD803EB2505E	2AF0F6BCE6DED7B5
A 17	0101010101010180	5555555555555555	7EDFAAA980158515	7EDFAAA980148515	070C7999A8C82036
A 18	0101010101010102	5555555555555555	451F0C33F24FB8DC	451F0C33F24DB8DC	7B5371F278975203
A 19	0101010101010104	5555555555555555	CAB8E849E0AB0C32	CAB8E849E0AF0C32	0F12A322BF72618B
A 20	0101010101010104	5555555555555554	7D34A65A0E2B62CE	7D34A65A0E2362CE	9B3DDFCEE0BB6B2A
A 21	5454545454545454	5555555555555555	3BCDD41E6165A5E8	3BCDD41E6175A5E8	19D27D342755BCF5
A 22	5454545454545454	AAAAAAAAAAAAAAAA	343A09F9B2EB5CCA	343A09F9B2EB5CCA	A0717E5B6EAD1379
A 23	ABABABABABABABAB	5555555555555555	CBC5F6064D34A335	CBC5F6064D74A335	477C929D97ACF4B0
A 24	ABABABABABABABAB	AAAAAAAAAAAAAAAA	C4322BE19E9A5A17	C4322BE19E1A5A17	D1C9D7EC695B9614
A 25	49BC26469EBA7304	0573CB52D6837492	3C2FBB40FC46DF20	3C2FBB40FC46DF20	FA099C3E5AF94054

the same key, two 64-bit data blocks that differ only in one bit position produces completely different cipher. Examples A18 and A19 show that DEA-encrypting the same data, under two keys that differ only in that a single 1-bit has been shifted by one bit position, also produces completely different cipher.

Examples A1 through A25 show that DEA-decryption behaves the same way. In each case the result of encrypting the item in the 'DATA' column under the key in the 'KEY' column is modified by inverting a single bit (in A1, bit 64; in A2, bit 63; ... in A25, bit 40) and then decrypted; it may be seen that the result of decrypting the modified cipher is completely different[18] from the correct value. For example, in A15, compare

     AAAAAAAAAAAAAAAA   (decryption of unmodified cipher)

with   85F784F1D183C1C5   (decryption of cipher modified by inverting bit 50)

> *Remark*: This test also confirmed that this emulator produced correctly all of the cipher values, and decrypted them correctly to recover the input plaintext data.

Garble Extension Performance

The Garble Extension concept has already been introduced. The fact that modern Strong Algorithms such as DEA and the stream cryptor described in reference 14 have the 'small change, large effect' characteristic discussed previously is responsible for their effective performance as garble extenders.

Table 10.1 shows that modifying even a single bit of the 64-bit block input to the block cryptor DEA causes complete change[18] of the 64-bit block output. Complete change of output at and after the point of any input change can be provided for a data string of any length by use of either of two of the Stream Cryptor Modes of DEA Usage (Cipher Block Chaining or Cipher Feedback).[20] The stream cryptor of reference 14 provides this characteristic in its native mode, in which it performs cryption on a byte stream of any length.

For either of these techniques, a small change early in a data stream is not suppressed by a long subsequent string of unchanged data. The *entire* output stream at and after the point of change is altered in a gross manner[18] by even a small change in input. Thus, for Content Authentication of a data segment of any length (see later section), one need only examine a crypted subsegment at the end of a data stream.

Block Versus Stream Cryptors

Once characterization of a modern Strong Algorithm is whether input data is processed as a unit or in sequence. On this basis these algorithms can be divided into two groups: block cryptors and stream cryptors.

1. *Block Cryptors*. Algorithms that perform true block cryption, including

DEA in its native block mode (called 'Electronic Code Book Mode' by NBS),[20] MIT-RSA,[15] and the double-cryption operators of one stream cryptor,[14] operate on an input block as a unit. Every bit of output is strongly affected by every bit of input. Each block of data is treated as an entity, independent of all other blocks.

2. *Stream Cryptors.* Cryption algorithms that process input data sequentially, or block cryptors[14] operated in a manner that causes them to process input data sequentially, are called stream cryptors. The nature and extent of Garble Extension may limit the kinds of applications for which such a process is useful; for Content Authentication, each element of input data must strongly affect all subsequent output data.

DEA may be used in any of several usage modes[20] that cause it to behave as a stream cryptor.

As noted earlier in this section, applicability of Strong Algorithms is affected by the usage mode and in particular by the nature and extent of Garble Extension. Where sensitivity to error or change is desired, Garble Extension may be mandatory. In certain kinds of communication systems it may be desired to minimize the disturbance of output data that result from input data error, and to have the data stream self-resynchronizing with minimum loss of data content after a temporary interruption of transmission; in such systems it may be desirable to minimize, or at least to limit, Garble Extension.

The two algorithms DEA and QIK-CRYPT offer the user the ability to choose and control the data span over which Garble Extension operates, for either algorithm, in block or stream mode.

One-Key Versus Two-Key Algorithms

Many publications have appeared as a result of a 1976 paper by Diffie and Hellman,[29] in which they proposed Public-Key Cryptosystems (PKS). That paper introduced the concept of cryption algorithms that would use different keys for encryption and decryption, as opposed to algorithms like DEA and QIK-CRYPT which use the same key to control both functions. The term 'public-key' came from their proposed constraint on as-yet-unavailable cryption algorithms, that it should be computationally intractable to derive one key even if one knows the other key and any amount of plaintext and cipher (i.e. the algorithm should resist Known-Plaintext Attack): under those conditions, one of the two keys could be made public. The term 'two-key' expresses a basic difference between PKS algorithms and 'one-key' algorithms such as DEA and QIK-CRYPT.

Many publications suggested applications of two-key algorithms. Several proposed algorithms to meet the Diffie–Hellman requirement. Others compared applicability of one-key and two-key algorithms. Some suggested attack techniques for breaking algorithms or systems (see the System Considerations section near the end of this chapter).

The most widely-known two-key algorithm, MIT-RSA,[15] has been subject to the largest number of attack proposals. Most of these attacks have been mathematically sound but economically infeasible; none has withstood public scrutiny. This algorithm is, thus, considered to be secure as of the date of this writing.

Several competitor 2-key algorithms have been shown to be vulnerable. The Lu–Lee (COMSAT) Chinese Remainder Theorem algorithm,[30] e.g., was broken within a few days of publication. In mid-1982, the second-best-known 2-key algorithm, Merkle–Hellman, was broken, as outlined near the ned of this chapter.

In a different context a COMPLAN group, retained by a commercial bank to give a 'second opinion' on the strength of a proposed message authentication algorithm, within one week showed both by analytic methods and by computer simulation that the algorithm was vulnerable to both substitution and transposition attack.[31]

Some application commentaries suggested schemes that putatively would work only with two-key algorithms. Generalized key distribution within a network, and point-to-point communication between two locations, have been discussed as two-key algorithm applications.

Within the last year an increasing number of writers have suggested that one-key algorithms could be used for most of the applications for which two-key algorithms had been suggested. Even in open networks, downloading of keys encrypted under remote-terminal Unit Keys permits a strong one-key algorithm such as DEA to be used safely. Two-point communication is a restricted case of this problem.

A few important problems—e.g. some aspects of key distribution in an insecure network—and some specialized problems seem to require two-key algorithms. Simmons[17] outlined several advanced two-key problems.

Publication in this arena prior to 1979 has been described comprehensively by three survey papers (Lemptel, Simmons, and Popek–Kline,[17]). The reader is referred to these papers for a compact overview.

'Public-Key' publication continues. An informal comment from Simmons is noteworthy: 'There's a lot less there than meets the eye'.

DEA, THE STANDARD ALGORITHM

The most widely known, and most widely criticized, cryption algorithm is the Data Encryption Standard Algorithm DEA, proposed in 1975 and adopted as part of the U.S. Federal Standard DES in 1977.[13]

Application of DEA has been inhibited by several usage and implementation issues. The Federal Standard applies primarily to bulk protection of point-to-point communication against wiretap; broader applications are now being examined. The rigidity of that Standard in rejecting software implementations, even though for some applications (e.g. for information in the open) security limitations are the same for Standard-conforming hardware as for software, has caused some confusion among potential users.

The fixed-size 64-bit data block has contributed some inconvenience, because adjustable-block-length operation is often required. There is a mandatory need for stream-mode operation by byte-stream data users and those whose primary needs are for data integrity/accountability/authentication. These considerations require that the algorithm be used under one of the Standard Modes of Usage,[14,20,41] to convert the native or 'Electronic CodeBook' (ECB) fixed-block usage mode to a stream mode. There is also a basic security requirement for avoidance of the native usage mode: As discussed below, ECB may be vulnerable to dictionary attack as a special case of Known-Plaintext Attack.[24]

The fact that the design principles for the critical S-transformation of DEA have been declared[13] to be military-classified has caused some concern. Several minor complaints have been raised: use in the algorithm of more than the number of interations required[32] to reach its limiting cryptographic strength; use of the IP and IP^{-1} fixed permutations, which add to complexity but not to security; and use of a linear key expansion process that was not justified in the Standard resulted in serious algorithm weaknesses for some values of Presented Key (see 'DEA-Defective Keys' section near the end of this chapter).

These objections, taken individually and collectively, have not been shown to justify rejection of the algorithm on grounds of inadequate security. Having survived critical review, DEA is gradually going into use.

A STREAM/VL BLOCK CRYPTOR ALGORITHM

Careful review of the DES technical and patent literature and of mathematical and other critiques of the Standard's cryptor algorithm, and limited analysis and testing, have led to the conclusion that the basic Feistel transformation is mathematically sound and cryptographically strong.

In 1976 a substantially different implementation of the Feistel mathematics was designed[14,26] with the following characteristics:

1. Operates directly on byte-stream data (Feature added in 1977: double-cryption operators to provide, as a user option, true variable-length-block-cryption capability).
2. Nonlinear key expansion (7040-bit expanded key); has no known 'defective keys' as discussed in §8 above.
3. Uses two-way presented key of 128-bit length (to make key-length debate unnecessary).
4. Provides asymmetry under complementation (avoids concern over an unproven potential weakness, avoids loss of 1 bit of effective key length).
5. Includes 'message-sensitive' (previous steam content) control in a Shannon –Vernam cryption step concatenated with iterative Feistel transformations.
6. Uses explosion (high-speed) techniques with precomputed-table transformations.
7. Emphasizes cryption performance (high speed, low space) at the expense of more time and space required at key-entry time.

8. Avoids inefficiencies such as fixed permutations and excessive iteration count.

The byte-stream orientation made explosion techniques feasible, because control tables need only be several kilobytes in size. The resulting algorithm is convenient for use in long-key-stream generation for indirect cryption, and also for use in content-authentication processes on information segments of any size. In software or firmware form it requires roughly the same space as DEA but crypts at higher speed. It is in daily use.

THE RIVEST–SHAMIR–ADLEMAN TWO-KEY ALGORITHM

One of the two-key algorithms that have been published has attained wider acceptance than most.[15] This scheme draws its cryptographic strength, measured as 'cost-to-break', from the high cost of factoring large numbers.

The RSA algorithm encrypts a message M (perhaps some binary representation of a character string, construed as a single positive binary integer) by raising M to a non-secret power e, and taking the remainder when the result M^e is divided by a non-secret product n of two large secret prime numbers p and q.

Let the message M (or a substring of the message) be a positive integer between 0 and $n - 1$. The encryption algorithm E computes the cipher (encrypted message) C from the plaintext message M by

$$C = E(M) = M^e \text{ (modulo } n),$$

and the decryption algorithm D computes the plaintext message M from its encrypted representation or cipher C by

$$M = D(C) = C^d \text{ (modulo } n),$$

where n is the product of two large prime numbers p and q.

The encryption key is the pair of positive integers e and n; the decryption key is the pair of positive integers d and n.

The product-of-primes n may be made public, because it is expensive to factor n into the two secret numbers p and q.

d is an integer that is relatively prime to the product of $(p - 1)$ and $(q - 1)$. e is computed from the relationship

$$e \times d = 1(\text{mod}(p - 1) \times (q - 1))$$

Care is required in the selection of several numerical values used in the algorithm.

The cost[33] to encrypt or to decrypt under RSA in software form in a general-purpose computer for a 512-bit message would be roughly that to perform 2^{24} or 16m multiplications, additions, and subtractions, which is several seconds of high-speed CPU time. It has been said privately that special-purpose hardware could perform such cryption at speeds of several kilobits per second.

CONTENT AUTHENTICATION

A very old problem, that of assuring that a particular information segment has exactly the currently correct authorized content (or is the right 'version'), is assuming new significance in the management of programming projects and in the use of distributed data bases. As explained in reference 34, this problem can be handled conveniently and economically by a 'non-security' application of modern highly nonlinear cryptographic one-key algorithms such as DEA and QIK-CRYPT.

The basic concept is that the information segment, together with an identifier field including date and time of authentication, is processed through a stream cryptor having Unlimited Forward Stream Garble Extension (see the section, Modern Strong Algorithms), under control of a cryptographic key assigned to the accountable person. An appropriate-length data substring at the end of the crypted output stream is designated the Authenticator Field (AF) and is stored or transmitted with the information segment. At any time, such as during preparation for subsequent use of the information segment, its correctness (freedom from accidental or purposeful unauthorized change) may be checked by re-crypting the segment and comparing the newly derived AF with the stored/transmitted AF.

Two usage choices are available:

1. Privacy protection (see earlier under Keyed Cryptography Concepts) may be required, or may be unnecessary or even unacceptable.
2. It may be necessary to provide security for the accountability aspect of authentication, to prevent unauthorized persons from performing the authentication process.

If privacy is to be provided, the entire output data stream produced by an encryption process is retained for use as cipher. If not, the output stream is discarded except its final L bits, which constitute the AF.

If a strong algorithm such as DEA (with a correctly chosen Usage Mode—see Strong Modern Algorithms) or QIK-CRYPT is chosen, whether or not privacy is to be provided, L is determined by the expression $L = \log_2 N$, where N is the acceptable number of random trials per false-duplicate AF. L should be at least 24 bits ($N \sim 10^7$); choosing $L = 64$ bits is often economically acceptable and avoids any significant chance of encountering a false-duplicate AF.

If accountability is to be protected, an appropriate key management scheme is required to permit users other than the accountable person to recheck authentication but not to re-authenticate. Such a scheme may involve use of higher-level system keys to encrypt the accountable persons' keys, and perhaps a tree-structured or matrix-structured control scheme that is isomorphic with the organization using the process.

Inter-site rechecking of content authentication can be performed[34] for an information segment of any length by communicating only a few hundred bytes between sites: segment *ID*, date-time index, *AF*, and an additional *AF* for the inter-site message itself.

DIGITAL SIGNATURES

A technique that is of great potential value in business is that of authenticating a message (assuring exact contents of it and confirming accountability for it). It should be possible to send the message by conventional telecommunication facilities.

One valuable aspect of such a technique would be *undeniability*; i.e. the message with its authentication code appended should constitute proof that it was originated by its sender and was received by its recipient. Authenticated parts of the message would ordinarily include a sequence number and a date-time-place preface to identify the message, as well as the names of other identifiers for sender and recipient. Ideally, a message confirmed by digital signature would not require use of a Trusted Archival Network Security Center.[35] or a Notary Public Machine.[36]

Signature techniques have been proposed for both one-key[30] and two-key[15] algorithms. As in many cryptography applications, if Strong Algorithms are used, the actual security limitations of the two classes of algorithms are similar; the limits on each process reside in other parts of the application rather than in the algorithm.

Despite much public interest in digital signature concepts, and several papers suggesting 'solutions' to the problems associated with them, it appears that no technique has yet been able to withstand public scrutiny as an ideal solution. Rabin,[36] for example, points out a basic difficulty in achieving 'undeniability': if certain critical information (i.e., the 'sender's key' in a PKS) is made public (presumably after the original 'signing' of a document), the sender can assert that another person could have originated the document. He can, therefore, deny that he is the true originator. In this aspect, one-key and two-key algorithms are not different in the security provided.

In certain limited application problems it may be feasible to achieve an acceptable level of security and acceptability for some digital signature techniques. Audited commercial bank records, for example, traditionally have been given great weight as evidence in legal disputes. Consequently, a highly secure message authentication technique in a bank's processing network can serve many of the functions sought for, and can have many of the characteristics of, an ideal digital signature scheme.

CRYPTANALYTIC ATTACK AND DEFENSE

This section provides a brief presentation of three cryptanalytic attack environments that are commonly used in discussing cryptographic strength of algorithms: Ciphertext Only, Known-Plaintext, and Chosen Plaintext, in increasing order of algorithm strength required to resist key-finding attack.

Assumptions

In Known- and Chosen-Plaintext situations it is assumed that a person or organization attempting to make unauthorized access to cryptographically protected information has:

1. Unlimited access to the computer hardware/software system used for encryption/decryption, and freedom to use the system for arbitrarily long periods of time.
2. Full knowledge and understanding of the application programs, files, and cryptographic control algorithms.
3. Ability to suppress all records of system usage during its application to cryptanalysis.

In Chosen-Plaintext, the attacker also has the ability to input and extract, at will, any desired Plaintext and Cipher information from the encrypt/decrypt processing configuration, with the (unknown) key in place.

Definitions

1. 'Plaintext' or 'clear' information is in a form understandable to man or machine.
2. 'Cipher' or 'scrambletext' is information that is cryptographically transformed into a representation that is not understandable without decryption back into Plaintext form.
3. 'Known Plaintext' is an attack situation in which the analyst has possession (in machine-readable form) of a specified amount of error-free Cipher and exactly corresponding Plaintext.
4. 'Chosen Plaintext' is an attack situation in which the attacker has the ability to choose or to specify Plaintext and to observe the exactly corresponding Cipher resulting from its encryption as well as to observe the result of any decryption. The encryption/decryption should take place under control of the key which is sought; until the problem has been solved, the key is unknown although the effects of its use are observable.
5. A 'deterministic' transformation used for encryption produces, for a given key and Plaintext data segment, one and only one Cipher segment, and the reverse is also true.
6. With an 'invertible' transformation it is possible to recover exactly the Plaintext corresponding to any Cipher, i.e., to decrypt, if the proper key is presented.

For more explicit and additional definitions, see reference 12.

Ciphertext-Only Attack; Huffman Encoding; Dictionary Attack

Monoalphabetic substitution schemes (and even polyalphabetic schemes, in which the value of one or more substitution transformation elements changes cyclically, usually with every character), are vulnerable to statistical attack methods. Tuckerman[37] showed mathematically that such schemes are thus vulnerable even when composed of an indefinitely long sequence of cascaded substitutions, and he demonstrated fully detailed experimental solutions of examples transformed with two cascaded substitutions.

All direct-substitution schemes are a special case of *encoding*, in which elements of Plaintext are directly replaced by elements of Cipher according to an established algorithm. More general methods, such as Huffman encoding[38] (in which the substitution scheme is derived from the characteristics of the Plaintext in order to minimize redundancy and length of encoded representation), may also be vulnerable to such attacks as statistical methods. Although it is a valuable communication tool, Huffman encoding is consequently of relatively low value as a cryptographic transformation tool. Its cost, when executed in general-purpose computer software, is strongly dependent on message content.

Known–Plaintext Attack (KPA)

As explained in reference 39, a simple algorithm (e.g. Vernam or Exclusive-Or) used to encrypt by combining Plaintext with a long Key Stream generated by a known algorithmic process, as in reference 40, as opposed to use of a truly random Key Stream or one generated by an unknown process, when successfully attacked permits the attacker to generate key stream and consequently to encrypt or decrypt information.

If the known stream-generating algorithm is reversible, it is possible to 'Backtrack', i.e. to calculate a Seed or other starting information for the key stream generator. The encrypt/decrypt action can then include any desired Cipher or Plaintext. Thus, in effect, the encryption key has been found and, in the words of reference 39, 'the game goes to the cryptanalyst'.

Known–Plaintext Defense

Two basic defenses can be effective against KPA:

1. The Key Stream can be interrupted or otherwise perturbed in some way that inhibits or completely frustrates Backtracing. Reference 39 shows limiting factors and gives an actual generating program to perform this frustration function with the TLP quasirandom stream generator[22] in the cryptopak™ software system.[14]
2. The Plaintext can be perturbed, prior to encryption, in some way that effectively multiplies the effort to cryptanalyze (known as 'Work Factor') by some large factor. Reference 39 shows how applying bit-within-byte permutation to the Plaintext alone, using continually changing permutation selection, can multiply Work Factor by $(8!)^N$, where N is the number of per-

mutations used. Use of $N = 3$ increases Work Factor to a level that would require over a quarter million hours of large-scale computer time to execute a successful Known-Plaintext attack on information encrypted under the high-speed Vernam algorithm.

Note that permutation of *Key Stream* prior to its use in encryption will not be useful in the defense against KPA, inasmuch as any algorithmically chosen sequence of permutations produces merely another not-really-random Key Stream, in the sense of Chaitin's approach.[21] Permutation of Cipher may have similar limitations.

Chosen-Plaintext Attack (CPA)

The ability for the cryptanalyst to design and specify test data, and to observe results of its use (i.e. to perform CPA), permits him to attack specific weaknesses of known algorithms.

If the Key Stream generating algorithm is known, and if a linear encryption algorithm such as Vernam (XOR) is known to be in use, a linear transformation may make the process transparent. After a few islands of corresponding Plaintext and Cipher have been found, direct machine comparison of information streams becomes practicable on a large scale. Thus, in one example in reference 39, relative sliding of Plaintext and Cipher data sets to detect exactly corresponding 'matched pair' segments gradually expanded to at least 33,344 bits of each, as required to perform Backtrack, offers negligible difficulty.

For more elaborate algorithms, it is useful to be able to design the test data. For example, all-ones and all-zeroes data streams, or patterns including a single one-bit among zeroes or the converse, may produce recognizable patterns that will characterize the nature of the encryption algorithm or combination of algorithms.

In particular, although permutation (resequencing) of Plaintext at the bit level can be useful against KPA, it can be transparent against CPA: a given one-bit or zero-bit retains its value even though it appears in a different sequence. Thus, repeating trials with carefully planned bit patterns may disclose the permutation(s) used. The Work Factor to accomplish this disclosure is small enough to be, again, negligible.

Thus, it is concluded that although Plaintext Permutation as discussed in the preceding section and in reference 39 can be useful in inhibiting KPA, it is an ineffective defense where CPA can be mounted.

Permutation of Cipher can, by disguising otherwise-recognizable patterns, provide increase in Work Factor, even for CPA. If the permutations used are selected and interchanged in an effective manner, the increase in Work Factor can be substantial.

The next section discusses a more generalized perturbation scheme which, used on either Plaintext or Cipher, will be a powerful defense against CPA.

Chosen-Plaintext Defense

The basic requirement for defense against CPA is that of providing a transformation from Plaintext to Cipher (an encryption algorithm) that has low 'cryptographic transparency'; i.e. the output does not have a readily recognizable relationship to the input.

One class of transformations that has low cryptographic transparency, and consequently when used in an encryption process resists both KPA and CPA, is said to have the mathematical characteristics of being non-affine.[42] For the present discussion let us consider transformations that are deterministic, invertible, and non-affine.

Such transformations are executed more economically, under usual assumptions for system characteristics, by processes that include table-substitution elements rather than by algorithmic manipulation alone. Generation of the substitution tables, which will be used many times in even a short encrypt/decrypt task, is a large processing task. Because, however, the tables are of modest size (hundreds of entries for one 8-bit-specified transformation), it is economically advantageous to pregenerate them and store them in the program that performs part of the transformation operation.

An advantage of this approach is that the non-affine character of the resulting transformations can be confirmed by testing the substitution tables themselves prior to their use in the working system. Careful design makes it feasible to use (fast) explosion techniques in implementing one byte-stream encryption/decryption algorithm (QIK-CRYPT, in reference 14). It consists of an iterative sequence of elemental non-affine transformations, substring interchanges, and interrupted-TLP-stream Vernam encryptions following and preceding generalized linear transformations. The overall transformation is non-affine and is resistant to all three attacks.

This algorithm requires, for control of its several kinds of transformation elements, a key that is 7,040 bits in length. Its software implementation includes a nonlinear process for key expansion from an external (presented) 128-bit key. Patent action has been initiated on a hardware version.

DEA Versus Cryptanalytic Attack

The National Bureau of Standards has concluded that the 56-bit-key Federal Data Encryption Standard DES Algorithm[12,13,14] is resistant to both Known-Plaintext and Chosen-Plaintext Attacks. Speculation and rumors about vulnerability have centered on brute-force attack schemes, using single blocks of Plaintext and Cipher, which would require on the order of 10^{17} random trials to be sure of finding a single key.

When used with a particular key, a block cryption algorithm such as the Standard algorithm DEA used in native or Electronic CodeBook Mode is a substitution enciphering process. The length of the substitution table or Dictionary is so long (about 10^{19} entries for each key) that cryption of truly random information by a dictionary scheme would be economically infeasible.

Use of (more typical) Plaintext having substantial amounts of repetitive content and cyclic behavior, or use of techniques such as that of Yuval[25], who suggests a DEA attack scheme based on a dictionary of 10^{10} entries, in cases where it can be assumed that the cryption key is unchanging, may make dictionary attack economically feasible.

With DEA, stream cryption Modes of Operation have been proposed[20] which avoid this weakness: the algorithm is converted into a stream cryptor for a data string of any length; and if the Initializing Vector IV is well-chosen and crypted substrings are kept reasonably long (say, at least as long as the 56-bit presented key), the number and lengths of dictionaries required can be made so large as to frustrate dictionary attack.

Complaints of inadequate key length (discussed above), and allegations of intra-government conspiracy leading to inclusion of a government-accessible 'trapdoor' in the critical S-transformation part of the algorithm, have been published in the popular press and in technical media. Neither of those complaints have been supported by hard data that would justify public rejection of the algorithm.

DEA-Defective Keys

DEA's linear key-expansion process gives rise to regularity properties that make this algorithm weak or even unusable for certain purposes. It is necessary to assure that particular keys to be used are not among those that bring on these weaknesses.

In the discussion below with its tables of keys to be avoided, we assume that the optional byte-parity feature of DEA is used, so that every eighth bit of a key is determined by the preceding seven bits. The 36 keys described below are particularly objectionable. If the algorithm is used without the optional parity-check feature and with one or more of their inactive byte parity bits inverted, those variants also are defective. Considering the entire key that can be represented by 16 hex digits, there are 9216 known keys that should be especially avoided with DEA.

For DEA, there exist sixteen known odd-byte-parity key pairs, called 'dual keys',[41] under which encryption of any datum under one key of a pair gives the same result as decryption of that datum under the other key of the pair. No other dual keys are known to exist.

The first four pairs (keys 1–4) are their own duals, called 'self-dual' by NBS.[41] Self-dual keys have the special weakness that under them any even number of cryptions returns the plaintext; the algorithm is its own inverse. Self-duel keys 1 and 2 are the all-zeroes and all-ones keys respectively, if the (optional) key-parity feature is ignored and all eight parity bits are reversed:

No.	Weak keys	No.	Self-Duals (Weak)
1	0101010101010101	1	0101010101010101
2	fefefefefefefefe	2	fefefefefefefefe
3	e0e0e0e0f1f1f1f1	3	e0e0e0e0f1f1f1f1
4	1f1f1f1f0e0e0e0e	4	1f1f1f1f0e0e0e0e

The next six key-dual pairs (keys 5–16) are distinct:

No.	Semi-Weak keys	No.	Duals (Semi-Weak)
5	e001e001f101f101	6	01e001e001f101f1
7	fe1ffe1ffe0efe0e	8	1ffe1ffe0efe0efe
9	e01fe01ff10ef10e	10	1fe01fe00ef10ef1
11	01fe01fe01fe01fe	12	fe01fe01fe01fe01
13	011f011f010e010e	14	1f011f010e010e01
15	e0fee0fef1fef1fe	16	fee0fee0fef1fef1

Jueneman[42] described the self-dual keys as 'weak', because their expanded-key components $C(0)$ and $D(0)$ consist of all zeroes or all ones; thus, the same 48-bit key component is generated for all sixteen rounds of the algorithm, and own-inverse cycling results.

He and Davies[42] called the other twelve (odd-parity) dual keys 'semi-weak'. For them, sixteen of the C and D components have 0101.... or 1010.... patterns throughout, and two each Cs and Ds are all zeroes or all ones. As a result, shift patterns for encryption and decryption have only two values and the algorithm is drastically weakened.

They called keys having repeated 0011... or 1100... patterns for C and D, resulting in slightly less cryptographic weakness, 'demi-semi-weak', and also discussed higher-order regularities:

No.	Demi-Semi-Weak Keys (have no duals)
17	e0e00101f1f10101
18	fefe1f1ffefe0e0e
19	0101e0e00101f1f1
20	1f1ffefe0e0efefe
21	1f1f01010e0e0101
22	fefee0e0fefef1f1
23	01011f1f01011f1f
24	e0e0fefef1f1fefe
25	fe1fe001fe0eef101
26	e001fe1ff101fe0e
27	1ffe01e00efe01f1
28	01e01ffe01f10efe

29	fee01f01fef10e01
30	e0fe011ff1fe01e0
31	fefe0101fefe0101
32	e0e01f1ff1f10e0e
33	1f01fee00e01fef1
34	011fe0fe01e0f1fe
35	1f1fe0e00e0ef1f1
36	0101fefe0101fefe

For nondefective keys DEA generates random sequences that have excellent statistical behavior. In particular, their periods are much too long to be observed experimentally. Gait[43] noted that when DEA is used as a random sequence generator the all-zeroes and all-ones keys yield periods of only 128 bits. The basic Power Spectrum test as used by Gait seems to be reliable and comprehensive. By that test, when used with nondefective keys, DEA performs well by comparison with conventional linear congruential pseudorandom number generators. Gait did not test the very-long-period (linear) TLP Sequence Generator of Bright and Enison,[22] which is based on a primitive generating polynomial of Mersenne Prime exponent degree. He did not have access to the QIK-CRYPT algorithm,[26] which uses DEA's Feistel nonaffine transformation and a highly-nonlinear key expansion process from the Bright–Enison TLP sequence generator.

Cryptographic keys for use with either cryption or authentication processes should be randomly and nonreproducibly generated; user-chosen keys tend to be mnemonic in nature and to be insecure because they can be guessed or otherwise discovered by unauthorized persons.

Random, nonreproducible generation and use of quasirandom keys can be supported conveniently and securely by cryptographic support software, as outlined in.[44] Such key management support processes can include checking of key-in-correctness and assurance that DEA-defective keys are not inadvertently placed in service.

Merkle–Hellman 2-Key Algorithm Broken

The second-most-widely known 2-key algorithm,[45] the Merkle–Hellman version of the Knapsack technique, came under question soon after its 1978 publication because of its use of superincreasing sequences to achieve processing economy. Those suspicions were only suspicions until April 20, 1982, when A. Shamir[46] broke the basic form of the Merkle–Hellman algorithm by use of the recently discovered integer programming method of Lenstra.[47] Faster break techniques, perhaps including Odlyzko's continued-fraction method,[46] may be expected.

At least one news wire service[48] jumped beyond the truth to conclude that The Knapsack Problem itself has been solved. Not so; Shamir broke the Merkle–Hellman shortcut, not The Knapsack!

Hellman now suggests,[49] however, that even the iterative form of Merkle–Hellman should now be considered to be potentially insecure.

System Considerations: HARD-NODE™ System Security Module

The discussion up to this section has centered on algorithm cryptographic strength, largely ignoring system security. Although cryptographically strong encryption can protect information in a generally accessible system or in the open, information so protected but without *system security protection* can be vulnerable to personnel (skilled programmers or operators) who are able to intercept keys or plaintext while either is in the system. Encapsulation of these sensitive data and of certain sensitive program elements in restricted-access hardware[9] also can frustrate such attack (see HARD-NODE System Security Module in the first section).

CONCLUSIONS

This overview has outlined the whole security problem (physical, personnel, system, and information-in-the-open) in order to place in its proper perspective the central problem of protecting sensitive information against accidental or purposeful violation of *privacy*, *integrity*, or *accountability*.

Physical security has been identified as a management problem area that is coming under good control in many organizations. *Personnel security* has been described as a difficult problem area where management control is losing ground; good information security techniques should minimize dependence on correct performance of persons.

ACKNOWLEDGMENT

In the early 1970s IBM supported fundamental mathematical work leading to the Feistel Transformation and to the Data Encryption Standard Algorithm. It later collaborated with government civilian and military agencies in making available to the computation/communication community this first practical application of a kind of mathematical technology that in the past had been available only in and for military-classified activities and for protection of diplomatic communications. These actions stimulated a large amount of interest and action in (and government-sponsored developments by) the academic community, commercial development of cryptographic products and application methods, and the beginnings of cryptography standardization.

In the judgment of this writer, this sequence of events will be recognized in the future as a major step forward in the orderly evolution of information processing.

REFERENCES

1. McPhee, W. S.: Operating System Integrity in OS/VS2. *IBM Sys. Jour.* **13/3**, 230, 1974.

2. IBM Programming Announcement, *Statement of MVS System Integrity*. May 3, 1978.

3. *Secure Operating System Technology Papers for the (first) Seminar on the DoD Computer Security Initiative Program*. Bound set of paper reprints distributed at a seminar at NBS in Gaithersburg, MD, July 17–18, 1979.

4. Denning, D. E., and Denning, P. J.: Data Security. *ACM Computing Surveys*, 11/3: 227, 1979.

5. Millen, J. K.: *Operating System Security Verification*. Report No. M79-223, The MITRE Corp., Bedford, MA, Sept. 1979.

6. Lampson, B.: A Note on the Confinement Problem. *Comm. ACM*, 16/10, 613, 1973.

7. Denning, D. E., and Denning, P. J.: Certification of Programs for Secure Information Flow. *Comm. ACM*, 27/7, 504, 1977.

8. Walker, S.: *The Advent of Trusted Computer Operating Systems*. Printed as an attachment to the Program of the Second Seminar on the DoD Computer Security Initiative, NBS, Gaithersburg, MD, Jan. 15–17 1980.

9. U.S. Patent No. 4,262,329 issued April 14, 1981 in the name of Herbert S. Bright and Richard L. Enison, assigned to Computation Planning, Inc., *Security System for Data Processing*.

10. COMPLAN Technical Note 913-30: *Outline of a Bandit Program: a Self-Effacing Trojan Horse Scenario*. Rev. 9/4/81.

11. Wilkes, M. V.: *Time Sharing Computer Systems*. 3rd ed. New York, Elsevier, 1975.

12. Bright, H. S., and Enison, R. L.: Cryptography Using Modular Software Elements. *Proc. NCC'76*, AFIPS Conf. Proc. **45**: 113, 1976.

13. FIPS PUB 46, *Data Encryption Standard*. NBS Jan. 1977; *Computer Security and the Data Encryption Standard*. NBS Spec. Publication 500-27, Feb. 1978; *Report of the (9/21–22/76) Workshop on Cryptography in Support of Computer Security*. NBSIR 77-1291, NBS Sept. 1977.

14. *cryptopak™, DESQIK™, and DESEM™ Cryptographic Application Support Software System Technical Product Descriptions*. Computation Planning, Inc. (COMPLAN®), Bethesda, MD 20814.

15. Rivest, R. L., Shamir, A., and Adleman, L.: A Method for Obtaining Digital Signatures and Public-Key Cryptosystems. *Comm. ACM* 21/2: 120, 1978.

16. Bright, H. S.: High-Speed Indirect Cryption. *Cryptologia* 4/3 July 1980 pp. 133–139; published version of COMPLAN® TN-913-35, High-speed indirect cryption. Rev. 10/5/79.

17. Simmons, G. J.: Symmetric and Asymmetric Encryption. *ACM Computer Surveys*, 11/4: 305, 1979; Popek, G., and Kline, C.: Encryption and Secure Computer Networks, ibid. pp. 331–356.

18. 'Complete change of data' in this chapter means that each output bit has 50% probability of being reversed.

19. Ehrsam, W. F., Matyas, S. M., Meyer, C. H., and Tuchman, W. L.: A Cryptographic Key Management Scheme for Implementing the Data Encryption Standard. *IBM Sys. Jour.* 17/2: 106, 1978.

20. Proposed American National Standard for the *Modes of Operation for the Data Encryption Algorithm*. ANSI-X3T1 Draft 5, May 25, 1981.

21. Chaitin, G. J.: Information-Theoretic Limitations of Formal Systems. *Journal, ACM*, 21: 403, 1974.

22. Bright, H. S., and Enison, R. L.: Quasi-random number sequences from a long-period TLP generator, with remarks on application to cryptography, ibid., pp. 357–370; republished in *Encyclopedia of Computer Science and Technology*. Belzer–Holzman–Kent, 15: 125, 1980.

23. Hellman, M., *et al.*: *Results of an Initial Attempt to Cryptanalyze the NBS Data Encryption Standard*. Stanford Univ. Info. Sys. Lab. Report SEL 76-042. Rev. Nov. 10, 1976.

24. Bright, H. S.: Cryptanalytic Attack and Defense: Ciphertext-Only, Known-Plaintext, Chosen-Plaintext. *Cryptologia* 1/4: 366, 1977; published version of COMPLAN® TN-913-14.

25. Yuval, G.: *How to Swindle Rabin.* Wiskundig Seminarium paper, Vrije Universiteit, Amsterdam, Nederlands, Oct. 1979 (in English).

26. COMPLAN Technical Note 913-33, *Some Considerations in the Design and Implementations of the QIK-CRYPT™ Algorithm.* Rev. 7/28/78.

27. Feistel, H.: Cryptography and Computer Privacy. *Sci. Am.* **228**, 15, 1973.

28. COMPLAN TN-920-15, *DEA Sliding-Bit-Change Test,* August 24, 1977.

29. Diffie, W., and Hellman, M.: New Directions in Cryptography. *IEEE Trans. on Info. Theory* IT-22/6 Nov. 1976, pp. 644–654.

30. Lu, S. C., and Lee, L. N.: A Simple and Effective Public-Key Cryptosystem. *COMSAT Tech. Rev.* **9/1**: 15, 1979; R. Rivest, informal communication, 7/19/79; also, unpublished memorandum, M.I.T. Electrical Engineering Department, July 1979.

31. Enison, R. L., and Bright, H. S.: private memorandum, *Analysis of Message Authentication Procedures for...,* 12/11/78, 17 pages; also computer listings, 12/14/78, 215 pages. Censored version of memorandum released for limited private distribution 1/15/79.

32. Meyer, C. H.: Ciphertext/Plaintext and Ciphertext/Key Dependence vs. Number of Rounds for the Data Encryption Standard. *Proc. NCC'78* AFIPS CP46 Montvale, NJ, 1978.

33. COMPLAN Technical Note 913-40, *Computational Cost of the RSA Algorithm,* 9/11/81.

34. Bright, H. S., Harris, R. A., and Moll, K. L.: Information Content-Authentication: A Problem and an Answer. *Computerworld,* In Depth Section, **4/21/80**; COMPLAN TN-913-37, *Method for comparing presumably-identical segments in a distributed data base.* 2/2/80; Bright, H. S.: Information Segment Content Authentication Using Cryptographic Algorithms. *Proceedings of NBS-IEEE Trends and Applications Symposium 1980: Computer Networking Protocols,* IEEE, Silver Spring, MD, **1980**.

35. National Bureau of Standards, Special Publ. 500-21, Vol. 1, *The Network Security Center: A System Level Approach to System Security.* NBS, Washington, DC, 1978.

36. Rabin, M.: Digitalized signatures. Chapter in *Foundations of Secure Computing.* Edited by R. Demillo, New York, Academic Press, 1978.

37. Tuckerman, B.: A Study of the Vigenère–Vernam Single- and Multiple-Loop Enciphering Systems. IBM Research Report RC 2879 (#13538), May 14, 1970 (Mathematics).

38. Huffman, D. A.: A Method for the Construction of Minimum Redundancy Codes. *Proc. IRE* **40**: 1092, 1952.

39. Enison, R. L., and Bright, H. S.: *Improving the Use of a TLP sequence as a Key Stream for Vernam Encryption with Cryptopak.* TN-913-8d issue of 8/26/76, Computation Planning, Inc. (COMPLAN™), Bethesda, MD 20814.

40. Carroll, J. M., and McLelland, P. M.: Fast Infinite-Key Privacy Transformatoin for Resource-Sharing Systems. *Proc. FJCC* **37**: 223, 1970.

41. FIPS PUB 74, Guidelines for Implementing and Using the NBS Data Encryption Standard, Nat. Bu. Stds, Page 10, April 1981.

42. Jueneman, R. R., Analysis of certain aspects of DEA...; Davies, D. W., Some regular properties of the DES Algorithm, draft papers, CRYPTO-82 Conf., UCSB 8/23–25/82.

43. Gait, J., A nonlinear pseudorandom number generator, *IEEE Trans. Softwe. Engrg.* SE-3, No. 5, 359, Sept. 1977.

44. Bright, H. S., and Knoble, H. D. Secure key-in of cryptographic key, COMPLAN

TN-913-43, 5/11/82; Bright, Enison, One-way ... cipher; nonreproducible cipher, TN-913-24, 2/25/77.

45. Merkle, R., and Hellman, M. E. Hiding information and receipts in trapdoor knapsacks, *IEEE Trans. Info. Theory* **IT-24**, Sept. 1978.
46. News item, New code is broken, *SCIENCE* **216**, No. 4549, 971, May 28, 1982, G. Kolatta.
47. News item, Advance in Integer Programming, *SCIENCE* **212**, No. 4490, 31 April 3, 1981, G. Kolata.
48. News item, Secret math code cracked..., Los Angeles News Service article in *Philadelphia Inquirer* 5/16/82 p 4-C, L. Dembart (Remark: This news article was brought to our attention by H. D. Knoble, Penn State University.)
49. Hellman, M. E., informal remark during CRYPTO-82 Conf., UCSB, 8/23–25/82.
50. The contents of the section, Cryptanalytic Attack and Defense, were drawn largely from reference 21. Parts of the Strong Algorithm Section were published in reference 14. Parts of other sections were presented orally and in the Proceedings to participants in the SHARE 54 Conference, May 1980. Copyrights to this entire chapter and its parts are held by Computation Planning, Inc. (COMPLAN®), all rights reserved, and have been released to those publishers and to John Wiley & Sons Limited for unrestricted publication in those media and in the present volume.
51. 'Affine' is a term used in linear algebra. The vector y is an affine function of the vector x if and only if there exist some constant matrix A and some constant vector b such that y can be obtained by multiplying A by x and adding b. In this context the vectors and matrices are binary and the operations are to be performed modulo 2. Because typical attack strategies that are economically attractive take advantage of the linear nature of many kinds of cryptographic process elements (e.g. permutation), the non-linear nature of provably non-affine transformations results in frustration of such attacks or in greatly increasing their cost.

Advances in Computer Security Management, Vol. 2
Edited by M. M. Wofsey
© 1983 John Wiley & Sons Ltd.

Chapter 11

DISASTER/RECOVERY PLANNING

J. Robert McGrael

Management Dimensions Corporation

The unparalleled technical achievements of the last three decades have changed the United States from an industrial to an information society. This age of global electronic networks, accelerating technological thrust, and the rapid synthesis of electronics and business has created a complete dependence on the computer for day-to-day operations of business, government, and, indeed, most areas of human endeavor.

While this blending of technology with business operations is a necessary and desirable maturation of the growing data processing industry, complete reliance can be a two-edged sword. The computer has become the corporate memory or main depository of records, and the telecommunications network has become the central nervous system of every major organization. This integration of man and machine interface really means that the users simply cannot function without the computer/network operation. Loss of the computer equates with loss of the business. In the vast majority of complex applications systems, no fallback is available in case of a disaster. Accidental fire, arson, sabotage, flood, chemical spill, power failure, earthquake, tornado, and a host of other man-made and natural disasters can destroy or interrupt data processing operations.

It should be remembered as more interdependent technologies develop that the very fabric that holds society together is becoming increasingly vulnerable and fragile. As technology becomes more complex, the exposures to disaster increase and the disasters will have a greater impact. This mounting potential for increasing disaster frequency and severity has made recovery the hottest non-technical topic of the past few years for MIS managers, top executives, and auditors.

Who has the ultimate responsibility for ensuring that the computer will provide uninterrupted service and that the telecommunications networks are operational? The final responsibility for planning lies with management, and it is management who must accept responsibility in the event of long-term interruption due to a disaster or contingency.

BASIC PLANNING

MIS management has four basic functions: planning, organizing, directing, and controlling. The vast majority of management activities fall into these four categories. It is not accidental that planning comes first. Organizing and directing without planning is like shooting without aiming. Strategic planning for management comes in two types; first is opportunities planning which is designed to further the missions, goals, and longer range objectives of the organization; second is contingency planning which is designed to prevent things from happening, or a preset plan that can be used as a fallback when 'things go wrong'.

While most current opportunities planning for MIS is uniformly below acceptable levels, it is the planning aspect of Disaster/Recovery, a subset of contingency planning, which is always put aside, never done, forgotten, or belittled by data processing managers.

If a DP manager uses opportunities planning to design the future environment of the data center and ignores threats planning, then he does not worry about the future—there will not be one.

Yet planning by top MIS executives in both large and small organizations is either done badly or not done at all. Is planning that mysterious or complex that only a few can do it? To initiate a project for threats planning requires answers for a few basic questions.

1. Where is the organization now? What are the vulnerabilities, exposures, and threats in the current situation? (Risk Assessment.)
2. Where does the organization want to be in 3 to 5 years? If all current security protections failed to protect the data center and network, would the organization be able to function? (Risk Assessment compared to Strategic Plan.)
3. What is the cost of control versus the savings potential to the organization in implementing security protection? If nothing were done, would these risks and exposures be acceptable to the organization?
4. If the risks are unacceptable, what are the organization's options, i.e. component failure plan, security protection, or disaster/recovery?

If management will address these basic planning questions, the need for a recovery plan is self evident. However, many executives would prefer to view the probability of disaster as extremely low, and not worth consideration for an investment of time and money.

This response to disaster ignores the hundreds or thousands of employees, stockholders, and other citizens who depend on the organization for jobs, dividends, or service. Certainly it is the moral and ethical responsibility of MIS managers to spend time in threats planning so that recovery techniques are in place and decisions made before, not after, the recovery incident. Further, the legislative, judicial, and executive branches of government have taken steps to ensure that planning action is effected and that those responsible for planning are held to account for failure to protect the assets of the organization and the services provided to the public.

Some major instances of these outside actions are:

1. The passage of the Foreign Corrupt Practices Act (FCPA) of 1977, whose accounting control provisions seem to indicate a requirement for recovery to protect financial systems.
2. The release by the Office of Management and Budget (OMB) of OMB Circular A-71 (Transmittal memorandum No. 1 dated July 27, 1978), which advises federal data centers to implement tested recovery plans, and a report (AFMP-81-61) by the Controller General to Congress recommending that Congress order each agency to comply with the OMB requirements.
3. The issuance of unfavorable Audit Review Reports regarding the lack of recovery capabilities of data processing organizations. These reports by government and other external or internal auditors often warn of a prolonged inability to operate computers or provide services unless threats planning is undertaken immediately.
4. Recently a court in the State of New York found that a company providing services can be sued by a receiver of those services if the defendant company could reasonably be expected to know of vulnerabilities and exposure and had not planned to protect itself from disaster. The plaintiff company won damages and also won on appeal by defendant.

With all that MIS and top corporate management has riding on the uninterrupted continuation of computer and network, why do so few have a written and tested plan? Analysis of organizations that have not addressed these planning issues reveals the following conditions:

1. Top management either is not interested, will not spend the money, or undervalues the computer operations generally.
2. MIS managers view the recovery project or the entire security areas as having no usable payoff equal to the successful implementation of application systems.
3. Lack of in-house planning experience.
4. Project started but set aside for higher priority projects.
5. Project started but personnel transferred, promoted, or terminated.

All these are symptomatic of poor planning. However, many companies are interested and will spend the money but have great difficulty in getting started.

START-UP PLANS

Many organizations have tried to design, develop, and publish a Disaster/Recovery Plan, and have assigned people for long periods of time, yet the project is not moving forward. This lack of forward momentum is frustrating to management, but often management itself is responsible. Inadvertently the top MIS executives 'script' the project for failure almost before the project is initiated.

If the current project for the development of a Disaster/Recovery Plan is not going well, management might ask these questions:

1. Is the person assigned to the development of the plan assigned to Disaster/Recovery *exclusively*, or has the person been assigned to numerous competing projects?
2. Was there a formal project 'kickoff' meeting held to assure that the project got the proper support from management, or did the project 'just happen'?
3. Has management strictly enforced the schedule for information input from personnel in MIS for inclusion in the plan; i.e. critical computer run information, or is the assigned person working in a vacuum and floundering?
4. Are status meetings between project personnel and management held monthly with Disaster/Recovery the exclusive subject of the meeting?
5. Has a project work plan been developed, and submitted to management. Has the work plan been reviewed and approved prior to the initiation of the project?
6. Are project status reports relating to the work plan submitted to management on a regular schedule?
7. Does the person assigned to the Disaster/Recovery Project have sufficient planning and MIS experience to build a comprehensive plan within schedule and budget?
8. Does the project have enough depth in personnel to ensure project continuity in case of catastrophic illness or terminations, or would the program have to start over?
9. Has management had some initial work sessions on the Disaster/Recovery planning project to provide direction on scope, writing style, plan organization, and other factors, or are the project personnel drifting?
10. Finally, has management requested recovery training, testing, maintenance, and other procedures so that the completed plan will be a living document, or did it just request a plan document?

If management is not comfortable with the answers to one or more of the preceding questions, and the project has not met expectations, perhaps it is time to regroup. Better yet, if the plan project has not yet started, then getting the project organized is the first goal.

ORGANIZATION OF THE PROJECT

Perhaps the easiest way to get organized is to take all of the ten questions above and 'script' the project for success rather than for failure. To rescript for success, management should turn each question into a positive point.

1. The project person(s) will be assigned exclusively to the Disaster/Recovery Project. The personnel will not be assigned to anything else until management is satisfied that the plan is complete.
2. A project kickoff meeting will take place to ensure that:
   a. Responsibilities are assigned.
   b. Authority is delegated so the responsibilities will be achieved.
   c. Sufficient resources are assigned.
   d. Project personnel can develop a project work plan for approval and that commitments to schedule can be made by the project personnel rather than having the dates dictated by management.
3. MIS management will assist the project personnel by enforcing the requirements for information and approvals, and if delays in securing information occur, the project schedule will be revised.
4. Project status meetings will be held by MIS management to monitor progress and assist the project personnel. These meetings will be exclusively devoted to the Disaster/Recovery Project.
5. A detailed project work plan will be developed. Tasks will be divided into controllable 40- or 80-hour segments. A person will be assigned to each task as specifically responsible for the on-time completion of the tasks. Task assignments such as Staff, All, Systems, Management, or other general names will be avoided, and be substituted by specific names or titles.
6. The project will submit a project status report each month 3 or 4 days prior to the status meeting. The status report on progress and problems will be the central agenda item at each meeting. The status report will be compared to the project work plan to ensure that the 40- to 80-hour task segments are being completed on schedule. Such statements as 'this task is 50%, 75%, or 90% complete' will not be accepted. The task is either complete or it is not. The report is a serious matter and remedial action must be taken when necessary.
7. The person assigned to the Disaster/Recovery Project will be at a high enough level in the organization to get tasks done, and have sufficient technical experience to write a comprehensive plan. The person will have enough planning and writing experience to feel comfortable in this assignment.
8. Management will provide sufficient trained personnel to take over the project in the event of illness, death, or termination.
9. Management will provide direction on plan scope, style of writing, organizational structure of the plan, and other items to indicate to the project person what management wants the plan to cover, and what items, if done well, will constitute success.
10. Management will define testing procedure requirements, maintenance items, and other activities associated with, but not necessarily contained in the plan. A separate documentation manual is to contain these items.

The DP manager can see that the foregoing ten points relate to the four basic management functions of planning, organizing, directing, and controlling. If management still has doubts about the organization's ability to meet the challenges posed by the ten points, perhaps it would be well advised to seek outside consulting assistance for a joint effort rather than relying on in-house expertise only.

THE RECOVERY PLAN PROJECT LIFE CYCLE

Like any other systems project, the Recovery Plan Project has a similar Project Life Cycle (PLC). To simplify things, one can divide this PLC into seven phases:

1. Initiation.
2. Evaluation.
3. Planning.
4. Analysis/Design.
5. Development.
6. Implementation.
7. Testing.

Initiation and *Evaluation* may start from a Risk Assessment Study, an Audit Report, or a request from management to proceed with a recovery plan to assure minimum disruption of service in the event of a disaster.

THE PLANNING PHASE

The Planning Phase of the Recovery Project is nothing more or less than a plan for a plan. The Planning Phase should settle basic questions about the Recovery Plan.

Plan Scope is one key item to be defined in the Planning Phase. Scope determines the beginning and the end of the project. Scope gives a size of magnitude to the work effort. More projects fail because of a lack of understanding of the scope than for any other reason. Experience shows that the best definition of scope for a recovery plan is as follows: Scope of the plan will be—from the point of disaster to the resumption of temporary processing—this definition seems so simple, so elementary, that it hardly needs to be mentioned. Yet, the scope as defined tells what to put into a plan and what to exclude. For example, if the starting boundary of scope is at the time of disaster, then all of the pre-disaster items are eliminated. These eliminated items can be safety items such as building evacuation procedures. CPR procedure, historical background, policies, and other pre-plan physical and data security procedures.

The eliminated items, while valuable, are items that will not assist recovery at the point of disaster. In a fire situation no one is going to retrieve the Recovery

Plan to see what procedures are needed for building evacuation, so why have the procedure in the plan?

At the other end of the boundary of scope is 'the resumption of temporary processing'. This aspect eliminates the early discussion of procedures to restore or rebuild the data center. Since concentration of all personnel will be on getting operations resumed, why waste precious resources during the 24- to 48-hour recovery on calculating computer cable lengths or adapter requirements in a front-end processor? In other words, a restoration plan should be separate from the recovery of temporary processing, and will be executed later.

The other major factor in outlining scope is to determine the amount of time the computer center could be out of operation before the organization is heavily impacted. Depending on the type of organization, and the type of service performed by the data center, the permissible time outage will generally range from several hours to several days. Now, both key factors to determine the scope of the Recovery Plan are present: the scope is from the point of disaster to the resumption of temporary processing, and recovery must be accomplished in N hours. Therefore, what is developing is an administrative-logistical plan for an N-hour period; that is all, no more, no less.

Defining scope to a specific time frame will limit the writing effort to procedures for each and every step toward resumption of processing and reduce the work effort to meet that object immeasurably.

When the project has been defined as an administrative-logistics plan to be used over a specific time period, it would be well to consider under what circumstances the plan is to be used. Of first concern is the fact that the computer will be out of service for a longer period of time than the permissible N hours defined in scope, but the plan should also cover:

1. *Minor Contingencies*: where the computer is not operational but the data center is still intact, e.g. machine failures causing long downtimes, power outages, component damage or failures. This situation is by far the most common problem and most commonly not mentioned in the plan.
2. *Local Disasters*: where the data center is not intact but the wider geographic area is unaffected, e.g. fires (internal or local), water damage, strike, or vandalism.
3. *Widespread Disasters*: where both the data center and the geographic area are impacted, e.g. earthquake, hurricane, flood, tornado, nuclear leakage, chemical spill, or civil strife.

In reviewing these three major conditions, it is apparent that different procedures will be used in each situation. Procedures for retrieving off-site data are unnecessary under a contingency incident such as long machine downtime. If the data center is still intact, it may be easier to gather data sets and documentation at the data center rather than at off-site storage. On the other hand, in the case of more serious disaster such as arson, many more of the plan security procedures will be activated than in a simple contingency situation.

Use of Scenarios

Many organizations start the recovery planning effort by giving consideration to the development of scenarios. Usually it is unnecessary to spend a lot of time trying to protect against everything and anything that might happen. Using the three major disaster conditions of contingency, local, and widespread should cover most types of incident. If the plan is written to cover the worst case of widespread disaster, then the procedures will cover most types of disaster incidents.

Why write a separate scenario of response for each type of disaster when one can address disaster incidents under the three major conditions. Instead, consider these factors: the data center is either intact or not; the estimated downtime will exceed permissible downtime hours or will not; the disaster has impacted a wide geographic area or has not. Just these factors alone will guide the plan procedures for comprehensive recovery in all situations. However, scenarios might be considered for the failure or destruction of special equipment, for example, equipment used in bank proof operations, data capture (MICR), or other elements of item processing. Many banks and other organizations cannot recover with computer hardware alone.

The next area of planning to be considered for this project is what other areas need protection. The first answer is the computer system and networks that run the critical applications. However, management must consider other areas that are data processing related:

1. Data Entry. Is the data entry section close to the data center? Can it be impacted by the same disaster?
2. Mail Room. Is the mail room in the same location as the data center? Is it used to mail bills or statements critical to cash flow?
3. COM. Does this organization use microfiche readers?

Are COM output support systems necessary?

Writing Style

In the Planning Phase you should decide on your writing style and keep it consistent throughout the plan. Nothing destroys the effectiveness of the plan more than long rambling sentences, bureaucratic language, or faulty organization.

Experience has shown the following rules work well:

1. Write from general to specific in each section. The writer can start with an

overview and by the end of the section pinpoint detail on procedures and resources to achieve the objective of the procedures.

2. Keep sentences short.
3. Use the sentences as 'bullets'; that is, do not overdo detail on how to do something.
4. Be brief.
5. Have each sentence tell 'who does what'.
6. Use the 'checklist' approach to writing.

As an example, the preceding suggestions are contained in the following sequence in a plan:

	TIME COMPLETED
Administrative Team Manager notifies Transportation Team to pick up data entry data.	_____
(*Who*) Administrative Team Manager (*does*) notifies Transportation Team Manager (*what*) to pick up data entry data.	WHEN

Terms

It may be well to define a few Disaster/Recovery terms prior to the creation of procedures.

A *Command and Control Center* is a large conference-type room which is used as a meeting place and a 'war room' headquarters for the Management Team. The Command and Control Center and alternates are established far enough from the data center so that the area will not be impacted by the same disaster.

The Local Command and Control Center is placed far enough from the data center so that it is not impacted by local disasters, e.g. fire, explosions, or water damage.

The Widespread Command and Control Center is located many miles away from the data center so that it will not be impacted by a widespread disaster. However, three points are worth noting about the widespread disaster.

1. After a widespread disaster, people may take a long time to assemble at the Command and Control Center because the employees need to ensure their families' well-being.
2. Transportation to the Widespread Command and Control Center may be difficult, if not impossible, so placement of this facility must consider this aspect.
3. If loss of life occurs, alternate team members or outsiders will have to be used. Documentation is important.

The Disaster Recovery Administrator is the person who maintains the plan and trains recovery personnel. In a disaster incident this person can be associated with the Management Team as a staff assistant to the Disaster Recovery Coordinator. During the incident this person usually maintains documentation and keeps the appropriate activities moving forward. The person selected for this position can be at a medium or low-medium level in the two organizations.

The Disaster Recovery Coordinator is the person who is responsible for successful recovery within the permissible hours which were defined in the Scope section of the plan. The Disaster Recovery Coordinator is the senior manager during recovery no matter what his normal position may be on the formal organization chart.

Alternates are either people or locations which can be used as a fallback for any reason. The Coordinator, Team Managers, Administrator, or team members could have alternates for three basic reasons. First, people cannot be notified in every case when a disaster occurs. Second, recovery is a 24-hour-a-day effort until temporary processing is resumed. People will need to be relieved for rest during recovery operations. Third, lives may be lost. The location alternates are used in case the primary location is not usable for any reason.

The next step in planning for the Recovery Project is to decide on Plan Structure and Organization.

Organization Structure

The Organization Structure is often determined by the size of the organization and strengths of the people. For example, a small organization of 10 or 20 people in data processing may look as simple as the example in Figure 11-1.

Because of the small size of this organization, few people may be available to recover in a disaster incident.

Under this structure, one or more people can be assigned to each function. The

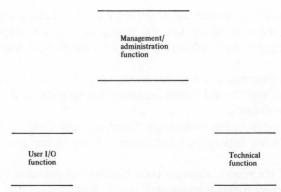

Figure 11-1.   Example of structure of small organization.

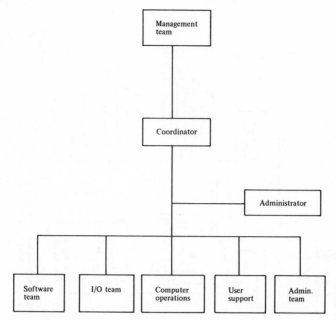

Figure 11-2. Example of structure of larger organization.

Coordinator (Supervisor) of recovery can be handled by the management/administrative function. Remember that even in this simple organization structure for a small company, alternate (replacement) personnel must be assigned.

If the reader is from a smaller organization, this structure should be optimally simple in order to effect recovery.

A larger organization can be broken into more recovery specialities, as shown in Figure 11-2.

An example of a large retail bank organization is given in Figure 11-3.

Larger organizations may require even more specialization, for example, an Administrative Support Team may be required (Figure 11-4).

Plan Structure

If the organization is large enough for a team approach, then the plan sections can be established as follows:

1. Introduction Section.
2. Management Team Section.
3. I/O Team Section (inlcuding Data Entry).
4. User Team Section.
5. Computer Support Team (including off-site storage sub-team).

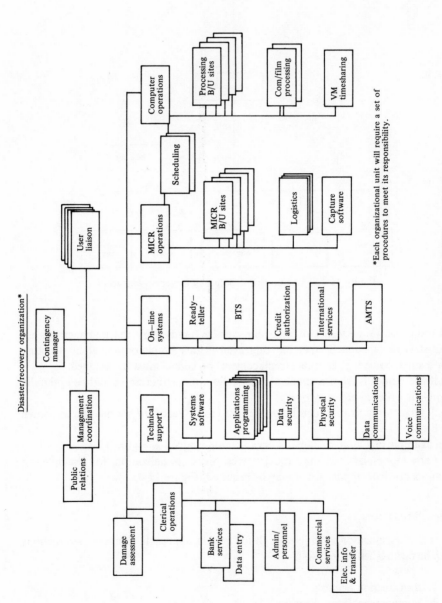

Figure 11-3. Example of structure of a large organization.

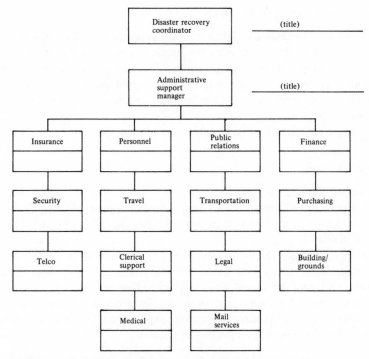

Note that many personnel assigned to this team are not always MIS
personnel; the loss of data processing is an organization-wide problem
and is not limited to MIS.

Figure 11-4. Example of Administrative Support Team for large organization.

6. Software Team.
7. Administrative Support Team.
8. Appendix Section.
9. Restoration Team.

Without belaboring the matter of writing, as in a style from general to specific,
each team section should have at the minimum the following subsections:

1. Team General Responsibilities (what—generally).
2. Team Organization (who).
3. Team Notification (when).
4. Team Assembly (where).
5. Detailed Procedures (what—detail).
6. Team Supplies/Resources (tools for accomplishment of the detailed procedures).

An example of a team General Responsibility section follows:

Computer Backup and Support Team

The Computer Backup and Support Team is primarily responsible for retrieving off-site (vaulted) data, activating the backup facility, assuring backup system integrity, and completing startup operations. The team will also be responsible for maintaining operational disciplines throughout the temporary processing period. Software program restoration and verification of systems integrity are completed by this team.

Following is an example of an Organization section:

I/O Support Team

Production Control Coordinator, Computer Operations Technician, Computer Support Coordinator, Senior Data Control Clerks, Control Clerks, Data Entry Operators, Senior Data Entry Operators, Schedulers, Mail Room Clerks, and Distribution Clerks.

In addition, special support personnel may be required *as in Bank operations*: Proof Supervisors, Proof Operators, MICR Operators, Microfilm Research, Reconciliation Group Personnel, and Adjustment Group.

This requirement for special equipment and personnel for financial operations support may also need a separate backup facility for the I/O operations group.

An example of a Notification Procedure follows.

DISASTER/RECOVERY—INITIAL NOTIFICATION
(LEVEL 1)

The Initial Notification is critical to the timely recovery of the data center. Due to the possibility of injuries or communications failure, a series of alternates have been established to ensure proper notification to a senior data processing manager.

1. In the event of a disaster in the data center, notification* will be made to:

MEMBER	NAME/TITLE
a. Disaster/Recovery Coordinator	————
b. Disaster/Recovery Coordinator Alternate	————
c. Disaster/Recovery Administrator	————
d. Disaster/Recovery Administrator Alternate	————
e. Management Team Manager	————
f. Management Team Manager Alternate	————
g. Management Team Member	————
h. Management Team Member	————

Notification* of a disaster will be made to the managers designated above by:

  a. Building Security
  b. Operations Personnel
  c. Police or Fire Departments
  d. Others
2. The initial notification of a potential disaster or a contingency will come from:
  a. Operations personnel
  b. Fire/Security personnel
  c. Other employees
  d. Alternate D/R Coordinator   _____
     The above personnel will notify:
  a. The Management Team Manager   _____
  . If not contacted, then call
  b. The Alternate Management Team Manager   _____
  c. Or continue calling team managers until contact
     is made   _____
3. Upon notification of a disaster, the manager initially notified will attempt to determine the extent of damage.
4. If the problem warrants the further notification of management, the manager initially notified will contact the other members of the Disaster/Recovery Management Team.
5. The Management Team will meet at the Command and Control Center:

  LOCAL: _____
  _____
  Entry Instructions:
  Key Location: _____
  Directions: _____

  ALTERNATE: _____
  _____
    Entry Instructions:
    Key Location: _____
    Directions: _____

  WIDESPREAD: _____
  _____
    Entry Instructions:
    Key Location: _____
    Directions: _____

Note: Office and home phone numbers have been listed in the Appendix of this Plan and in the wallet-sized plastic cards provided to Disaster/Recovery personnel.

The following is an example of an actual detail procedure.

ADMINISTRATIVE SUPPORT TEAM
D/R PURCHASING PROCEDURES CHECKLIST

NOTIFICATION/REPORT	TIME COMPLETED
1. Upon notification from Administrative Support Team Manager, report to the Command and Control Center	_____
2. Report to the Administrative Support Team Manager	_____
3. Review Damage Assessment Report with the Administrative Support Team Manager and D/R Coordinator	_____
a. Determine forms, paper, and supplies needed	_____
b. Contact supplies vendors* and inform them of disaster	_____
c. Request expedited order handling	_____
d. Inform vendor of new delivery address	_____

CONTACT/ORGANIZATION PROCEDURE

	TIME COMPLETED
1. Using the appropriate requisition form** create the correct supplies orders	_____
2. Contact Administrative Support Team Transportation personnel for pickup of supplies	_____
3. Monitor supplies status during recovery operations	_____
4. Maintain copies of supplies requisition and other expense (audit) items	_____
5. Forward all audit items and final report to the Disaster/Recovery Administrator	_____

*Note: See Appendix for Telephone Listing
**Note: See Appendix for Forms Examples
Following is an example of an Assembly Procedure.

ACCESS TO COMMAND AND CONTROL CENTER

ITEM	TIME COMPLETED
1. Notify XYZ (Building Manager) as directed by Management Team Manager, J. Doe, Director of Information Services	_____

2. To gain permission (Bldg. Mgr.) to enter 000 Main Street Building, obtain XX (Alarm Company) elevator passcard and keys to BBB Building, 20th Floor, Room 2000 contact Building Manager:
   a. _____ HOME:
       OFFICE:
   b. _____ HOME:
       OFFICE: _____
3. Proceed to BBB Building, 000 Main Street and enter building from South Street entrance   _____
4. Press buzzer on left side of door to notify building security guard   _____
5. After entry to the lobby, sign in on guard log   _____
Note: Open the door to the BBB Building with YOUR key; otherwise the guard will NOT let you in
6. Walk down the hallway, passing all elevators until you reach the Red telephone room on your right   _____
7. Pick up the phone. No need to dial—this phone is directly connected to XX Alarm Company   _____
8. Give XX Alarm Company your name, passcard number, number of people going up with you, and what floor you are going to   _____
   Use your XX elevator passcard to get to the 20th floor   _____
   a. Press UP button to open elevator door
   b. Insert card with mag strip facing up in the direction of arrow
   c. Press button for 20th floor and *leave card in* until you reach your floor   _____
9. Turn on electricity and lights at hallway power panel   _____
10. Open 20th floor, room 2000—The Command and Control Center   _____
11. Go to room storage cabinet and obtain keys to Room 2005 where off-site storage cabinets are located   _____
12. Transport boxes located in storage cabinets back to Command and Control Center Room 2000   _____

Examples of supplies and resources are: keypunching instructions, data entry stations, scratch tapes, program cards or tapes, formats, keying instructions, logs, transmittals, schedules, card stock, daily production schedule, a 9-track 800/1600 bpi tape drive, data terminal switching unit, computer printer ribbons, tape racks, DP technical library, initialized disk packs, off-site retrieval checklist, systems supplies checklist, computer output forms, computer printer carriage control loops, tape labels, library restore procedure, copy of library tape listing, operator procedures, operations documentation, backup of current operating system on tape, JCL cards of critical jobs, operable communications network, power, lights, air conditioning, telephones, carts, air travel cards, car rental cards, data center security badges, dial backup telephone numbers, operating system manuals, software products, check requisition form, travel plan, statement of expense, status media, water, food, and clothing.

ANALYSIS PHASE

The next phase of the recovery project is to gather the data. The data gathered in the Analysis Phase are utilized during the Plan Development Phase.

The Analysis Phase is also used to complete the detailed design of the plan. For example, items of information needed will include the following:

1. How many hours would your computer have to be down before your organization was impacted to the point that a disaster would be declared? 4–8–16–24–48 hours or more? (If not previously decided.)
2. From whom would the initial notification of a disaster come? (If not previously decided.)
3. In the event of a building evacuation where would your on-site staff assemble? This place could be a nearby company-owned facility (parking lot if necessary) or a nearby 24-hour restaurant.
4. What are your Critical Applications?
5. What critical runs are supported by your network?
6. What other major (non-critical) systems are supported by data processing?
7. What organizational divisions/functions and other users are assigned to support each critical application?
8. What software is required to support your critical runs?
9. What communication front-end (e.g. 3705, or other) requirements are needed to support your critical runs (e.g. adaptors, line sets)?
10. A Command and Control Center (an area designated for meeting of ALL D/R personnel) must be created. This chosen site should be a conference room, hotel room, or other facility far enough away from your data center so that it is not impacted by the same localized disaster. It must have telephone, power, water, sanitation, a locked file with supplies and materials, and the capacity to accommodate many people for an extended period of time.
11. This Command and Control Center will have to be supplied with resources, such as telephone, D/R plan manuals, writing material, food and water, clothing, status media boards, radio, clock, CB radios, portable lights, first-aid supplies, tape recorder, typewriters, accounting forms, and accountability documents. What will you need?
12. You will need to have the hardware configuration of your computer

backup facility. Check, DASD, modems, front-end, peripheral gear. Check to ensure other special features—PCM users, please note.

13. The backup facility must have an adequate equipment configuration and an availability sufficiently complete to allow processing of data for an extended period of time. You will need to be completely knowledgeable of the procedure required to bring-up the backup site computer including software restoration. Include software restoration procedure.

14. List the requirements of the backup site, such as scratch tapes, computer printer ribbons, tape racks, technical manuals, disk packs, tape labels, stock paper, stock form cards, operator procedures, forms used by operators, copy of the D/R plan, program listings, backup of the current Program Library on disk, copy of the Library, Job Control Language, copy of the Procedures Library, off-site retrieval codes, DIAL backup telephone numbers, data entry supplies, run documentation, backup data center security information, list of accommodations, gas, airport, hotels for the backup center, air travel cards, office supplies, and adding machines.

15. List addresses and phone numbers for hotels and restaurants located near your Command and Control Center, data entry facility, computer backup site, and other areas. Also provide maps showing backup site(s), Command and Control Center site(s), and other important areas.

16. Where is your collection point for input to the backup computer center?

17. Where is the distribution point for output reports from the backup computer center?

18. Where is the collection point for input to the backup data entry facility?

19. Where is the distribution point for output from the backup data entry facility?

20. Where is your off-site storage facility?

21. Where are the keys to the off-site storage facility and the storage containers located?

22. Where is your data entry backup facility located?

23. What critical runs does data entry support?

24. What data entry equipment is required?

25. How many data entry shifts are worked?

26. What is the total number of data entry employees for your organization?

27. How many pieces of data entry equipment are needed for critical runs?

28. How many data entry employees are needed to support critical runs?

29. Are all data entry program formats, documentation, support schedules, and other supplies stored off-site? Where; directions to location?

30. Based on the location of your data entry backup facility, will data entry personnel have to be transported? Who is responsible for arranging travel?

31. Do you need food service at data entry backup site? Who is responsible, how delivered, who is responsible for cost, who has the food monies?

32. The data entry backup site will require supplies/resources, such as entry machines, scratch tapes, program cards or tapes, formats, keying instructions, logs, transmittals, schedules, and card stock.

33. Who will be the Disaster/Recovery Coordinator (Manager of Recovery)?
34. Who will be the Disaster/Recovery Administrator (person maintaining the plan)?
35. List the names of personnel you are assigning to your Management Team.
36. List the names of personnel you are assigning to your I/O Team.
37. List the names of personnel you are assigning to your Data Entry Team.
38. List the names of personnel you are assigning to your User Support Team.
39. List the names of personnel you are assigning to your Computer Backup and Support Team.
40. List the names of personnel you are assigning to your Administrative Support Team. Include home and office phone numbers for team personnel.
41. The I/O team will require supplies/resources, such as automobiles, dollies, carts, cartons, scratch tapes, forms, disk packs, card stock, ribbons, and tape racks.
42. The Computer Backup and Support team will require supplies/resources, such as scratch tapes, disk packs, tape racks, Technical Library, forms, carriage loops (if used), ribbons, tape labels, card stock, keypunch machine, Operator Procedures, Program Listings, JCLs, power, lights, air conditioning, and telephones.
43. The Administrative Support team will require certain skills as follows but not limited to: Insurance/Risk, Security, Finance, Personnel, Public Relations, Purchasing/Supply, Legal, Facilities, Telephone, Clerical Support, Medical, Internal Auditing. Identify the personnel responsible (the responsible people need not be in Data Processing).
44. List critical internal software jobs e.g. daily save of operating system).
45. List operations schedules for critical jobs.
46. List your report names, report numbers, and frequencies of reports (volumes).
47. List the following types of forms used by your organization: Travel Plan and/or Statement of Expense, copy of the Check Requisition Form, and any types of Operations Documentation Checklists.
48. Will you use on-site transportation or do you have a preferred truck rental company? List the name of your preferred truck rental company and its telephone number.
49. If your backup data center is not in the city where you are now located, how do you plan to get there? Airline, automobile?
50. List the telephone numbers of key vendors, forms vendors, telephone company, communications equipment vendors, fire, police, gas company, electric company, alarm company, armored car company, private guard service, and hospitals.
51. You will need a schematic of your present hardware configuration.
52. You will need a list of all equipment and special features.
53. You will need a schematic of the present network configuration.

54. You will need a list of all communications equipment and special features used for critical runs.

The preceding list is certainly not all of the points to be covered in a plan but provides a brief idea of the information required to flesh out the plan structure built in the Planning Phase of the project.

Questionnaires and requests for information may have to be distributed among several people who have the specific information needed. This allocation of information requests to several experts will also shorten the time required to complete the Analysis Phase.

During the Analysis Phase it is particularly important that management provide increased support to the Disaster Recovery Project personnel. The project schedule is highly dependent on ensuring that questions are answered completely within the allotted time. MIS personnel usually are busy and will want to procrastinate on answering the Analysis Phase questions. The higher level MIS managers will have to enforce the schedule for replies. One way to hasten replies is to insist that all late responses to Analysis Phase questions be listed in the status reports by person responsible. The people responsible for supplying information to project personnel should be requested to attend the meeting. In the status meeting, management should stress the need to complete the questions and provide data on schedule. If the project has been delayed by poor response, the schedule should be revised accordingly.

THE DEVELOPMENT PHASE

As information is gathered during the Analysis Phase, project personnel can be preparing for the Development Phase.

In the Development Phase of the Disaster/Recovery Project, the plan draft is organized, detailed procedures written and supplies allocated.

Decisions in Development

During the Development Phase minor points will occur that were not addressed during the Analysis Phase. If one has been thinking through the disaster recovery steps, decision points may be hit fairly early in the game. For example, assume that a fire or explosion hits the data center during working hours. The preplanning (security) procedures may describe the building evacuation techniques, but where do people assemble and what are the first actions taken?

Conversely, if a disaster occurs during non-working hours, who gives the initial notification and whom do they call? If the fire, police, or security personnel are aware of the disaster situation, how do they contact the coordinator or alternate? Suppose the first calls are not answered? Did the people assemble where a phone was available for 24 hours a day? In other words, what is the fallback?

Next assume that you got out of the data center building, assembled people outside, made your phone calls, and received a response. How will the personnel get to the Command and Control Center? Once you get there in off-work hours, is it locked? How do you get in? Did you write an entry procedure and train the people on how it is done? Assuming the surviving people got in, what do they do first, second, third? What supplies and resources have you stored at the Command and Control Center; how are they used and by whom? Is the supplies storage cabinet locked? Who has the key; how do you open it? Are there provisions for water, coffee, and restroom facilities at the Command and Control Center? If the phones and power are inoperable, how do you notify people? What points do you cover in the Damage Assessment meeting, who attends the Damage Assessment meeting, and who personally surveys the damages? If you must go to off-site storage to retrieve the last of your critical run data sets, are you sending the very person who first destroyed your data center to retrieve it? (Do you need additional security?) How do you protect the old data center from looting? Who is in charge of salvage and how do they relate to the insurance company? How do you activate the Disaster/Recovery Plan? What do you do first? When should users be notified of the disaster?

My point is that hundreds of small decision points will appear as the plan develops. It is much better to address these questions in the plan before a disaster rather than in an actual disaster situation.

Without plan procedures, each of these decision points could cause a delay, and the recovery could take several additional days to implement—assuming that all the right decisions were made and everything thought of under the stress of disaster.

It is important to have a 'siege mentality' to cover every aspect of what might happen during a disaster, and during the Development Phase each of these aspects must be addressed.

One of the major advantages of engaging a qualified Disaster/Recovery consultant is to ensure that the plan is comprehensive and will cover all current exposures and vulnerabilities. There are perhaps five qualified Disaster/Recovery firms in the United States, that is, consulting firms that do nothing but recovery planning. It is not that they are any smarter than you, but planning for recovery is their only job and they have developed that siege mentality.

Equipment Backup

With the increasing complexity of data centers it is necessary to consider more than just the computer if the operation is to be recovered. For example, banks may have to consider a Plan Section for proof teams and equipment, and MICR personnel and equipment. MICR equipment is complex and the backup cost is quite prohibitive for all but the larger banks or multi-data center bank. Yet solutions for MICR processing can be used in part to solve the problem. Two major banks and at least one hardware vendor have a commercial backup offering for item processing under consideration. Also mutual agreements in this area may work if the host bank has time available.

In analyzing equipment backup, the experienced person will look not only at the data center computer configuration but also at *all* input and output operations that are required to keep the data flowing. Equipment commonly found in or near data centers are data entry, mail rooms, or computer output microfilm (COM) processing. During development of the recovery plan procedures points will be uncovered that will assist in completing the detailed procedures and produce supplies/resource requirements.

Data Entry

Data entry functions, accomplished either by the data center staff or by users in the same building, can heavily influence a recovery if the input is vital to the update of data sets used in a critical application. This problem is now compounded by the elimination of data entry devices (card, key to tape, key to disk), and their replacement by on-line local (direct connect) terminals.

The major problem with local terminals is the difficulty in re-establishing communication lines to a computer backup site many miles away. Solutions available in this case are:

1. Have entry personnel travel to the computer backup site to continue input.
2. Fall back to older equipment and create or utilize the old update program or create an interface program.
3. Use a local commercial entry site off-shift to create data and ship the tapes to the backup site.

Following are a few data entry plan considerations.

1. Are all documentation, operating systems (where applicable), or program formats stored off-site?
2. Who is in charge of the team, who is the alternate manager?
3. Where is the data entry backup site?
4. Is a firm contract signed?
5. How does the backup data entry site hardware configuration compare to the destroyed site?
6. If a local disaster took place in the data entry area, can the plan cover this situation as a stand-alone recovery?
7. What is the collection point for input data?
8. How will input data be transported to the data entry backup site and to the computer backup site?
9. What supplies and resources will be needed at the data entry backup site, e.g. cards, schedules, logs, and scratch tapes?

10. Who is notified at the data entry backup site? What if that person cannot be contacted? Are home phone numbers available?
11. Given requirements for data entry devices, will the site be on third shift at backup? Does this fit the critical run schedule?
12. Given the distance, geographic location, and the hours that the entry devices are available, is it realistic to expect the data entry and user personnel to travel to the backup, or are they the family's second income earners with baby sitting and other problems? If so, then develop the alternative procedures.
13. If the personnel can travel to the data entry backup site, how are they transported? Where do they meet? Are they paid portal to portal or do they work shorter hours?

These and many other questions about data entry alone can require many decisions and procedures.

Mail Room

Just as all input areas must be considered, so must the output area. It does no good to recover computer operations if no one is going to supply input to keep operations current and no one has planned for output handling. If the mail room is located near the data center and can be destroyed in the same disaster, this function should be considered in the plan.

Many of the questions that apply to Data Entry also apply to the mail room.

1. Is a backup available locally? What hours can it be used?
2. Are supplies available, e.g. window envelopes for statement or billing runs, mail trays, file distribution racks, mail folder, stuffers, slitters, postage meters, and scales?
3. How is the mail output transported?
4. How do the personnel who may use public transportation get to the mail room backup?
5. Has a team been designated, who is in charge?

Computer Backup

In reviewing computer backup, the major consideration has been the CPU mainframe and memory size. While these questions are vitally important, many other points must be reviewed. Before looking at detailed questions concerning the backup equipment, a review of the types of computer backup available is in order. These backup types are: mutual agreement or mutual contract, shells, hardware vendors, service bureaus, consortiums, Disaster/Recovery services, sister organizations, and duplicate sites.

Mutual Agreement or Mutual Contracts

Such arrangements are used by companies who would like to have the auditor believe that backup protection is available. The major advantage of mutual agreements is that they are low cost or no cost. The major disadvantage is that mutual agreements are worth exactly what you pay for them—nothing! Other disadvantages are that changes in hardware and software between each data center must be coordinated. Testing is difficult, and establishment of telecommunications for both organizations cannot always be accommodated in the same front-end processor. Each data center may need telecommunications at the same time of day, and the host data center cannot make the lines and equipment available. With the rapid proliferation of fixed disk drives it is difficult to guarantee that sufficient drives will be available for your exclusive use. Also, if data bases must be unloaded and reloaded to make fixed drives available, the time loss may impact the host data center schedule.

Shells

A shell is an available building suitable for installing computer equipment. The shell is often referred to as a 'cold site' since it contains little or no equipment but has electrical power, raised floor, and air conditioning. The three major advantages of a shell are:

1. Many organizations offering shells will permit a lengthy stay, sometimes several months, while a destroyed data center is reconstructed.
2. The cost of a shell is considerably less than that of a 'hot site' which has the computer hardware installed. The cost savings are 50% or more over many hot sites.
3. Depending on the type of computer manufacture, the shell is the only alternative available. This unavailability may occur when using computer manufactured by companies that have only a small share of the computer market, and 'hot site' services for this vendor are not offered.

The major disadvantages of a shell are:

1. Testing the plan is difficult or very costly if it can be done at all. A plan not tested is not a plan.
2. With the increase of multivendor data processing center shops and Plug Compatible Machines (PCM), doubts would exist about the delivery of equipment within the time specified for recovery.
3. Other doubts would involve rebuilding a data center during a disaster situation. A resumption of temporary processing in a short time frame would seem to be enough challenge for most organizations.

4. A widespread disaster may cause several organizations to activate their plan at the same time. This situation could put a data center in competition with others that may want to create a different hardware configuration in the same shell.

Computer Hardware Vendors

These suppliers will agree to make their 'best effort' to replace equipment as rapidly as possible. Hardware vendors (e.g. IBM, Honeywell) will usually give verbal or written assurance that the company 'will make a best effort' to provide equipment.

The major advantage in using a hardware vendor is the low cost or lack of cost. The major disadvantages in using a hardware vendor's nearby facilities are:

1. Many vendor accounts may wish to use the facility in a widespread disaster.
2. The vendor's facility may be impacted by the same disaster.
3. The vendor may have difficulty providing an approximate mix of equipment to satisfy all customers.
4. Telecommunications and network capabilities at the vendors may not be suitable for your use.

Service Bureaus

The major advantage of using the Service Bureaus is that cost may be lower depending on the contract. The main disadvantage is availability. Some serious concerns have been expressed about the availability of a computer dedicated to day-to-day users. However, it is possible to use a service bureau for computer backup if space and a computer are made available solely for the use of Disaster/Recovery subscribers.

Consortiums

These affiliations of organizations consist of many data centers, each of which pays a portion of the cost for a data center. The advantage of the consortium is the availability of the data center and ease of testing. The prime disadvantages are the difficulty in getting all organizations to agree on requirements, high cost, and the danger of the impact of a wide area disaster where many organizations may want to use the data center at the same time.

Disaster/Recovery Services

Since 1976, the critical need for computer backup has been recognized. Companies have been formed to provide this service through the establishment of computer 'hot' sites coupled with shells or 'cold' sites. Based on cost, service, availability, and security, this approach has been most popular for companies seriously interested in uninterrupted computer service to internal users and the public.

The disadvantage of commercial Disaster/Recovery services may depend on the contract; however, it should be pointed out that a subscription fee covers a specified hardware/network configuration, and any added equipment will increase cost.

Sister Organizations

Such companies have two or more DP complexes that ultimately report to the same person or group. Ostensibly each data center will use others within the same organization as computer backup locations. While cost may seem to be an advantage, this approach is losing popularity. One of the major problems is that each division subsidiary, or company, has a high degree of autonomy and cannot or will not cooperate with the others. Another problem is the varying technical and hardware growth rates at each data center. These growth differentials can cause compatibility problems.

Duplicate Sites

Surprisingly popular, replicated sites have been built by large corporations for two major reasons. First is the need for very rapid recovery of highly complex networks, i.e. financial or credit card institutions. The second major reason for building a duplicate data center is sheer size. Many major organizations have data centers far larger than the commercial disaster service centers.

Other Aspects of the Computer Backup Site

Once an organization has selected the type of recovery service (i.e. service bureau, sister organization, or commercial disaster recovery service), then other aspects of the computer backup site can be reviewed. It may be useful to build a matrix of all significant technical, administrative, and physical factors which will impact the data centers. In the first column of the matrix, these factors should be listed. In the other column, list how each vendor reflects the organization's needs as well as how one vendor stacks up against another. Table 11-1 is a sample matrix.

The preceding items are only a *few* examples of factors relating to the type of computer backup services to be selected. The purpose of the comparison matrix is to permit a balanced review of all options. Additionally, one can quickly eliminate those options which are unsuitable, and can professionally present an unbiased relationale to management.

To improve the results of the matrix, add a weight to each factor depending on its importance to you. The weighted factors can also be scored according to how

TABLE 11-1
Vendor comparison matrix

Factor	Your organization's requirements	Backup 'A'	Backup 'B'
CPU type			
CPU memory size			
Stand-Alone CPU			
Shared CPU			
Operating System			
Tape drives			
Disk drives			
Test hours per year			
CPU available (days)			
CPU available (hours in day)			
CPU available (shared hours)			
Front-end processor Type			
Front-end processor Size			
Front-end processor Adaptors			
Line sets			
Modems available			
Dial backup modems			
Local loops available			
Printer requirement			
Bursters			
Decollators			
Office/work space			
Forms storage space: Locked storage Off-site storage			
Security Personnel control Guards Delivery of data/reports Protection of Personnel			
Security airport pickup COM available			
Data entry Type of machine			
Number of machines			
Hours available			
Personnel available			
Food cost available			
Hotel available			
Hotel reservations			
Technical manuals			
Software			
Special equipment			

well the backup service meets your needs. For example, a score of 0 indicates that the factor is not available or not offered by the backup. A score of 1 indicates that the factor may be addressed but is not satisfactory, a score of 2 indicates that the factor is addressed and is satisfactory, and a score of 3 is awarded when the factor exceeds your requirement. The score can be multiplied by the weighted factor to improve the accuracy of the analysis.

IMPLEMENTATION TESTING

When the plan is written, and the computer and other backup sites are selected, final testing can begin. However, even if a computer or other types of backup have not been selected, certain test phases can still be accomplished. However, this early testing outside of the computer backup will improve the plan rather than prove recovery capability. Suggested tests phases are: notification, resource, organization/responsibility, in-house, software, telecommunications, application, and systems test. The use of phase tests rather than a full-blown systems test will ensure that each step is correct before proceeding to the next one.

Notification Test

This test can be conducted on the weekend or at night at very little cost. The objective of this test is to make sure that the team phone numbers are correct and that enough people with the appropriate talents can be contacted to support the various recovery functions. If notification fails, there is no point in going to the next step.

Resource Test

This test is a review by physical inventory/audit of all resources, supplies, forms, and other material which are stored at the various locations designated in the plan. This test can be conducted during normal business hours at low cost. It is important to assure that Disaster/Recovery and operational resources are available prior to the full systems test.

The first two tests proved that sufficient people and resources are available to effect recovery.

Organization/Responsibility Test

This test measures two additional points. The test is held after training of team personnel is completed. All team personnel and alternates are notified to assemble at the Command and Control Center. After arrival, the team personnel are tested as to their responsibilities. The test measures the time required for assembly at the Command and Control Center, and the second measurement is the knowledge that the Disaster/Recovery team personnel have concerning the procedures covering their responsibilities in a disaster incident, real or simulated. The test normally takes 4 to 5 hours.

In-house Tests

This test is a scenario wherein all tapes and discs currently in use at the data center are not used for recovery. The tape library is off limits to the recovery team. The teams are notified and assembled; then the off-site stored material is brought to the data center and used to restart the system. The backup data sets are used to run the system and, depending on their age, can be compared to the runs made when the data were current. By comparing previous runs, no effort need be expended in reconstructing recent transactions.

Software Tests

These tests are normally done in situations where the organization needs an I/O generation or wants to practice loading software, either stand alone or under V.M. Please remember to ensure that the tape is readable by testing it before departure for the backup site.

Telecommunication Testing

This type of testing is often conducted in conjunction with software tests. This test ensures that dial backup modems, other hardware and software are operational between terminals of RJE sites and the backup computer location.

Application Tests

These tests are often used to concentrate all recovery efforts on one highly critical application. The concept here is that all of the bugs can be worked out of complex systems on a system-by-system basis.

Systems Test

This complete test of all applications and telecommunications takes place at the computer backup site. It is this test that most people have in mind when Disaster/Recovery Testing is first envisioned. Based on long and bitter experience, however a controlled step-by-step approach to testing is suggested.

CONCLUSIONS

Because of the space limitations of this chapter, only highlights of Disaster/Recovery concepts were reviewed. Still, the areas that have been discussed should be summarized.

The two types of strategic planning are opportunities and contingency planning. Data center Disaster/Recovery is a subset of contingency planning. To get started on the recovery plan, one must script the project for success. To achieve success people must be assigned to the project exclusively. It is also important to conduct project kickoff meetings, enforce schedules, hold project status meetings, develop detailed project work plans, insist that project status reporting be performed, assign high level responsibility for successful completion of the project, assign backup people in case of termination, provide close direction to maintain scope, and ensure that project personnel have a good chance of completing the plan successfully. Finally, the procedures ancillary to the plan, but not used in a disaster incident, should be requested by management. These ancillary procedures are training, testing, and maintenance procedures which are all important to project success.

The example project life cycle and control system that was suggested included seven phases: initiation, evaluation, planning, analysis/design, development, implementation, and testing.

The initiation and evaluation have already been discussed in this summary.

The Planning Phase is a combined effort of MIS management and the Disaster/Recovery Project personnel. Some basic topics are plan (project) scope, plan distribution, areas to be included in and excluded from the plan, measurement for the successful completion of the plan, a definition of the data center restoration program, and finally the types of disasters and the time frame covered. Mainly the plan must protect against any contingency, local or widespread disaster that could bring computer service to a halt from a time period exceeding the pain threshold of the organization. Writing style, plan structure, and team organization should be established in the Planning Phase.

In the Analysis Phase for the Disaster/Recovery Project, the majority of plan data is collected as well as some design refinement.

The Development Phase is used to insert the data gathered in the Analysis Phase into the plan structure determined in the Planning Phase.

The Implementation Phase of the developed recovery plan can be improved by testing with or without a computer backup. Those tests which can be conducted without a computer backup are: notification, resource, organization/responsibility, and in-house tests. The tests requiring a backup computer site are: software, telecommunication, application, and operations tests.

THE FUTURE

The future for data centers is fraught with danger. As organizations depend more and more on the computer to assist in the successful completion of day-to-day functions, the need for each data center to have a tested recovery plan in place will become mandatory. At the very time that this dependence is increasing, technology is becoming increasingly vulnerable to intentional and accidental occurrences which would have financially serious or fatal consequences.

As a result, MIS will lead the way in recovery planning, and in the future the rest of the organization will realize that other segments must also have the same recovery capabilities as do the data processing group. For example, in many companies the data center is located in or near corporate headquarters or in key critical work areas. Even if the computer operation were to be quickly recovered, it would still be necessary to recover other functions to create input and utilize output. Because of this vital need for total recovery planning, the corporate contingency planner, whether an in-house or outside consultant, will have a bright future.

In regard to computer backup services, currently ten organizations are offering computer centers for backup. Over the next 5 years the number of companies offering the service for most major maxi-computers and most of the viable super-minicomputers will increase. The current subscribers to computer backup services will increase tenfold or more in the 1980s. Surprisingly so will the number of mutual backup agreements increase as data centers move from a no backup situation to a mutual support agreement. Even though support agreements provide little real protection, data centers tend to go through an evolutionary thought process about recovery planning as they mature. Many organizations will move into a mutual agreement and then in a few years will sign a contract for a commercial computer backup service.

Consortiums will have little growth during the next decade; on the other hand, duplicate or replicated data centers will be a fast growing solution for computer backup. The main reason for this phenomenon is that these large company data centers are often three, four, or more times larger than the typical commercial backup services, and must seek other means of recovery.

Shell sites will not grow quickly because of the high cost versus the low protection offered and the fact that most commercial backup computer services also supply shells as a part of their offering.

Telecommunications backup will be immensely simplified by less dependence on land lines, improved commercial offerings by private network companies, and improved hardware/software. The dark side of the future indicates increasing violence, fraud, terrorism, and more polarization between those who want to destroy society and the security personnel trying to protect it.

One area not completely clear at this time is how government agencies intend to provide backup for their data centers. Thus far the government data centers are using mutual backup agreements which are entirely inadequate. It would seem that the federal government, which was the leader in Disaster/Recovery in the 1970s, would look toward duplicate sites for backup to assure continuation of critical operations.

The future for Disaster/Recovery is this: Virtually all data centers will have to have a tested Disaster/Recovery Plan in the next 5 years; as smaller data centers mature and become vitally important to their organization, then they also must plan.

Finally, Board of Directors Audit Committees, top management, and data processing executives who are aware of the need for a tested recovery plan and do nothing have a dim future indeed—and, if a fatal disaster occurs, will have no future at all.

Advances in Computer Security Management, Vol. 2
Edited by M. M. Wofsey
© 1983 John Wiley & Sons Ltd.

Chapter 12

FUTURE DEVELOPMENTS IN DATA PROCESSING SECURITY

Stanley C. Mashakas

U.S. Department of Justice

In 1789, Benjamin Franklin stated, 'In this world nothing is certain but death and taxes'. Today, another thing is certain: data processing is constantly changing and those involved in it must maintain an awareness of the state of the art and where technology developments will lead.

This chapter explores the future of data processing, projects expected developments, and extrapolates the impact of these expected developments on ADP security requirements. The reader should keep in mind that this projection is based upon an increasing demand for reliability and availability of data processing and could be seriously altered by economic, social, or political pressures on data processing developments. For example, a worldwide shortage of natural resources could cause substantial emphasis to be placed on the efficient use of available resources and the preservation of the environment rather than on the development and improvement of data processing in associated areas of natural resource control. The result of this chapter is an attempt to project the automated system of the next decade and the interrelationships of the major security issues facing this new technology.

As a rule, the broad scope of computer technology—processors, memory units, peripherals, communication equipment, and software—makes forecasting a task requiring knowledge of the design and operation of component subsystems, as well as understanding of underlying principles, design, and processes of the components. Whether it is necessary to involve all the associated technologies depends on the context in which the forecast is to be used and the level of detail needed to make a determination. Assessing the state of the art and forecasting future developments in computer technology is used here only for the purposes of ADP security planning, development, and administration.

The method of forecasting selected is a mixture of associated component and subsystem techniques which should become standard in future systems. The present uses, inherent advantages and disadvantages, technological barriers, physical limitations, and alternative technologies are considered. Forecasts, therefore, are quantitative and directed to the effects of changes on the cost, performance, and security factors in that the changes may restrict system utilization.

Forecasts need not come true or be positive in outlook to be valuable. Forecasts, if prepared and acted upon by management, may have a chance of becoming a reality. Forecasts, in the case of pessimistic or negative projection, may predict issues which can hinder organizational progress and contingencies that are prepared to sustain organizational growth. Even if forecasts prove to be erroneous, the efforts of management may aid in surpassing planned objectives. But overly optimistic forecasts, which lead to the allocation of scarce resources for goals that are technically, administratively, or operationally unattainable, are not valuable. The reader is reminded that the critical issue of the effects of technological developments centers on who will have access to the data and what kind of controls and safeguards will be established.

In order to maintain technical stability in data processing, numerous conditions, including management awareness, improved system reliability, and a sound program of standards, are required. These requirements are derived from the fact that as systems increase in complexity and capability, the successful implementation of security can be enhanced, to a greater extent, through timely development of reliable hardware and software, system standards integrated into the life cycle development of component systems, and, finally, a management commitment to protection, prevention, and recovery mechanisms for data processing.

Computer technology, although relatively new, has its share of forecasting errors by persons capable in the field. It has been stated that Tom Watson delayed IBM's entry into the computer industry with his belief that ten computers would suffice for the entire United States. A forecast in 1951, by England's foremost computer expert, predicted that all the computations that would ever be needed in England could be performed by three computers under construction, and no one else would ever need computers nor could they afford them.

COMPUTER SYSTEMS IN THE NEXT DECADE

Hardware

An important factor in determining the architecture of tomorrow's processors derives from the desirability of manufacturing circuits in the most standardized form possible. One of the most significant developments in computer technology has been the decreased cost of such circuitry for logic and memory. It is predictable that each advance in density technology will result in a visible trend to decentralization of many data processing functions. Thus, in the next decade, with advances in super density packaging coupled with dramatic increases in speed and performance, hardware suppliers could build mainframes with an internal performance rating of 50 million instructions per second (50 MIPS), 64 thousand (64K) bytes of cache memory, and 16 million (16M) bytes of main storage on a single chip. But, negative predictions suggest that computers will not become faster by orders of magnitude because of the difficulties and high research costs encountered in the development of the needed circuits. I remain positive in my outlook to hardware development because, if a desire for faster computers exists, research will achieve such capabilities.

Additionally, as high density technology advances, computer systems will probably be based on multiple independent processors that operate under a standard operating system. When a component fails, the operating system directs the work load to other resources and the processing continues. Reliability is also enhanced in that two or more processors should be able to detect and react to an error situation and contain its effects better than a single, possibly faulty, processor attempting self analysis. Such redundancy or fail-safe, will result from hardware innovation as opposed to software because of the continual needs for software maintenance.

Architecturally, to the degree possible, modules at the microprocessor and even higher level will be used in preference to designing new specialized circuits. The intrinsically high reliability of such modules, in controlled environments, will significantly motivate manufacturers to replace electromechanical interfaces. The specialized processors are likely to have their functions determined by microcoded stored logic to facilitate standardized manufacture and maintenance.

Increased parallelism is likely to be used to reduce the wait times encountered in interlink data transfer and manipulation operations. By increasing parallelism, the hope is to achieve orders of magnitude for program needs. Such parallelism is likely to be realized in the form of other specialized processors dedicated to I/O, file and data base management, memory and interrupt processing, and security administration. For example, front-end processors for telecommunications and remote terminal access capable of interchanging data with the main processor should become standard. Also, back-end processors for such functions as interpreting user authorization levels, scheduling accesses, and managing storage hierarchies are all potentially available. Data should only leave the system being archived and transported on-line to a disaster processor or off-line to mass storage for emergency backup.

Predictably, multi-level hierarchical storage systems, automatic data migration, and multiple error correction should become a necessity of memory design. Because of very large real and virtual address spaces available, different levels of storage should be transparent to the user. Each major level will be subdivided according to speed, access time, and cost into a schema to address memory storage for primary, secondary, disaster, and archival functions. The various processors within the mainframe should be able to access large memory blocks in such multi-level memories. Enhancements will include cross-memory services, which allow a large program access to additional space, and multi-level memory search.

A trend to keep all data on-line should force manufacturers to ensure archival and backup memory capabilities that are inexpensive, and physically immune to any system failure that might destroy its contents. Disaster and archival functions may be combined or remain separate depending on the advances in circuitry. Magnetic bubbles, holograms, and other features may be preferable for this type of requirement.

Also, one distinct advantage of computers in the future is the environment required. Power and cooling required for large systems today are significantly different from those required for smaller systems. Most minicomputers are air-cooled while mainframes, as a rule, are liquid cooled. The disadvantages of liquid cooling are that it requires special plumbing and makes it more difficult to move the processor once it has been configured. Power is another distinction between mainframes and minis. Mainframes tend to operate with three phase power, while minis can generally use standard power. With the modular approach to expanding from a small system to a larger configuration, only minimal differences should occur in power and cooling requirements. Environmental problems will persist, though, owing to the number of peripherals tied to a system.

Software

Demands will escalate to increase the efficiency and effectiveness of system software. While hardware technology continues to improve dramatically, software technology continues, as always, to lag behind it. The result of such lag has been computer systems that utilize only a fraction of their capabilities. The trend for the future should be toward removing core robbing, inefficient systems software and replacing it with products designed to improve performance of the hardware, the application the system is processing, or the relationship with the user.

For purposes of this chapter, software is defined as the collection of programs, however created and subsequently translated, that are executed by the hardware. These programs can be divided into four generic classes: systems operation, systems control, programming languages, and applications.

Because of the innovations in hardware technology, a trend will be to increase the availability of software functions in hardware and firmware. Many of the system control functions now performed by operating system software are likely to be embedded in microcoded instruction for uniform, logical, and stable extension of the hardware. The storage used for operating system execution will be isolated from access by the user through some architecture to apply program verification, similar to the security kernel concepts for providing uncircumventable, shared systems. Rather than try to prove that the entire operating system meets all the specifications, developers can centralize all the operations affecting reliability or integrity into the nucleus of a software security kernel. The correct functioning of a kernel implies a secure system.

The major system operation functions of today's operating systems, i.e., job scheduling, error monitoring, recovery, system management, and control, should be performed by relatively simple monitors dedicated to specific modes of operation and operating in some form of virtual machine environment. Although these functions are expected to increase steadily in importance, they are also expected to decrease in sophistication and become clearly separated from the operating system proper. The goal of operating systems in the future will be toward development of a multi-user, shared resource operating system which by constructive means is certifiably secure and highly reliable.

Computer systems should automatically log and report the data needed to control related external activities, e.g. user accounting, billing, and references to protected files. The logging system, protected by the security schema and inaccessible to the users, will log all references. Performance measurement facilities will become more desirable so that system managers can observe the performance of users and programs and balance system resources accordingly.

Job control or command languages should become simpler because of the degree of automation within the computer system, meaning that users will be able to provide less detailed instructions. Simplifications will include higher level symbols closer to natural language and interactive command facilities to aid users in defining their requirements. Command and programming language should be combined so that the user will not be conscious of using one or the other, but will address the machine in a combination of both.

Some of the basic improvements of emerging software technology will be in the development of newer and more powerful programming languages such as ADA, Forth, C, and Lisp. The functional capabilities of programming languages, such as COBOL, FORTRAN, and PL/1, should not change dramatically. The use of precompiliers to augment these languages will reduce the time to develop and maintain applications by accommodating structured programming techniques. Therefore, an improvement in programmer productivity should emerge.

If one looks at the type of applications being developed today, large programming efforts oriented toward the use of data bases, remote processing, real-time, on-line, networking distributed systems are visualized. The major effort of applications development in the future will be to improve application reliability and maintenance through enhancement of the original application.

No control of applications can occur unless discipline and accountability can be installed in the operational environment. Accountability will become the measurement of provable software. By accountability, one can identify the programmer who wrote each line of code. When an error occurs, the programmer whose code was the source of the problem is easily identified. Accountability should not remove the requirement to produce easily understandable and maintainable software. The use of programming tools should readily aid in satisfying the next decade of software requirements.

Present efforts for data base systems involve improvements in system functions or improvements in system performance. System function design addresses data languages and data dictionaries. System performance design addresses workload descriptors and design, plus optimization of files. No matter how inexpensive the hardware becomes, data base systems will require designs for improvements in efficiency. Look to the future for data base systems that are easier to use, are more powerful, and optimize programmer efficiency through ease of use.

For smaller systems, cross compilers should become available and should aid networking. For medium- and large-scale machines, compiling will be done on the central processor and complete sets of languages should be available.

Finally, one thought must be added concerning software costs. The trend toward separate pricing of software should continue. The operating system should not be expected to be software priced because the basic system should have fewer functions and be less visible to the user. On the other hand, separately sold or developed software will be measured by performance and quality if it is to remain competitive. User requirements, program development, and maintenance costs will force standard improvements in all areas of software development. Message control software could be priced separately to offset the low hardware costs.

Communications

Input/output controllers, teleprocessing controllers, multiplexers, concentrators, and modems will become more independent, self-checking, and asynchronous. Small computers and intelligent terminals should be provided with a limited degree of communications control capability, since they will be connected to communication lines. Although they should cost less to implement than larger computer stand-alone alternatives, many minicomputer-based local networks should rival the processing power of typical time-sharing systems. Small, local networks also expand more easily, provide better reliability, and are more immune to response time variations than time-shared configurations. The most significant advantage of such local networks is that they put computing power at the discretion of the user. Again, a significant opportunity to boost productivity and applications development is available.

Fiber optics is a technology that will prove to be a practical, easy to handle means of communicating large amounts of data at faster rates with increased integrity. Since fiber optics is the transmission of light, the absence of copper conductors with electrical impulses makes this technology impervious to electromagnetic interference (EMI) or radio frequency interference (RFI). Since the generation of such interference is the basis for the TEMPEST phenomenon, fiber optics provides low cost and unmatched transmission security. This added benefit will not be the reason for widespread acceptance. Rather the lightweight, compact, high data rate handling capabilities over their electrical counterparts will force the acceptance of this technology.

Satellites offer additional flexibility to data communication services in terms of routing capabilities, contingencies, and costs per service. In addition to acquiring leased or dial-up services, users will have the alternative of using packet-type switching. Packet switching technology allows improvement in data communication services and makes possible network performance capabilities tailored to user requirements. Such capabilities are rapid response time, high reliability through redundancy, low error rates, dynamic allocation of transmission capacity through node sharing, and finally charges proportional to traffic volume.

With large processors, embedded communication controllers or front-end processors will be used for telecommunications. The host-dependent controllers now used will be superseded by this design. The new system controllers will route, sequence, and account for streams of message traffic, similar to the Department of Defense Automated Digital Network (AUTODIN). Automatic data compression will be accomplished within the front-end processor.

Secure communications in a physically vulnerable network depend upon cryptography to pass data between two machines. Encryption and decryption will become standard requirements within the devices, and their overall security functions will be similar to those performed by comparable cryptographic devices but their costs are expected to drop dramatically. Conventional encryption algorithms like the Data Encryption Standard (DES) and those employing public key encryption algorithms will be the basis for this security.

SYSTEMS ENVIRONMENT

The successful operation of EDP in the future will be heavily dependent on a resource sharing network environment. The advent of such an environment is likely only if a number of known networking problems are resolved. But if one were to realize the breadth of the field of computer applications and the requirement to access geographically remote computer resources, such an environment, as described, is not totally unlikely for the future.

The four aspects to consider for the systems environment of the future are administrative or office automation, data processing, data base administration, and telecommunications. These four disciplines must be combined for efficient performance. Local networks will allow these functions to communicate back and forth.

This section, therefore, describes a general-purpose computer system in a network environment. The mechanism used to communicate data from point to point will utilize fiber optics cabling for short distances and satellite communications utilizing packet switching techniques for long distances. In a network environment, the problem of accessing resources is totally different from that in the traditional stand-alone computer system. Also, if one were to list the many threats to the integrity of the computer system, Figure 12-1 would illustrate this concern. In a network, the number of weak links increases dramatically if the security problem is not addressed initially during the design of the network.

Typically, all access path functions are centralized in the host computers front-end communications processor. At the remote end, all the network interface functions are in the intelligent terminal or, in the case of computer-to-computer interface, in the remote communications processor. The key reason is to make available processor resources for application processing and still satisfy the functions that the network needs to provide for an effective access between two users. The operating system of the host computer supports all office functions—from word processing to application design and the way users interface with the

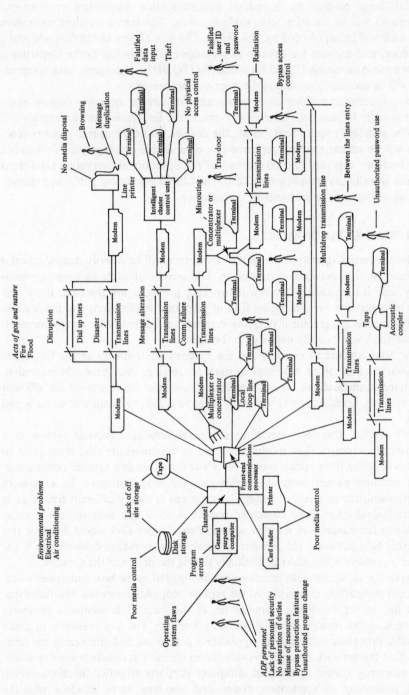

Figure 12-1. Network configuration vulnerability diagram.

system. The end user is required to learn a single operating system to control multiple operations on multiple machines, for functions ranging from manipulating letters within an organization to assessing the host computer for data base manipulations.

To give the remote user access to processor-based resources after log-on and authentication, the host front-end processor satisfies the following network functions:

1. Makes sure a transmission path exists utilizing the links available, bypassing failed circuits.
2. Accommodates buffer sizes and flow control with economies for intermittent use utilizing packet switching and fast circuit switching techniques.
3. Satisfies error checking and correction functions.
4. Accommodates end-user format language requirements through protocol conversions and session dialogue management.

A log of all processes conducted in the transaction processor is maintained. Authorization and semantic integrity rules for such transactions are under the purview of the operating system security kernel. Execution of the transaction may involve several application programs. The applications library is maintained by an administrator responsible for control and development of all programs. In the multi-level memory concept described previously, the data base resides in different levels based on user profiles. Authorization rules control access to resources, objects in the data base, and the applications library.

The back-end processor is designed to assist the host processor in data base management. The back-end processor receives requests from the host, does the necessary search and retrieval, returns the requested data to the host, or makes the specified changes to the data base. The data base processor is specifically designed to be a slave to the host CPU. It employs microprocessors for each track on a cylinder so an entire memory may be read in parallel, and it contains a pipeline processor architecture so that many processes may be performed on data simultaneously. A security filter processor embedded in the design can reject requests which do not conform to the data base access controls. The ability of the back-end processor to provide adequate security against malicious or accidental access to the data is enhanced by its linkage to the transaction processor. Therefore, there are no paths through separate file management or holes because of memory protection breaches. The basic advantage to this approach is that the hardware and data base software can be specialized for the data base functions. This approach eliminates general-purpose operating system software, develops smaller programs requiring less processing time, and results in a smaller on-line system requiring less core.

A policy of least privilege is maintained throughout the transaction. Data can only leave the system after being encrypted and archived. Figure 12-2 illustrates the operation of the remote user in this network with identified security mechanisms within the environment.

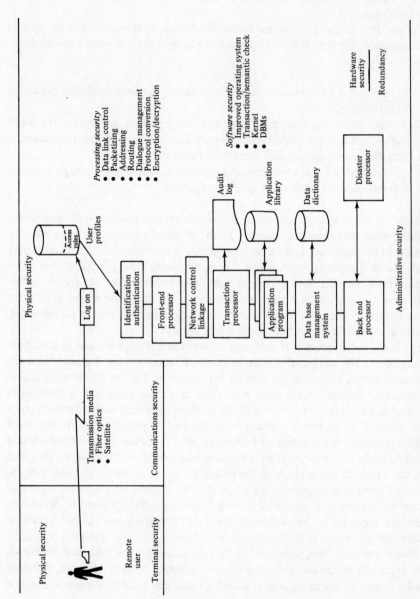

Figure 12-2. Security mechanisms for network application processing.

ARCHITECTURE FOR SECURITY

If security features are incorporated into the design of future computer systems, the architectural features, as described, should be feasible at reasonable cost. The increasing importance of sharing information among different users of a common data base and limiting damage in case of errors or malfunctions contribute to the growing pressure on developers to design better computer systems. The desired security architectural features are as follows:

1. Controlled access to resources through adequate access permission incorporated into description mechanisms. A description should contain the access permission to the object level which has been determined by the security processor. Access privileges are granted only to perform stated functions.
2. A permanent security level maintained for each object. (This feature is proposed in the security kernel discussed previously.) Hardware implementation of this concept would extend to the storage devices so that instructions to any device would have to include a security level attribute verified by the hardware. Data access requests would be verified with respect to the security level of the process requesting the information transfer.
3. Different user access capabilities to the same object in an environment of controlled sharing. The requirement for multiple access capabilities to the same object implies that the access capabilities cannot reside with the object itself but must be represented in descriptors residing with the process accessing the object.
4. Continuous access permission checking and transaction logging. Access controls that operate at the external level verify that each user attempting to access the system is authentic. Access controls that operate at the internal level verify that each running program generates references only to authorized segments of memory. Ideally access controls operate each request in a domain of least privilege. (This feature is designed against the Trojan Horse security problem. This security problem results from an authorized and trusted user supplying a routine that, in addition to performing its stated function, creates a data communication path to transmit additional information back to the user.)
5. Control over all memory space, particularly in a multi-memory level hierarchy. Flow controls regulate the dissemination or copying of information by prohibiting derived data from having a lower classification than the original data accessed. (This feature offers a partial solution to the Confinement security problem. Confinement is the problem of ensuring that a program will not transmit information to another program unless authorized to do such a transfer.)
6. A security processor to enforce all the security rules in the system. This processor must be isolated from other processes by varying degrees of com-

plexity through hierarchical concepts of capabilities (security being the highest capability).

7. Access controls applied to all storage devices or channels. A method for controling access to devices is through dedication of certain portions of memory. Therefore, access to devices is relegated to each user based on his profile. Inference controls prevent 'leakage' through programs that produce summaries of groups of records. This technique reduces the risk that a user, restricted by access and flow controls, can deduce the data denied him by correlating the response from many summaries. (This deduction of data from correlation is known as the 'Census' security problem.)

8. Transfer from one processor to another. Such transfers are controlled through the semantic integrity checks of the security kernel. Cryptographic controls protect information stored or transmitted in the system.

EDP SECURITY MANAGEMENT

The conclusion of this chapter is devoted to identifying a range of security issues and discussing the considerations that must be given to these concerns. As discussed previously, a very large research effort is engaged in designing computer security to various aspects of EDP, i.e. operating systems, data base management systems, and others. Resolution of the known security weaknesses in present computer systems will allow computer security practitioners to address newer problems or resolve areas that were considered unsolvable.

An obvious need is to apply the principles of sound security management to the emerging developments of EDP. The speed of technological advancements and the increasing sophistication of software mandate that organizations that lack computer security basics catch up and implement measures now to avoid disaster or obsolescence in the future. Although most organizations are aware of the need for traditional physical security and internal access controls, they are oblivious to many of the other aspects of computer security. Management awareness is slowly emerging with regard to the additional effort needed to reduce the potential from other, ignored and significant security weaknesses. Only through a total EDP security program can management feel reasonably secure that its efforts to reduce risk potential to an acceptable level are satisfactory. Only with an ongoing effort can an organization react with a practical approach as new security problems arise. The focus will be on those additional issues which will face EDP management in the future, namely, liability, accreditation, authentication, auditing, personnel, and disaster recovery.

Liability

The question of legal liability will certainly become an issue of the future. The Foreign Corrupt Practices Act of 1977 places a particular responsibility on the management of an organization for the correctness and control of an organization's data. Applying an even broader principle of law, a director of a corporation is legally obligated to use the same degree of care in the performance of his duties that a reasonable, prudent man would use in his own private business. Because of such guidance as Office of Management and Budget (OMB) Circular A-71, which addresses minimum security requirements for government EDP operations, the question of liability will also move into the government sector. What then is the legal liability of the management official responsible for EDP who fails to apply adequate security for a computer system? In the private sector, the management officials of corporations are subject to derivative suits by stockholders. The answer to liability in each sector will be decided on a case-by-case basis.

When considering that this question of liability would only surface after a loss of processing capability, it is quite likely that decisions could go against management. Questions as to 'What is reasonable?' will likely be answered by comparing the security techniques applied in a similar competitor's EDP environment. Questions as to 'What is prudent?' will be resolved by considering those security policies and techniques that were implemented after a risk assessment of the organization's EDP operation.

Probably no defense exists for a management that has not conducted a risk assessment or implemented a basic computer security program. Again, it will be very difficult to defend one's lack of action if management, through a formal risk analysis, had received documented evidence of the potential threats and vulnerabilities to his operation. One possible defense centers on 'assumption of risk' in which the plaintiff states that he was aware of the risks inherent in the situation but chose to ignore them or decided that the cost of protection outweighed the risks involved. A word of caution is offered for those who propose this line of defense; some legal scholars maintain that 'assumption of risk' is but a form of 'contributory negligence', in that one is negligent by assuming the risk. The best possible defense is the 'state of the art' defense used in product liability. If one can prove that a product (in this defense, the product is EDP operations) is as safe as the current state of the art permits, there can be no strict liability by the plaintiff. This approach is similar to the 'super due care' defense, which states that the system operates at a time when technology allows no safer product.

A legal body should surface that will specialize in computer related issues, i.e. violations of software, patent or design, violations of privacy, computer fraud and embezzlement, legally admissible evidence, and liability or damage claims.

Standards/Accreditation

Because of the liability issue, many management officials will want assurance from their staff that the company's security efforts are adequate. Therefore, the future holds major efforts to develop formalized, standard processes for certification and accreditation of systems. Minimum standards for application areas will be proposed so that systems can be approved for operation in a specific environment with a particular type of application, e.g. payroll disbursement, personnel, and others. It will be imperative for organizations to develop objective criteria in the form of standards to identify sensitive data and establish effective controls to protect such data during processing. The lack of accreditation will not prohibit an organization from implementing its systems, but it will be a benchmark of the risk to secure operations. Accreditation will be the management defense that its efforts have been reasonable and sufficient to counter the known threats to the environment. Therefore, minimum standards and policy for acceptable levels of risk will be identified. Rather than measure a single attribute of a system, a list of the minimum required safeguards will be evaluated, i.e. level of sensitive data and processing, capabilities of users, personnel, physical, operational, technical, and administrative security practices.

It should not be the role of the proposed standards to specify or recommend a specific set of protection mechanisms, whether they are in hardware or software. The standards should be a clearly desirable set of attributes and approaches whose presence would at least indicate that the system administrators are familiar with applying state-of-the-art techniques for computer security. Only after evaluating all the attributes of a given system can one identify the security requirements needed to operate in a given environment.

The best example of the possible use of security standards for certification can be described in a recent Lloyd's of London insurance policy for Electronic Funds Transfer (EFT). Essentially, the normal policy on bankers bond largely prohibits coverage for EFT theft. Specifically, banks cannot obtain insurance for EFT thefts except for cases of direct employee dishonesty. One specific bank management, disturbed about the weakness in coverage, approached Lloyd's. After determining that there was a need for electronic and computer crime coverage indeed existed, the insurance company developed a detailed application procedure for coverage. The application for coverage involves the following characteristics:

1. The applicant must provide a lengthy audit guide prepared by a data security officer.
2. The applicant must provide system control documentation and a description of the EDP environment.
3. The applicant must allow an on-site risk management survey by independent auditors.

The uniqueness of this insurance is that it is non-standard coverage, and the underwriters can be restrictive in areas in which they feel uncomfortable with the controls.

Table 12-1 illustrates the protective mechanisms that will lead to the accreditation process.

Table 12-1
Accreditation matrix

	Physical safeguards	Administrative safeguards	Data Sensitivity controls	Terminal security	
Authorization • Resource control assurance mechanisms					Contingency planning
EDP security policy • System requirements for EDP	Identification of users	Access controls	Authentication scenario	Security administration	
Detection • Security assessment tools	Audit monitoring	Security officer monitors	EDP security assessment	Risk analysis	
Prevention • Mechanisms to support security policy	Data security controls	Verification of system operation	Security policy enforcement	Personnel security	
Hardware • Verification of secure operation	Software checks	Fault detection	Component redundancy		
Software • Support for security policy	System design specifications	Off-site storage	Accreditation of design	Verification of implementation	Security kernel
Operation • Maintenance of security confidence	Configuration control	Resource management	Formalized verification	Separation of duties	
Development • Use of standards	Structured programming	Automated testing	On-line auditing		

Authentication

Because research continues to remove hardware and software weaknesses and therefore tightens up the computer itself, the problem of verifying the individual user will generate much renewed interest. If a computer system is to provide controlled access to resources, the overall control mechanism associated with this system must have some technique for determining and verifying the identity of the user. Identification is defined as the process of determining who the user claims to be. Then, authentication is the process of verifying the user's identity. All users can affect the security of the system and must be uniquely identified and subsequently authenticated. In the most ideal situation, a user would have a universal unique identifier and an appropriate unique authenticator.

Traditionally, a resource-sharing centralized computer system is concerned with providing controlled user access to resources through identification, authentication, and authorization scenarios. In the normal access control mechanism, this procedure is accomplished through the User ID/Password/ Authorization format. The following discussion highlights the security weaknesses of such an approach.

In a single computer system, alphanumeric passwords are typed by the user to authenticate the user identifier. Authorization is granted upon valid submission. The inherent security disadvantages of this method of authorization are as follows:

1. Generation of passwords can be from two sources: the user or a security administrator. If a user generates the password, analysis reveals that it will be very short, easily remembered, seldom changed, and often distributed to other users so that it loses the property of being unique. To resolve these concerns, the responsibility for password generation and change can be delegated to a security administrator. Again, analysis reveals that such generation only resolves the problem of infrequent change and this method of generation suffers from the weaknesses described previously.

2. Some method must be provided to hide passwords when they are being submitted to the system for authorization. Overwrite routines have been employed on hard-copy terminals to obliterate an area before typing in the password. On CRT terminals, this practice is not always possible. Therefore, an over-the-shoulder observation can compromise the password before it is accepted by the system and removed from the CRT screen.

3. Some form of identification of the device must be made, in addition to identifying the user, especially when the weaknesses of passwords are known. All remote terminals require physical security and procedural controls to prevent theft and unauthorized use. Assurance that such restrictions are in effect is also required. Experience has shown that physical security and procedural controls are weak to non-existent in most remote terminal areas. To verify the terminal location, call-back routines were employed. Once a user logged on and identified himself, operator intervention took

place. A phone call was placed to a predefined number where the user was to be located. If verification was made, the user was allowed to continue with processing. Such a technique is administratively and operationally impractical because of the constant changes to the user community. Coded cards, for terminal unlocking and physical identification, were proposed and utilized to resolve this issue. Essentially this proposed solution suffers from the same problem that keys have—soon everyone has one. The card is no longer unique to the system because everyone now possesses the capability. Also, the card is seldom recalled when a person is transferred or their requirements for usage change. Techniques which rely on the use of cards or keys are also vulnerable to being compromised by a counterfeit copy of the original.

4. Authentication of the user must be continuous. Once a user logs on and authenticates himself, a procedure must exist to assure that he remains the original user. The answer lies in some type of physical connection to the terminal. The need for unlendable passwords and continuous authentication has led to the development of measures to include physiologic identifiers, i.e. fingerprints, voiceprints, handwriting analysis, and even polygraph-type techniques. No such perfected technique is in place because of the difficulty of performing precise, repeatable measurements. In order to perform repeatable measurement of a personal attribute, reference profiles on associated identifiers have been utilized. A central file containing identifiers unique to the individual is established. Once the user enters a request to access the system, the file is accessed and a random number of identifiers is used for vertification. The main disadvantages of this method of authentication are:

   a. This technique is not intended to satisfy the need for continuous identification but rather makes repeatable measurement more precise.

   b. The method employs data processing to support identification. The EDP functions required are the same as needed for any application, i.e. a computer program, processing, storage, maintenance, and others. These requirements could be extensive considering the number of users and the attributes. An advantage is that this method may be derived from or be used in conjunction with other security programs, i.e. access controls.

5. Communication line security should be available to protect the password transmission from the terminal to the computer. Cryptographic techniques and devices have been proposed and utilized. Unfortunately, the mystique surrounding cryptography has led many DP managers to believe that the authentication issue has also been solved with the implementation of such sophistication. What has been implemented is really a technique intended for the larger overall system design for security.

But advancements in authentication should result in standards for persons and devices involved in accessing single resource computer systems. However, networking creates problems which are beyond those discussed previously. In the network environment, the user may be a person, terminal, a host computer, or a combination of all three. Also the resource may be a data item, data file, program or a host computer system. So the authorization mechanism in a network environment must satisfy the following functions:

1. Controlled access to the resources.
2. Controlled usage of the resources.
3. Assurance that the desired level of protection is maintained through monitoring, surveillance, and auditing of proper functioning. Therefore, the requirements for network security expand to: identification/authentication/authorization/access control/monitoring/auditing/integrity checking.

Internal Auditing

Each change or technical advance in EDP has brought new challenges to the role of the internal auditor. External auditing, by definition, has excluded itself from the detailed audit which the internal auditor must perform. Additional auditor capabilities are required to function effectively in the EDP environment. If one can accept that computer security is an underdeveloped capability, computer auditing has not been overdeveloped. Because of publicity concerning computer abuses and the failure of controls, management is becoming increasingly aware of computer audit shortcomings. In the next decade, management is going to be more aware of its organization's vulnerability to computer-related failures and losses, and the auditor's inability to assure the adequacy of computer system controls.

For discussion on this subject, computer auditing will be generalized into two broad categories. The first category is an audit of what is done by the computer, i.e. auditing of an application such as payroll. Primarily, organizations are concerned with this type of work because of the requirement to verify financial statements. Generally, the auditors have been able to respond to this requirement. The second category, however, is a Pandora's Box of areas beyond that of just auditing the computer system, i.e. systems design and development, resource management, installation management and operations, and even computer security. Both categories are very much within the province of computer auditing. Who else is responsible to management for assuring that EDP operations are being run economically, efficiently, and effectively in accordance with management's stated policy? Auditors have not actively accepted the second role because of the EDP expertise required.

If many future audit situations will require a level of EDP knowledge beyond the capabilities of the audit staff members, where will this skill be obtained? In the 'Standards for Audit of Government Organizations, Programs, Activities and Functions', the Comptroller General states that the audit staff must possess the appropriate skills and obtain the necessary staff members or consultants required for review of computer systems. Look then for systems analysts, programmers, DP managers, and security specialists to become part of the internal audit staff.

Traditionally, the responsibilities of the auditor include:

1. Protecting the assets of an organization.
2. Assuring adherence to stated organizational policy.
3. Assuring adequacy of controls and procedures.
4. Determining the reliability of management information.
5. Recommending operational improvements.

In evaluating the effectiveness of the organization, the auditor can identify and help solve problems, improve controls and security, and reduce intrinsic high risk EDP activities. These tasks seem very much in line with the responsibilities assigned to the computer security staff, and one may question how problems could possibly arise.

The auditor would request the following in order to evaluate computer security:

1. A workable definition of computer security to allocate audit resources.
2. An organizational computer security policy statement to assure compliance.
3. Standards of computer security to determine adequacy of controls.
4. Access to EDP to measure performance and reliability.
5. Tests and the examination of results to measure accuracy.
6. The ability to communicate the findings to maximize management understanding and acceptance.

Although computer security is a widely discussed subject, a definition can refer to many different subsets of the total computer security effort specifically, if the definition is obtained from management. For example, computer security has been defined as protection of the 'computer' from attack or destruction by a variety of threats ranging from natural disaster to acts by disgruntled employees. Recently, definitions have been expanded to include the protection of software and data against accidental or intentional disclosure, modification, or destruction. A preferred definition would be a state or condition that a system possesses in its computer hardware, software, data, and personnel based on the risks, threats to the environment, and the evidence of trustworthiness in technological safeguards and managerial procedures applied to the life cycle operation of the system.

From submission of this type of definition, the auditor and his relationship with the EDP components would be moving in different directions. Armed with such a definition, the auditors would be evaluating security in terms of absolutes; i.e. the presence of a control or procedure is good, and its absence is bad. More often than not, the auditor will find that an organization has no total system computer security policy or overall assignment of security administration. In dealing with security standards, checklists have been produced and adopted by auditors for their evaluations. The auditor will find a wide discrepancy between organizational practice and standard operating procedures as described in his checklist. The guidelines that are used by auditors and even the actual operation in the organization are often reflections of practices for early generation computer systems, rather than the adaptation of prudent techniques through the evolution of technology. Thus, the auditor is utilizing outdated guidelines that are inadequate or useless for evaluation of the actual operation. When access to the computer is granted, the auditor is usually assisted by the component being evaluated. The results and conclusions of such tests are often biased from both views. General disagreements will exist on the value of the resources to be protected, the threats to which the resources are exposed, the rate of threat occurrence, the rate to which the system and its applications are utilized, and the level of compliance with security policy or available safeguards that are in place. Finally, without doubt, EDP and security managers believe that an audit of their function is an adverse reading of their ability to perform. Also, the audits have disappointing results since top management finds general disagreement within the organization about the findings and auditors see a lack of implementation of their recommendations.

The audit of computer security practices as an issue will become more intense. Several directions in technological development will have impact on the auditability of computer systems and the security measures provided. As larger quantities of data are being put on smaller volumes of storage, the threat of theft or the loss of data from a single event is going to increase. Data security, data backup procedures, and recovery operations will become more important. Audit data will become more difficult to obtain as more capability is distributed over geographically remote areas without centralized control. A key issue will be management's ability to provide an audit capability over the operation in a distributed system. Auditing computer security is going to force the auditor to develop new approaches to keep abreast of the state of the art. Much of what appears to be a reluctance on the part of management to implement needed controls and audit capabilities into system development and designs for new applications is in reality the institutionalization of bad or outdated practice. Interactive programming tools will have to be developed appropriate for the environment being evaluated. The single most important issue for auditors will be to concentrate on those applications associated with high value data and resources. Such concentration should lead to better standards and guidelines to be used to determine:

1. Acceptable levels of risk.
2. Sufficiency of protection provided.
3. Operation of security mechanisms.
4. Reliability and recovery requirements.
5. The interface with physical and procedural controls.

Personnel

People are the most important component of the EDP environment. No organization can implement the security requirements without a staff dedicated to achieving its goals. Good security practices must be concerned with the people in an organization, their capabilities, their continuing employment and termination. This approach necessitates a proper organizational framework, continuing attention to employee relationships, and a constantly aware enforcement mechanism.

The selection of EDP personnel includes an effort to determine a candidate's qualifications based on training, talent, and experience to do the duties required. The selection for sensitive positions should include a verification of trustworthiness by pre-hire screening and continual re-evaluation throughout the employee's career. The risk analysis of the EDP environment should reflect the sensitivity of each position. Wherever checks and balances on employee activities are missing, the position is even more sensitive, for example, when the person responsible for the system input of payments is the same person who verifies and authorizes payment. Procedures for designating one or more levels of position sensitivity and the screening applied to each level of sensitivity are required. The organization must emphasize personnel selection to include security criteria that determine employee character, i.e. integrity, loyalty, discretion, and trustworthiness. This description is not a support for the methodology employed in national security screening of applicants but rather is an attempt to suggest that an organization must extend personnel security requirements to its personnel management program as part of an ongoing computer security effort.

In the future, personnel problems in EDP are going to be significant. Even today, much is being written about 'turnover' and 'burnout' of EDP professionals. One example of the cause centers around the basic requirements of the job. In any organization, key personnel are given more and more systems to maintain based on their ability to manage them. At the end of a few years, these people are doing nothing but maintenance. Rather than being assigned to new technologies and applications, they are stuck with the old ones. Finally, management must hire someone from the outside with the new, required experience. Such confinement to specific jobs contributes to job dissatisfaction, low morale, turnover, and general unhappiness. Both top management and security practitioners are concerned, but for different reasons.

Management will strive to move employees to greater job challenges and opportunities for advancement to avoid personnel problems. More and more allowances will be made; in fact, key programmers may even be allowed to stay home and resolve problems from their portable terminals. Job rotation will be utilized to keep personnel challenged. Rather than have a smaller number of employees knowledgeable about the system and capable of causing serious harm to the organization, the number of potential problems will increase.

This personnel approach to resolving problems will severely limit the security officer's ability to function. Many executives do not understand the relationship between security and the rest of the organization. As a result, the security professional's chances of being successful will be seriously limited unless he can develop a security-conscious environment. The personnel problem for the next decade will be a combination of providing the needed technical and security training, obtaining the leadership from top management, and changing from short-term fire-fighting techniques to long-term approaches.

Contingency Planning

Since every computer system is vulnerable to accident, disaster, malicious damage, as well as plain mismanagement, security measures encompassing contingency planning must be considered in advance of need. In view of the large investments that organizations have in the automation effort, contingency measures are absolute necessities. The major concern about contingency planning is economic justification. Phrased another way, if your organization could continue to function for days or weeks after a loss of processing, it is probable that much of the EDP function is not needed. A concern about contingency planning should be the determination of how much is necessary?

Several proposed approaches for contingency are:

1. Manual operations.
2. Mutual aid agreements.
3. Service bureaus.
4. Shared contingency facilities.
5. Multiple corporate sites.

Because this chapter has predicted a computer system in the next decade that relies heavily on an on-line network, the discussion of alternatives pertains to that environment.

A return to manual operations is usually available only on an application-by-application basis and is heavily dependent on the volume of transactions and manpower required by the application. Small batch-type systems may be able to use this alternative but not the real-time environment proposed.

Surprisingly even today, organizations rely heavily on mutual aid agreements. The problem of incompatibility and time availability makes such agreements questionable. Attempting to maintain compatible hardware and software configurations for two computer systems for agreement purposes is expensive and risky. Even if hardware were compatible, differences in the operating system would require massive conversion efforts to implement the contingency capability. In time of need, is the agreement enforceable? That period is not when an organization would want to go to court for its processing requirements.

Service bureau availability for contingency suffers from many of the same problems as a mutual aid agreement. Conventions unique to the service bureau must be identified and resolved prior to contingency implementation. Testing can prove to be quite expensive.

A recent trend is an attempt to ensure quick recovery through the 'empty shell' or shared contingency facility. This concept has a number of companies sharing the cost of building and maintaining a stand-by facility. The facility usually is complete with a raised floor, water cooling system, power, fire and security systems, and telecommunications. *Only* the computer is missing. While this proposal may sound sufficient to some organizations, a number of disadvantages are apparent:

1. No testing of the contingency program can be accomplished without the computer.
2. No two companies can occupy the facility at the same time. If the facility is twice as large as necessary to handle the largest requirement, it is now twice the expense originally proposed.
3. The liability of partners to assume the expense of supporting this concept must be long term. This feature prohibits an organization from using any new concepts in the future. A penalty for dropping out of the agreement is probably implied and places an additional expense on the remaining partners.
4. The concept revolves on the hardware vendor supplying the equipment in the necessary time frame to sustain operations. What are the vendor's liabilities if he is late in delivering the equipment?

Ideally, the best approach for distributed processing is in a multiple or two-site computer network. Certainly, the second site hardware is ready to be implemented. In such a configuration, the first site primarily controls all message traffic and computer functions, with the second site, the backup, acting in a mirror capacity. Off-site storage of all transactions is automatic to the second site. In case of primary site failure, switchover to the backup can occur quickly. Apparently such a concept is extremely expensive but provides for adequate contingency if cost justified. The testing for this type of capability would require a rigorous exercise of all possible failures and the establishment of a step-by-step sequence to assure switchover.

No matter what alternative is chosen, a well-thought-out contingency capability is vital. To ensure the availability of critical functions and to facilitate continuity of operations, a well-documented and tested capability is also required. The challenge of the next decade will be to provide a contingency capability throughout the EDP advances experienced by the organization. Insurance protection for vital assets and loss of business will supplement the inability of most organizations to address their contingency requirements adequately. This method offers nothing more than a false sense of security and an avoidance of the responsibilities assigned to top management.

CONCLUSION

To the EDP security professional, the computer environment has offered many challenges. To compound the problem further, advances in technology will bring about unforeseen vulnerabilities to an environment that is anything but stable. To top management of an organization, the challenges to address the operational requirements adequately seem to be in conflict with the needs to apply security to the resources. Computer security and the auditing of computer security have not been given the highest priority because of the urgency to convert to more sophisticated systems needed to maintain business and the expense, budget and manpower, involved in bringing this sophistication on-line. To compound matters, the results of a security program are not highly visible and can be regarded as overhead.

Computer security is necessary today, and will be more so in the future. Organization dependence upon EDP will create unique vulnerabilities. Decentralization of functions will increase the need for protection and increase the awareness of management concerning overall lack of control. More technology and methodology are available today than are needed to make quantum improvements toward improving computer security. The missing ingredients are people trained to use the techniques available and an overall understanding by top management of the long-term implications of reluctance to implement an appropriate security program. The future will determine the reliability of the forecast presented.

BIBLIOGRAPHY

Heinrich, F.: *The Network Security Center: A System Level Approach to Computer Network Security.* NBS Special Publication 500-21, Volume 2, January 1978.

Cole, G. D.: *Design Alternatives of Computer Network Security.* NBS Special Publication 500-21, Volume 1, January 1978.

Belford, G. G., Bunch, S. R., and Day, J. D.: *A State of the Art Report on Network Data Management and Related Technology.* University of Illinois at Urbana-Champagne, April 1, 1975.

Needhan, R. M., and Schroeder, M. D.: Using Encryption for Authentication in Large Networks of Computers. *Comm. ACM,* 21/12, December 1978.

Walker, B. J., Kemmerer, R. A., and Popek, G. J.: Specification and Verification of the UCLA Unix Security Kernel. *Comm. ACM,* 23/2, February 1980.

Audit and Evaluation of Computer Security. Edited by Z. G. Ruthberg, NBS Special Publication 500-19, October 1977.

Audit and Evaluation of Computer Security II, System Vulnerabilities and Controls. Edited by Z. G. Ruthberg, NBS Special Publication 500-57, April 1980.

Denning, D. E., and Denning, P. J.: Data Security. *Computer Survey,* 11/3, September 1979.

Goetz, M. A.: Advanced Commercial Applications in the 80's. *Datamation,* November 1979.

Senkop, M. E.: Data Bases: Past, Present and Future. *IBM Systems Journal,* 16/3, 1977.

Wood, C., Fernandez, E. B., and Summers, R. C.: Data Base Security: Requirements, Policies and Models. *IBM Systems Journal,* 19/2, 1980.

Fenroth, Y., Franceschini, E., and Goldstein, M.: Telecommunications Using a Front-End Processor. *Comm. ACM,* 16/3, March 1973.

Canady, R. H., *et al.*: A Back-End Computer for Data Base Management. *Comm. ACM,* 17/10, October 1974.

Landwehr, C. E.: Formal Models for Computer Security. *Computer Surveys*, 12/3, September 1981.

Seltzer, J. H.: Protection and the Control of Information Sharing in Multics. *Comm. ACM*, 17/7, July 1974.

Guidelines on Evaluation of Techniques for Automated Personnel Identification. FIPS Publication 48, U.S. Department of Commerce, National Bureau of Standards, April 1, 1977.

Computer Auditing in the Executive Departments: Not Enough Is Being Done. Comptroller General Report to Congress, FGMSD-77-82, September 28, 1977.

Hoag, E.: Safeguarding Your Computer. *Output*, **March 1981.**

INDEX